OPENING THE
DOORS OF WONDER

Reflections on Religious Rites of Passage

ARTHUR J. MAGIDA

UNIVERSITY OF CALIFORNIA PRESS   Berkeley   Los Angeles   London

University of California Press, one of the most distinguished university presses
in the United States, enriches lives around the world by advancing scholarship
in the humanities, social sciences, and natural sciences. Its activities are
supported by the UC Press Foundation and by philanthropic contributions
from individuals and institutions. For more information, visit www.ucpress.edu.

University of California Press
Berkeley and Los Angeles, California

University of California Press, Ltd.
London, England

Library of Congress Cataloging-in-Publication Data

Magida, Arthur J.
    Opening the doors of wonder : reflections on religious rites of passage /
Arthur J. Magida.
        p.   cm.
    Includes bibliographical references (p.   ) and index.
    ISBN-13: 978-0-520-24545-7 (cloth : alk. paper)
    ISBN-10: 0-520-24545-8 (cloth : alk. paper)
    1. Ritual.   2. Rites and ceremonies.   3. Religions—Customs and
practices.   I. Title.
BL600.M28   2007
203'.82—dc22   2006007729

Manufactured in the United States of America

15   14   13   12   11   10   09   08   07   06
10   9   8   7   6   5   4   3   2   1

This book is printed on New Leaf EcoBook 50, a 100% recycled fiber of which
50% is de-inked post-consumer waste, processed chlorine-free. EcoBook 50 is
acid-free and meets the minimum requirements of ANSI/ASTM D5634–01
(*Permanence of Paper*).

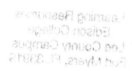

We can only see as far forward as we can remember back.

AFRICAN PROVERB

Memory is the diary that we all carry about with us.

OSCAR WILDE

CONTENTS

PROLOGUE

When I was ten years old, my fifth-grade teacher used to make an announcement every week that I never quite understood. It had something to do with "catechism class." The second word was a cinch. Even I comprehended it. But "catechism"? It seemed like another language, maybe from another planet.

The announcement would always come around two o'clock, usually on a Wednesday or Thursday. Almost two-thirds of the class would tidy up their desks, bolt out of their seats, and just about skip out of James Madison Elementary School, a two-story brick building surrounded by a chin-high metal fence painted a not-very-attractive lime green. At James Madison, hoisting the American flag to the top of the pole in front of the school early in the morning was a high honor, almost as distinguished as carrying the erasers down to the basement at the end of the day and sucking gusts of chalky dust out of them with a vacuum cleaner that some goofy inventor had devised for that very purpose. But in my eyes, the greatest honor of all was to be among those lucky kids who dashed out of this school in bleak Scranton, Pennsylvania. I admired how clever they were. Clearly they were privy to a secret, and they were keeping it to themselves: not just how to get out of school ninety minutes early but also how to escape our teacher, Miss Dyer, whom we feared and loathed. A bully and a tyrant, she humiliated at least one of us every day in front of the entire class—teasing, scolding, or just plain chewing out some poor sucker. Her class was a gulag, a stalag, a slammer for fifth graders. From 9:00 in the morning until 3:30 in the afternoon, we held our breath, never knowing when she would strike or whom she would pounce on. Anyone who figured out how to get away from Miss Dyer, even for something I did not comprehend—like "catechism"—automatically went up in my esteem.

Many years later—decades later, in fact—I'd learn that catechism was more of a mystery than I'd dreamed back in Scranton. In their church a few blocks from school, within thick stone walls and beneath a spire so tall it seemed (from my short grade-school perspective) almost to touch the sky, the Catholic kids were being instructed in the fundamentals of sin and salvation, two lofty abstractions that exceeded the cramped comprehension of most fifth graders. Most likely those kids knew only that they were hearing serious words with serious implications. Beyond that, such ideas were better left to adults to figure out, which was pretty much how we felt at that age about anything that was grave and somber and had the weight of the world resting on it.

Of course, I didn't know that the way the catechism was learned—committing to memory volumes of questions and answers and being drilled on them again and again—could be traced all the way back to the ancient Jewish rabbis and teachers, who were fond of posing and then answering questions, in a sort of one-man Socratic dialogue a few centuries before Socrates was even born. Jesus, who was well aware of the power of questions, often used the same approach in the impromptu sermons he delivered in villages and synagogues throughout ancient Palestine: "What think ye of Christ?" "Who do men say that the son of man is?" "Who do ye say that I am?" Question after question challenged Jews' lack of faith, their corruption, their dull inability to realize that they were living in apocalyptic times, that Armageddon itself might break out before sundown. Jesus wanted to shake people up, make them change their ways before it was too late: "O thou of little faith, wherefore didst thou doubt?" "Why do ye transgress the commandment of God by your tradition?" "O ye hypocrites, can ye not discern the signs of the times?" Even as Jesus' strength drained while hanging from the cross, one last question was left in him: "Eli, Eli, lama sabachthani?"—"My God, my God, why hast Thou forsaken me?" Then he was quiet, but far from forgotten.

The question mark, then, characterized Christianity from its start, a mode of learning and preaching that Christians inherited from their Jewish brothers. Questions took people on quests; occasionally, questions actually led to answers. I didn't know any of this, not in fifth grade and not in Scranton. All I knew was that these kids left school much too early once a week and that I was stuck with Miss Dyer—all . . . day . . . long.

Somehow, with time and effort, I figured out that this catechism stuff was bringing these gentile kids to an essential juncture in their religious life, just as Hebrew school was bringing the Jewish kids to a similar juncture. The Christian kids had communion and confession and confirmation, and the Jewish kids had bar and bat mitzvah. All of us were lurching toward some kind of destiny at our respective altars, although few of us really knew where the ritual led. "Lurching," in fact, was the best description for this journey. As newcomers to religion, we were only doing what we were told to do. And whenever obedience exceeds comprehension, there is confusion, and there is uncertainty, and there is lurching.

We were reasonably sure that wherever we were heading would satisfy clergy and parents and grandparents. It might even satisfy God Himself, and what could be better than making God a happy God? But the *deeper* reason for the satisfaction that we were so diligently sowing among our elders and our beloved deity was really beyond us: we were passing from one phase of life to another, learning secrets and wisdom that stretched back generations, maybe to the Creator Himself. How could we know this? At that moment in our young lives, about all we were capable of grasping was the simple, elementary tautology that you did *this*—whatever it was—because you were your parents' child and you wanted to be "good" in their eyes and in the eyes of God. There were no choices. There were only imperatives, mandates, expectations, and assumptions, with little leeway and scant latitude and not much of what I would later learn was called "free will."

Still, I never quite forgave my Christian friends for abandoning me to Miss Dyer. Maybe, I figured, their luck had something to do with the messiah they worshipped and the Bible—the "newer" one—they read. It was all so frustrating. After all, *their* God was giving them a free "Get Out of School" pass. *That* was divine intervention, although maybe not the kind that was really needed in that sere and devastated region of northeastern Pennsylvania, with scars upon the land and the heart. Unemployment almost rivaled that of the Great Depression, streets built over abandoned coal mines were caving in daily, the air was filthy and blackened from burning culm dumps along the perimeter of the city, there was an unwanted incandescence in the middle of the night—with all that going on, the *best* God could do was to get the *Catholic* kids dismissed from Public School No. 33 a few hours early every week? What about *us*—the *chosen* people? A few thousand years before, God had freed hundreds of thousands of Jews from slavery after punishing the Egyptians with one plague after another—killing their firstborn, ruining their crops, turning the Nile into blood—and now He was freeing someone else? I needed no further proof that the Lord moves in strange and mysterious ways. I'm sure that He had His reasons—His very wise reasons—for letting the Catholic kids troop out of my fifth-grade classroom. But at the tender age of ten, the reasons sure as hell eluded me.

In certain ways, all of us, Christian and Jewish, had embarked on different versions of the same adventure: the Catholic kids were memorizing catechism; the Jewish kids were memorizing their *aleph, bet, gimmel*—the Hebrew *ABC*s. Everyone was learning Bible stories: Abraham smashed idols in his father's house. Joseph wore a coat of many colors. Moses descended from Sinai with two extremely heavy tablets. And of course, for the Christians, there was the matter of a certain virgin birth and a miracle involving loaves and fishes and a resurrection that resounded throughout all eternity. Everyone studied, and studied hard. No one wanted to risk the wrath of God, clergy, or especially parents. The world was scary enough without that.

Being Jewish, I had a bar mitzvah—for me, a great disappointment. My most lasting memories of it have nothing to do with the thrill of reading from the Torah for the first time or the pleasure this gave my parents. Rather, I remember being yelled at a lot and wearing a suit that never stopped itching.

For months, I was drilled, coached, scolded, and intimidated by a man I didn't like—the cantor at our temple. He had bad breath and a short temper and wore rumpled clothes, and every year he had to perform a miracle: turning boys whose voices were still changing—they were equipped with the vocal equivalent of a yo-yo—into halfway competent singers. While teaching, he shook his head in dismay, knowing that regardless of how bad we were (and most of us were *very* bad), we would still have a bar mitzvah, since the ceremony had nothing to do with musical talent and everything to do with a kid turning thirteen. My dear cantor had been around too long. He knew the ridiculously small odds of a boy chanting his Torah portion with soaring glissandos that echoed through the stone arches of the synagogue's massive sanctuary while congregants and guests from afar thrilled at the young Caruso, honored to be in his presence, stunned that they were witnessing musical history.

Of course, that never happened.

The other major memory from my bar mitzvah involved a gray flannel suit. My parents and their friendly haberdasher had decided that this stylish garment was "ideal" for the occasion. The problem was that it itched. Nonstop. At the bar mitzvah itself, every itch was a nudge, a reminder to stand up straight and enunciate precisely and make everyone proud of me. For all I know, it worked. I'm not sure because I have no idea how well I said my Torah portion or my "learned" talk to the congregation about that portion. I don't remember any of that. I do remember the itching.[1]

I figured that, years later, I would look back on this moment—one *possibly* fraught with holiness—as the one when I started becoming who I was meant to be. For now, though, it was hollow. If I'd been more reverent or had better understood those commandments I was now obliged to follow, maybe the rite would have nourished me, even changed me. And if my parents had practiced a different kind of Judaism, then maybe *that* would have rubbed off on me. True, they brought me into the temple and they brought Judaism into the house. But it never seemed to sway or inform them. Their Judaism, quite simply and quite annoyingly, was a functional Judaism. Prayers were said and candles lit, maybe as obeisance to their parents or maybe, to go way back, as obeisance to Abraham, Isaac, and Jacob. I don't know. No one ever talked about it. This stuff was off limits: too sensitive because it was too personal, although the personal was where truth lay.

There was no questioning, no discussing. You did this stuff, this religious stuff, because that was who you were and what you'd been born into. My parents, Florence and Paul, knew the mechanics of religion—the gestures, the words: when you light candles and when you say prayers; the proper demeanor at synagogue and, especially, at a Passover Seder, where neither a giggle nor a smile was allowed. But the spirit behind these gestures and genuflections—what Judaism calls *kavvanah,* the intention behind an act—was missing. Who knows? Maybe no one ever exposed my parents to *kavannah*—a lapse not unlikely, since their lives were filtered through duty and obligation, not spirit and joy.

So in the end, I couldn't relate to my Torah reading or even to the Torah itself. The pity is that a day so loaded with meaning and imagery and majesty was, in the end, a complete and devastating dud. The attention was great and the presents were grand. I still have some of them. But in the end, this rite took me nowhere. There was no passage.

From many friends, I've heard similar accounts about their rites of passage. In virtually every faith, things seem amiss and people are perplexed that the day—*their* day!—didn't reach further into them, that it wasn't more conclusive, more decisive. Few people are transformed. There's no reworking of the soul and there's nothing profound. For that, the heart must move in tandem with the grain of circumstances, the sacred circumstances, and that may be too much to ask: miracles don't occur on demand.

Decades later, a Zen monk in Berkeley helped me figure out what may have happened at my bar mitzvah. Every day, the monk meditated for hours. It was always torture—difficult and intractable, especially when there were so many other things he could be doing, like cooking and shopping and being a good husband and doting father. Then one day he realized that his meditation wasn't changing, but his life was. Those sessions of quiet, intense focus were transforming how he experienced the world. Meditation was subtly enhancing his compassion, his wisdom, his patience. He *was* "progressing," although not as he'd anticipated.

Expecting something magical from a ritual—a bar mitzvah in Pennsylvania or meditation in California—could mean that you're looking in the wrong place. The gradations of life are too slow for these instant transformations. True: *satori* (Zen enlightenment) arrives in a flash, but only after years of preparation; and *kavannah* (Hebrew for directing your heart toward God) animates prayers, but only after the heart has been humbled. "Magic" takes a nanosecond to strike but a lifetime to nurture. Placing it on a timetable guarantees disappointment.

That is why I wrote this book. I wanted to see who isn't disappointed, who is changed, how they're changed, why they're changed—who, if anyone, is rescued from a probable familiarity with the crushing hand of fate; who is blessed with an exciting and extravagant psychic charge. Depending on our religion, we get dunked, sprinkled, lectured to. We read, we sing, we chant. We make promises and we take vows. We wear white robes or orange robes or brand new suits or dresses that we may never wear again. We might think about heaven or hell or God or messiahs, about this life or the next one. Or, to be more honest, we might just think about the party following all the mumbo jumbo.

And when it's all over, have we "arrived," whatever that means? If someone didn't have one of these events, did they compensate in any way? Is a rite of passage a rehearsal for the competence and general bravura we need to get through life, with all its disruptions and annoyances and exasperations?

Each of us has our hunches about these questions. After all, life is a series of hunches and guesses strung together into a story—our story, a story that's perplexing, charming, entertaining, confusing, confounding, and maybe best of all, unexpected as hell. It's a story riddled with rites and with passages and with destinations we have yet to reach, a story that we're making up as we go along and whose ending we haven't figured out yet.

A few words on stories and on the structure of this book: Every world religion gets its own section—a chapter that explains the evolution of its coming-of-age ceremony with its elements and their theological meaning. This is followed by several interviews with famous or influential individuals about the rites of passage they had in that faith. Here you will find a Nobel laureate, a *New Yorker* cartoonist, an internationally renowned holistic guru, a former rock star, a Zen roshi, a college president, a TV anchor, two rabbis, a psychedelic pioneer, a novelist from Africa, a comedian who became famous on *Saturday Night Live,* and more.

Hearing their stories is a privilege. These people are smart, savvy. Some are devout; some want to be devout. A few are cynics; a handful have no use for religion. But let's put what they say into perspective. While, in one way or another, the people I interviewed have shaped our culture and our times, in the greater scheme of things our stories are just as valid as theirs. We *all* have stories. In fact, we *are* our stories. They're indispensable to who we are and who we've been and who we want to be. Stories rescue us from the chaos of the everyday. Without them, our birth would mean little, our death might mean less, and everything that happens between those two goalposts of our lives would be blurry and inchoate.

The Harvard psychologist Jerry Bruner understood how stories structure our lives. "The self," he said, "is a perpetually rewritten story." We're constantly making narratives, he said, narratives about ourselves. In the end, we become these stories, stories which tell our lives and hint at a conclusion that we're still shaping.

If every life is a story, then rites of passage are pivotal chapters in them. The key may not be *how* we remember them, maybe not even *if* we remember them. The key—the real key—is that, at some obscure level, these rites have etched a new story for us among the tales that buoy and sustain us. In ways known and unknown, they make a dent on who we are and who we may yet be.

Few people understood the power of memory better than the German poet Rainer Maria Rilke. "Ah," Rilke wrote, "poems amount to so little when you write them too early in your life. You ought to wait and gather sense and sweetness for a whole lifetime . . . and then, at the very end, you might perhaps be able to write ten good lines. For poems are . . . experiences. For the sake of a single poem, you must see many cities, many people and things, you must understand animals, must feel how birds fly, and know the gesture which small flowers make when they open in the morning. You must be able to think back to streets in unknown neighborhoods, to unexpected encounters, and to partings you had long seen coming. . . . And it is not yet enough to have memories. . . . For the memories themselves are not important. Only when they have changed into our very blood, into glance and gesture, and are nameless. . . . Only then can it happen that in some very rare hour the first word of a poem arises in their midst."[2]

To affect us, rites of passage don't necessarily have to hit a bull's eye, forever wedding us to a faith, a God, a tradition. But just like a memory or a poem, they enter our blood and our glance and our gesture. As they become part of us, they provide another story for our narrative, a story that will exult, proclaim, exclaim, confuse, and befuddle. For all stories, all good stories, enlighten and bewilder and hold a truth that is holy and sacred and blessedly contradictory: elusive, fleeting, and above all, eternally and enduringly momentous.

A postscript: The day after I wrote the above section, an old friend called from Florida. I'd seen Ronni only a few times since graduating from high school, but some ties don't fade. She wanted me to know that Sheldon was dying. I'd been good friends with Sheldon from fifth grade through our second year in college, when he went his way and I went mine. That happens to all of us: the years intervene, experience intervenes, life intervenes. The funny thing was that in the end—and for Sheldon, it *was* the end—none of that really matters. He was dying and he was in pain, and after Ronni's call I was anxious to let him know that I remembered him and cared about him.

I called Sheldon the next day. It was as if no time had passed. We talked and joked, *not* with the awkwardness of not having seen each other for years, but with the ease of having known each other for a long time. Most impressive was Sheldon's courage: blind from diabetes, one-legged after an amputation, he'd told his doctors to disconnect him from his dialysis machine. In a few hours, he'd be in a hospice; in less than twenty-four, he'd be dead. Even so, we barely talked about death. Rather, we talked about growing up in Scranton and about old friends and about attending Temple Israel and about once seeing a movie during Passover, when Sheldon sinfully ate a hot dog on a roll while every other Jew in the world was eating matzo. And maybe because Sheldon was on the verge of going through the ultimate rite of passage, we talked about another journey—our bar mitzvahs. We both admitted that, at the time, we hadn't understood what they meant. What *was* important was that the memories of having had a bar mitzvah had stayed with us all these years. These memories abolished time. They rescued the obscure and the forgotten. They obliterated oblivion. Our bar mitzvahs—inconsequential though they had seemed—weren't mere blips on our childhood screens, something we did because we were nice Jewish boys. No, our bar mitzvahs were part of us. Without them, I would not be Arthur and he would not be Sheldon. And neither of us would be Jewish.

With these memories enjoying such longevity, who could deny their power, their grandeur, even if, for some people, people like Sheldon, their truth remained a mystery that lingered all the way unto death.

INTRODUCTION

SOMETIMES, THE MAGIC WORKS

Catholics don't remember their baptism. Muslims don't remember their baby welcoming. Jewish men don't remember their circumcision. Water is sprinkled, a relative says a few words about the newborn, a foreskin is cut. These are all done *to* babies, who have no say about any of this and no idea what's going on. A decade or so later, after several years of religious education and many visits to a church, mosque, or temple, children may know what they're doing and even *why*. They are conscious and they are awake and that, along with so many other reasons, is why rites of passage during puberty are so different from what we have as babies.

But consciousness doesn't necessarily guarantee wisdom. A nineteenth-century best-seller, for instance, a children's Bible primer written by a repressed, miserable, and possibly insane English woman, woke kids up to the world around them. It also scared the bejesus out of them. *The Peep of Day*, by Mrs. Favell Lee Mortimer, was translated into thirty-eight languages, including such tongues as Yoruba, Malayalam, Marathi, Tamil, Cree, and Ojibwa. Despite phenomenal sales, over one million copies worldwide, *The Peep* is one of the most sadistic books ever intended for children. Consider this snippet from its first chapter:

> How kind of God . . . to give you a body! I hope that your body will not get hurt. . . . If it were to fall into the fire, it would be burned up. . . . If a great knife were run through your body, the blood would come out. If a great box

were to fall on your head, your neck would be broken. If you were not to eat some food for a few days, your little body would be very sick, your breath would stop, and you would grow cold, and you would soon be dead.[1]

How *The Peep* helped anyone is a puzzle. Most likely, it sent kids squealing to their mothers for protection from the evil God who'd designed a body that could be diced, chopped, or pulverized any minute. What they heard from that loony Mortimer woman could make them swear off religion forever: we are all refugees from an avenging God who takes sinners, even the smallest of them, none too lightly.

Obviously, being aware isn't necessarily reassuring: readers of *The Peep* were chilled to the bone. Yet awareness can confer knowledge; it can provide context; in the best of all worlds, it can bring wisdom. We may advance through life in fits and starts—few paths are direct—but wacky Mrs. Mortimer had the wrong idea: you don't scare kids into compliance. Guide them gently, treat them kindly, and they'll be open to the possibilities you're offering them. A rite of passage isn't a horror show. Religion should bring kids into the light, not make them cower in their beds, scared of life and happy to get away from it.

The words and images of a rite of passage guide parents and children from one plateau to another: children venture further into the world, where they'll have many adventures and make many mistakes, and parents try to cling less to their sons and daughters, knowing that their "career" as parents is being reshaped. With grace and ease and, hopefully, little disruption, these rites ease families from one role to another, from one phase to another: parents become elders; children are on their way to becoming adults, eventually becoming parents themselves. As the world changes, it stays remarkably the same.

Life is full of rites of passage. Mastering a challenge, coming to terms with ourselves or with someone else, learning a new skill—a new language, a new swimming stroke, a new whatever—all fit under a fairly porous, generous definition of "rite of passage." But in this book, we focus only on the really powerful ones—those that provide connections and links and opportunities to sense that our wisdom and knowledge and place in the world are broader and deeper and more timeless than we would otherwise suspect. The rites of passage in this book traverse the ordinary. Many experiences deliver us to a new and unanticipated realm, to a place that was only rumors and fictions for us. But just as Melville in *Moby-Dick* speaks of "reality outracing apprehension"—apprehension in the sense not of fear or disquiet but of understanding—a profound rite of passage can be our threshold to a land with illimitable borders, to a territory that defines us even as it defies definition, sometimes even as it defies words themselves.

Common to all the lessons that can be extracted from these events is that they make us more comfortable in the world and extend our horizons. A woman I know in North Carolina never had one of these ceremonies. Raised a Christian but as unaffiliated as could be, she was never baptized or confirmed and always sensed that something was missing, that other people possessed a moment, a certainty, an understanding that she didn't. Now a teacher in high school, she has never missed a graduation at the end of the school year. This is her students' rite of passage as well as her own. Watching her grinning students, in their caps and gowns, diplomas in hand, reminds her why she teaches; indeed, this moment teaches her that she has a mission and that every June she watches it reach fruition. In a sense, there's a certain timelessness at stake, just as with a religious rite of passage: she's connected to the future, to those marching before her out of the commencement auditorium on their way to college or their first job. But compared with a more traditional rite of passage, the sort she missed as a youngster, what she experiences is fundamentally one-sided: the future may spread before her, but the past doesn't recede, other than maybe the past four years of the students who are graduating. She is connected in one direction, bereft and adrift in the other.

The timing of a traditional coming-of-age ceremony has two main influences. One is historical. For centuries, children were essential to the livelihood of their family. They worked in the fields, in the kitchen, at looms, in barns and, in their early teens, they took on even more work. At around eleven or twelve, childhood, which was no great lark anyway, was essentially over. In addition to having more chores and responsibilities, children were now considered capable of making religious commitments affecting the rest of their lives, maybe even their eternal lives. If their young bodies were reasonably mature, went the reasoning, then so, too, were their souls.[2]

The other reason for the timing of a traditional coming-of-age ritual is biological. In our early teens, weird things happen to our bodies. Hair appears where there wasn't any. Voices deepen. Breasts develop. Girls menstruate. Boys ejaculate. This isn't the body we were born into, and we're scared, excited, thrilled. If bodies can change, then everything can change. Nothing is fixed. Panic, curiosity, bewilderment set in. Just as it seems that everything is coming undone, we participate in a rite, an initiation, that honors who we've been, recognizes what we are, and tells us who we just might be.

The elaborate theater of a rite of passage constructs a spiritual shelter, a refuge to protect us in bad times and bless us in good. But we can't be too sure about this. As the Indian grandfather says in *Little Big Man,* "Sometimes the magic works; sometimes it doesn't." When it works, it grabs us by the lapels, forcing us to pay attention. Then we have an urge, a curiosity to see the invisible, to touch the untouchable: to know that there is more to "us" than us. One of Jean Cocteau's nieces had this same instinct. When asked if she wanted to see the new brother an angel had just delivered, she said, "No! I want to see the angel."

When we *do* see the angel—when an initiation really works—it can unsettle us even as it reassures us. As we separate from one role, we move along to another, stepping into a new and, for us, unexplored terrain. We learn—possibly even understand—arcane, esoteric stuff: the secret names of ancestors or deities or the mythical history of our tribe or barely pronounceable incantations and hardly understood creeds.

And when it doesn't work, we get peeved and we can't figure out why. This is working for everyone else, we might think, so why not for us? A Baptist woman, years after her minister asked, "Do you love Jesus and want to follow him?" realized that "They might just as well have asked me if I loved Panky [her stuffed panda]. It would have meant the same thing to me." If they're going to ask you deep theological questions—well, "deep" for a twelve year old—then they had darn well better explain them to you beforehand.

There's a reason that every culture and faith has these ceremonies: we demand pauses and breathers along the arc of our lives. Without them, life would be a blur, a shapeless, endless stream of time and energy. These ceremonies provide the lulls, the repose, the time out, if you will, to consider where we're going and why; and where we've come from and why; and what the rhythm of life is and why. As the hurdy-gurdy of life accelerates in our ever more "modern" age, it's a relief to be thrown back—at least momentarily—on the steadier rock where time slows down to a sweet, lovely crawl and we are almost palpably certain that we are not alone, that countless generations before us have said the same prayers and been blessed in the same way, as will countless generations after us. The brilliance of these ceremonies is how well they connect us to an almost infinite DNA of time and space. They are our antennae outward, inward, and God-ward.

It's tempting to mistake these coming-of-age events for transformations, instant or otherwise. They're not. They can teach us and they can inspire us. (They can also bore the hell out of us.) What really matters is not how they instantaneously transfigure us—a specious claim, anyway—but what they're asking: "Who are you?" "Where are you?" These questions, says the Jewish philosopher Martin Buber, are "the beginning of the way. . . . We can let God in only where we really stand, where we live, where we live a true life. If we maintain holy discourse with the little world entrusted to us, . . . then we are establishing, in this our place, the Divine Presence."[3]

Without a way—a Muslim way, a Christian way, a Jewish way, a Hindu way, a Buddhist way—there's a chance that we will lose our way. These rituals are the maps to ourselves: they are an atlas of our soul. They introduce us to a Presence, and they introduce us to our self.

Around the globe, this introduction is done in many ways. In Zaire, teenage girls in the Bemba tribe catch water insects with their mouths and kill a tethered chicken by sitting on its head. In Gabon, ten-year-old boys drink a nauseating potion. If they vomit, adults chase them through the village, yelling, "You must die! You must die!" No one is actually killed, but a village full of grown-ups running amok is sufficiently scary to convince the boys—it's sufficiently scary to convince *anyone*—to drink the potion. Next, the boys are locked in a house full of ants. As the bugs bite the boys, their elders stand outside, chanting, "Now you must die. Now you must die," and the terror from the ants and the chanting and the pitch-blackness of the night and the boys screaming from their pain reaches an almost intolerable crescendo. But there's still no reprieve. For the next three months, the boys live in a cabin in the jungle—naked. They're painted white—the color of death for these people. At night, they can join the dances in the village, but they have to sleep back in the cabin. By the time they return to live in their village, they've proved their courage. They've faced death, and now they're ready for whatever comes before death.

And in Northern California, teenagers in some Native American tribes stay awake for several days. This is more than just not falling asleep. As the philosopher Mircea Eliade wrote, fighting exhaustion really means you're "being conscious, present in the world, responsible." The boys pull this off splendidly, largely because they help each other: talking and teasing and nudging each other and doing just about anything they can think of to stay awake. This is the power of community, of friendship, of having comrades who care about you as much as they care about themselves.[4]

We Westerners are proud of how we transmit religious culture. We like to think that we're kind, gentle, compassionate, that we don't harm anyone, that we're "civilized." We don't scare anyone out of their minds, like those kids in Gabon who are stuck in a cabin in the middle of the jungle for three months. And we don't circumcise teenagers, a painful practice common in Africa. We don't require teenage boys, as they do in the Ndembu tribe of Zambia, to drink powder made from the burned foreskins of previous initiates, thought to contain their ancestors' virility and to bestow energy, wisdom, and strength. Jews cut the foreskin of a boy when he's eight days old, certain that this seals the infant to his eternal covenant with God. But the Ndembu believe that a foreskin actually *contains* an inheritance— a covenant, of sorts; that it possesses the same substance that nourished the warriors and sages and chiefs who came long before them.

Initiations into today's world religions are much more tame. We induct youngsters by reading and studying and reciting texts and chanting prayers. Of course, we don't call these "incantations" or "spells" or "charms." That might sound much too "superstitious" from a Western perspective.

In his wonderfully tender memoir, *North toward Home,* the writer Willie Morris points out how faith can wear out after a while, especially for a boy like him—smart and ambitious and raised in a small town in Mississippi, where the only real exposure to religion came from weekly visits to the local Methodist church. "As a boy gets older," Morris wrote, "unless he has special inner resources, or a tailbone made of sheet-iron, or unless he gets saved by Billy Graham at twilight in a football stadium, the simple small-town faith starts wearing thin. . . . With me, the older religion gradually began to wither not as a result of the exercises of brain cells, or the enlightenment of civilized discourse, for I would not have known what that was, but from plain human boredom."[5]

We all get bored, and we all wonder from time to time what religion can really offer us, if the solace and comfort it sells is the genuine article, fit not just for eternity but for the present. In fact, eternity has vastly different meanings for youngsters whose faith and parents and community are all clamoring for an initiation of some kind, something that will signify the seriousness of this endeavor we call "life," with all its confusion and frustration and hope and disappointment. Sometimes, we find the answers we seek without religion, and without ever having one of these rites of passage. And that's fine. But when done right, and experienced right, and understood right, these events can be incorporated into our lives, maybe not the day they're celebrated, but slowly and almost invisibly—days afterward, years afterward. Then, the day *can* be a true turning—a turning toward God, toward ourselves, toward those "inner resources" that Willie Morris recalled so sweetly and so gently.

That's where the real power of these days lies, not so much in their pomp or their ceremony, but in what they transmit and endow. They can fill us with grace and maybe with understanding. They can help us embrace life and shape life—our life. Minus this grace and understanding, we muddle along, doing the best we can. When these events work—really work—when they shift our awareness and our psyche and cohere us to our faith and our people, when they open the door of wonder that's waiting for us, then we have the wind at our backs—the wind of our God, our traditions, our people. That's better than walking upright and alone into the nonstop gale we call "life."

PART ONE

CHRISTIANITY

Soldiers for Christ

Come Holy Ghost, Creator blest,
And in our hearts take up thy rest;
Come with thy grace and heav'nly aid
To fill the hearts which thou hast made.

CATHOLIC HYMN

As I went down to the river to pray,
Studying about that good old way
And who shall wear the robe and crown,
Good Lord, show me the way.
Oh brother, let's go down,
Let's go down, come on down.
Oh brother, let's go down,
Down in the river to pray.

TRADITIONAL AMERICAN GOSPEL SONG

1

THE DESCENT OF THE SPIRIT

Sarah Fisher was a happy fifteen year old. The week before, she'd rejected a friend who'd offered her marijuana. It's tough: when you're in high school these days, pot is everywhere—people are smoking and dealing and whispering about what's better, the stuff from Mexico or the stuff that someone's cousin grew in his basement. This is the currency of hip youth, yet all Sarah wanted to do was say "no." She wanted to say "never." She wanted to say "not me, not you, not anyone." But that's so uncool, so dorky. Geeks say that. Moms say that. Narcs say that. Not sophomores. Not friends. Which left Sarah pretty much on her own. Not quite a pariah, but not in the in-crowd, either. Sort of in between. But now, Sarah had finally found her ally, her confidante, her friend for life: the Holy Spirit.

Turning away her buddy because of pot was hard enough: they'd been pals since sixth grade. But Sarah knew that life would get harder: it always does. Ahead was college, love, marriage, children, heartache—all the reckonings that life either blesses us with or denies us. To some extent, we all move in our own orbits, our own tracks, and now Sarah, reinforced by the Spirit, was alone no more. She was ready for the long haul, and she knew she would always have a companion—a divine companion—by her side.

Minutes before I met Sarah, she'd been confirmed with sixty-five other teens in a church in the Virginia suburbs of Washington, D.C., a spacious house of worship with exposed wooden beams and lots of light streaming through the windows: a pleasant and unassuming place, where magic was struck whenever there was a confirmation. The previous week, Sarah hadn't yielded to her pot-smoking friend, and already, a few minutes after her confirmation, strengthened and emboldened by the Spirit, she was ready for "mortal combat" with *anyone* foolish enough to try to lead her astray. *That* was magic.

One sign that Sarah had been infused with the Spirit was that she was already anticipating the future. Most teenagers can't see beyond the present—their sights don't extend over that horizon. Unlike them, Sarah had perspective. "If I didn't do this," she said firmly, "I'd feel empty when I got married." With that declaration of ultimate intent, one that looked down the road of her life with a maturity a few leaps ahead of her relatively scant decade and a half, Sarah, her parents, and some family friends went to a nearby Outback Steakhouse for dinner—steaks for two people, surf and turf for two others, a thick piece of salmon for the lone semi-vegetarian. Over dinner, Sarah's father said how much her confirmation pleased him. "It fulfilled an obligation that I, as a Catholic parent, had to my daughter," he reflected. "It was also really the first opportunity for Sarah to have any meaningful say in deciding her religious identity, in deciding how she will acknowledge that there are deeper levels of reality. Coming to grips with this is crucial for truly centering your life. The spiritual need—the divine spark—in each of us must be nourished or our lives are barren."[1]

Forty-nine years separated Sarah's confirmation from her father's—his was in Grosse Point, Michigan, in 1955. It was inevitable that they'd prepared for their confirmations differently—the church had changed immensely in that half century. "Sarah studied more Scripture," he said, "and she had more discussions aimed at understanding. I memorized more questions and answers, virtually none of which I can remember now. I was happy that I answered all the questions and very impressed with the light slap on the cheek from the bishop, a symbol that we may have to go through hard knocks, and even be a martyr, to be Catholic. Now I think 'martyrdom' can be so much more subtle and insidious than simply being physically persecuted for the faith. Spiritual martyrdom is real in our society, especially today."[2]

The Spirit that descended into Sarah Fisher was formerly known as the

"Holy Ghost." The name was changed because, as one priest told me, "it sounded too much like Casper," the friendly cartoon ghost. Apparently, "spooky" is not a desirable quality when trying to convince youngsters that the religious life is the good life.[3]

Whatever it's called, at any confirmation, the Spirit descends as a bishop lays his hands on the youngsters, asking God to send His Holy Spirit upon them to be their helper and guide. As he gently presses oil onto the forehead of each confirmand, the Spirit's seven gifts descend—wisdom, knowledge, understanding, courage, reverence, wonder, and awe—all buffering the teenager against the ways of the world.[4]

Sarah Fisher may have been the exception: she felt that Spirit, wanted that Spirit, needed that Spirit. But sitting next to me at the rear of the confirmation hall were three twelve-year-old girls, all confirmed the year before. They hadn't necessarily enjoyed it, but it was part, they said, of being Catholic, and that's what Catholics did. And their parents insisted on it anyway. It was as simple as that.

"But did you feel the presence of the Holy Spirit at your confirmation?" I inquired, pressing them gently for some sense of how they'd responded to the ceremony. Wasn't the Spirit what this was all about? Being strengthened, fortified, armored against the world, protected against sinners and temptations, inspired by the Good News and the Holy Presence? They all giggled, thinking me silly. "Of course not," said one girl, whose skimpy skirt was slightly out of place in a church on a lovely Sunday afternoon. "That stuff's for little kids."

Then she ran off, catching up with her friends, who were sauntering along to the modest reception in the banquet room. They were trying to look sophisticated while intuiting that at least a decade lay ahead of them before they really had a claim on sophistication—with or without the intervention of the Spirit.

The year before, in England, I met a much younger Anglican who had a healthier perspective on the descent of the Spirit. "I really expected to be suddenly enlightened," admitted nine-year-old Lauren. "This did not happen, and I came to realize that the influence of the Holy Spirit is not felt immediately, but over time." Indeed, and that time varies for everyone. For all we know, by now little Lauren may be completely enveloped by the Holy Spirit—a veritable warrior for Christ before she's even reached her first decade. Or she could be as patient and wise as she was on the day of her confirmation, knowing that all comes in due time and with due reason.

One problem when talking about Christian initiations is that they are the most varied of all the major religions. And they're held at different times, which does not ease the confusion. Only Catholics and Anglicans have confirmations, and they're invariably for no one younger than nine or older than sixteen. Every denomination has baptisms—some reserve them for newborns, while others only baptize teenagers. A few baptize younger children or baptize people as often as they want. Every branch of Christianity offers first communion, and most have a first confession. Quakers, being perennial outsiders, have absolutely nothing that's mentioned in this paragraph.

This variety has much to do with how Christianity evolved. To create their new religion, Christians borrowed three rites that had been buried deep in Judaism. For centuries, Jews baptized either new converts or Jews who had sinned or been sick as a way to welcome them back into the community. Communion can be traced back to an ancient Jewish custom: communing with ancestors through a meal. And confirmation is a version of the ancient Jewish tradition of anointing males with oil to their foreheads when they become mature.

Christians took all this and made something new. Baptism became more miraculous and penetrating: a way to reach into the soul and purge the sin and transgression of rebelling against God, of balking at God's rightful rule over His creation and forgetting that we're mere stewards and caretakers—cogs, if you will, of his great plan. Baptisms cleansed and refreshed and renewed: you were beginning a new life, a fresh life, a life radically different from before.[5]

The first generations of Christians took the Jewish ceremony of anointing with oil and laying on of hands and turned it into their confirmation ritual, which was eventually reserved for young adolescents. What was being confirmed were the promises that a proxy for these children had made at their baptisms. These babies hadn't been able to swear that they would be faithful to God; they didn't even know who God was. So adults did it for them. Now the babies—all grown up—could make their own commitment to Jesus.

And communion became a way to bring people closer to Christ—closer, in fact, than anyone had been when Jesus was alive. Wine and wafer transubstantiated into Jesus' own blood and body, and people literally absorbed their Messiah into themselves. Catholics still believe this and still rely on this. As the Southern writer Flannery O'Conner said: "If the Host is only a symbol, I'd say the Hell with it." She never did. And then there was the young girl in Belfast who took communion for the first time in the 1970s. Furious that the day was ruined when a boy threw a water balloon at her pretty new dress, she vowed revenge—on Jesus, who should have protected her. Messiahs are supposed to do that. How can you say you're saving the world if bullies are still picking on little girls? The next week, she promised herself, she would give Jesus' flesh a good chewing when the priest handed out communion. Apparently, she figured that would teach Jesus not to slack off.[6]

Let's look at these initiations one by one, starting with baptism and working our way back to confirmation, where we'll rejoin Sarah Fisher and her anti-drug campaign of one. That way, we'll get a sense of how each plays out with Christians at different moments in their lives—cleansing their souls, strengthening their resolve, readying them for this world and the next one with a succession of charged illuminations and blessed transportations.

Baptism—the one almost-indispensable initiation for joining Jesus—is central to becoming a Christian; for Christians, in fact, it's almost central to being human. After a particularly unpleasant experience, someone might say, "I need to take a bath—I feel dirty all over." After murdering Duncan, for instance, Lady Macbeth complained that "all the perfumes of Arabia will not sweeten this little hand." We want to be "sweet"—clean, worthy, pure (even after murdering someone)—and baptism reaches where words, prayers, and wishes cannot travel and penetrate. Sweeping away the detritus, it refreshes and renews us. It makes us whole again.

Baptism has been called the "door of the sacraments" and "the door of the church." Cynics have other names for it. H. L. Mencken called it the "water route to the celestial city," which sounds like a travelogue about Venice; and in the 1960s, Radio Moscow called it a "dangerous health menace" and blamed it for the short life span of Russians—an average of thirty-two years—under the czars, an era when nearly every Russian baby was baptized. If these children weren't among the thousands who soon died of pneumonia, then they suffered from "weak hearts" and "weak lungs" as adults—all, of course, stemming from their brief dunking as babies.[7]

It all started, as most things do in Christianity, with Jesus. John the Baptist, Jesus' cousin, suddenly appeared out of the desert, proclaiming "a baptism of repentance for the forgiveness of sins." John was a wonder—"clothed in camel's hair, a leather belt around his waist," and feeding only on "locusts and wild honey." People from throughout Judea, including, according to Mark, all the inhabitants of Jerusalem, came to see John and hear him preach and be immersed in the Jordan, a broad but otherwise unimpressive river in what is now northern Israel. Joining them, Jesus emerged from the water and saw "the heavens break open and the Spirit descend on him, like a dove. And a voice came from heaven: 'You are my beloved Son; in you I take delight.'" From there, the Spirit drove Jesus into the desert, where for forty days and forty nights, he held off the temptations of the devil, readying himself for the battles that lay ahead. Finally leaving the desert, he began his ministry, telling the people of Nazareth, "The Spirit of the Lord is upon me." Jesus preached, and he suffered, and the day before his crucifixion, he promised his disciples that the Spirit would not depart with his death. They, too, would sense, feel, and know it. It would not disappear with him: "You will receive power when the Holy Spirit comes down on you; then you are to be my witnesses." Forty days later, at the feast of Pentecost, exactly that happened: the Spirit filled the apostles, who began proclaiming "the mighty works of God," and anyone who accepted their preaching received the "gift of the Holy Spirit" upon being baptized.[8]

For the first three hundred years after Jesus' death, the relatively few people born as Christians were baptized on their deathbed, ensuring that no last-minute transgressions screwed up their afterlife. But after Christianity conquered the pagan world, baptisms flipped from the end of life to its beginning. The church, turning its attention inward, was infatuated with "original sin"—the new idea that everyone came into the world contaminated by the sins that Adam and Eve had generated when they disobeyed God. Suddenly, baptisms were touted as the cure for this cosmic infection.[9]

By the middle of the third century, church leaders weren't debating *whether* babies should be baptized. Baptism was now an infallible proposition of the church. Rather, church leaders had to figure out *when* babies should be baptized: two days after birth or eight days, which is when Jewish males were circumcised. They voted for the earlier time. Holding off baptism, even for a few days, was too risky: Who knew what kind of mischief those little tykes could get into? And finally, went one of the arguments, *every* baby was literally crying out to be baptized. The wailing that we usually associate with being hungry or soiled was really a plea to be baptized—*fast*—so they would be purged of the stain from that first sin. Those little babies, so new to the world, understood that life without baptism was really just a way station to hell. They might be newborns, but they weren't dummies.[10]

The severity of this damnation proved to be too much by the Middle Ages, when more compassionate theologians proposed the idea of limbo for unbaptized babies. Here, the tots would spend eternity in total happiness although they would be denied the presence of God and perfect communion with Christ. Protestant reformers eliminated limbo from their theology, but this imperfect, incomplete afterlife remained a staple of Catholicism until 2005, when the Vatican signaled that it, too, was excising limbo from its architecture of the cosmos. This was a nod to reality: few Catholics were taking limbo seriously. As Rev. James Martin, the editor of the Jesuit publication *America,* said, "I've rarely baptized a baby where [limbo] has not come up, at least as a joke." It was also done as an empathic gesture: In 2004 Pope John Paul II had charged the church's International Theological Commission with devising "a more coherent and enlightened way" of describing the fate of blameless, innocent infants who die without a baptism.[11]

One possible unintended side effect of this newfound grace is that the urgency that previously enveloped baptism may fade. And with that, the generosity of Rome may eclipse the indispensability of a ceremony that assured endless generations of Christians that they were more than the elect. They were the saved.

As Christianity developed, so too did styles for baptizing. Catholics, Lutherans, and Episcopalians are sprinkled with water; Baptists (and many other Christians) are immersed in it. These differences started with the Roman emperor Constantine. On the eve of a major battle in 312 C.E., Constantine had a vision of a cross bearing this inscription: "Conquer with this!" He won the battle, Christianity won his heart, and Rome had a new state religion. Almost overnight, it was mandatory to baptize babies, a policy so successful that, by the close of the fourth century, nearly 90 percent of the empire's population was Christian. Most had been baptized as infants. Not Constantine. It was common for Roman generals and politicians, the kind of people who fought military campaigns or carried out capital punishments, to delay their baptisms until close to death so *all* their sins would be expunged. Constantine did the same. On his deathbed in 337 C.E., he was too weak to be moved and too fragile to be immersed. Instead, water was sprinkled on him, the drops rinsing away sixty-four years of scheming, warring, plotting, and killing. Hours later, he died.[12]

This new form of baptizing caught on, although the vocabulary didn't change: *rantizo,* Greek for "sprinkle," has never displaced *baptizo,* Greek for "immerse." Whether one is sprinkled or dunked, the meaning is the same. The ultimate difference lies in the timing, not in the quantity of water. For Baptists, the "age of accountability"—when they can begin to understand Jesus—is usually somewhere between nine and twelve years old. At this point you can be baptized, although as a Baptist minister half-jokingly admitted, "You can be baptized at any age, as long as you can hold your breath." Predictably, the younger the child, the more reluctant the minister is to baptize him. A few years ago, for instance, when a five year old in Baltimore came forward to be baptized, his minister was not sure what to do: five year olds have little sense of salvation and sin and Jesus' sacrifice at Calvary. In the end, the minister followed a colleague's advice: "Baptize the boy. He's making a commitment with everything he has right now. If you don't do it, you'll be rejecting him, and that pain will be with him the rest of his life."[13]

The boy, who is still a good member of his church, taught his minister, a truly humble man, that the spirit moves at its own pace, one that may confound the usual ways of the church but pleases, as far as we can tell, a Creator who, apparently, has an impeccable and unknowable sense of timing.

The staging of baptisms can be grandiose or simple. Some Baptist churches feature a baptismal seat poised on a lever—down and up, in and out, and presto! You have been cleansed. The baptismal font in one Southern church could have doubled as a prop in an Andrew Lloyd Weber play: a black light—black for "sinner"—shines after someone enters the font; a red light—red for "blood," since the prophet Isaiah said, "Your sins be as scarlet"—blazes as sins are being washed away; and a white light—white for purity—dazzles with the glory of salvation as the newly baptized person leaves the font, pure and clean. More low-budget, rural churches have baptisms in shallow streams or rivers, which may vaguely resemble the Jordan River where Jesus was baptized. The imagery is potent: nature can do more for any soul than black and red spotlights. But outdoor baptisms can be risky. In the 1960s in Kentucky, a preacher scurried downstream with a long stick to retrieve a wig that had floated away from a woman he'd just baptized. Apparently, even people seeking salvation want to look their best.

Oddly, macabre dangers lurk in indoor baptisteries, the large fonts that you'd think would be safer than streams or rivers. In late October 2005, a minister standing waist deep in the baptistery in University Baptist Church in Waco, Texas, was fatally electrocuted as he adjusted his microphone. Rev. Kyle Lake, who was only thirty-three years old, left behind a wife, a five-year-old daughter, and twin three-year-old boys. Luckily, the woman being baptized had not yet stepped into the water. The congregation, shaken and shattered, was determined to carry on. "I don't know how, when, why, where or what's going to happen," Ben Dudley, an administrator of the church, told a thousand people at a remembrance service for Rev. Lake, "but we will continue as a church in this community because that is what Kyle would have wanted." Despite such rare tragedies, Baptists have given no thought to adopting the Catholic mode of baptism. Sprinkling may be safer, but it is surely less authentic than the immersion method, used by John to baptize Jesus in the shallow currents of the Jordan River.[14]

Ordinarily, the Vatican recognizes Protestant baptisms, but not for Jean-Jacques Rousseau. In 1728, when he was fifteen, motherless, and abandoned by his father, Rousseau ran away from his apprenticeship to an engraver, a mean old man who physically punished him for the slightest infractions. Maybe because of his age or maybe because of his temperament, Rousseau appears to have impetuously decided to leave his homeland and his faith. Stealing away from Geneva, he meandered through the duchy of Savoy, where a Catholic priest whom Rousseau impressed suggested he head to the cathedral town of Annecy, where a benevolent lady might take him under her protection as well as lead him toward the Roman Church. In Annecy, he stayed briefly with Françoise-Louise-Éléanore

de la Tour, the baroness of Warens, who was delighted that such a precocious lad from Switzerland, a nation steeped in Protestantism, was so interested in Catholicism, the sworn enemy of the Reformation.

The authenticity of this overnight religious turnaround can be doubted.
As Leo Damrusch says in his definitive biography *Jean-Jacques Rousseau:
Restless Genius,* "It was a major step to desert Calvinism in favor of the enemy it routinely denounced as the Whore of Babylon. Strictly speaking,
this was not apostasy, since . . . [Rousseau] had not been confirmed and
admitted to communion in Geneva. . . . All the same, it was a striking re-
pudiation of the culture in which he had been raised, and in his unfinished
last work he was still brooding about his defection. He settled on his favorite explanation of submission to external pressure: 'Still a child and left
to myself, enticed by caresses, seduced by vanity, lured by hope, forced by
necessity, I became a Catholic.'"[15]

The baroness sent Rousseau to Turin, the capitol of the Savoy, to complete his conversion. The city—three times larger than Geneva, its opulence
and wealth taking their cues from its elegant court—stunned Rousseau,
who was unaccustomed to such show and glamour. He was immediately
taken to the Hospice of the Catechumens, the place for persons seeking
religious instruction. The large wooden doors were locked behind him,
not to be opened until priests determined that his conversion was complete. An aged priest set to work on Rousseau, but since the young Gen-
evese had some theological knowledge and was prone to argue, he was
quickly passed along to a younger, brighter priest, who countered Rousseau's quibbles with quotes from Saints Augustine and Gregory. Rousseau
later claimed that he had stayed at the hospice for two months, but records
show that he abjured the Protestant faith a mere nine days after arriving
and was baptized two days later. Then, the vicar general of the Holy Office
of the Inquisition quizzed Rousseau on his new faith. Dissatisfied with
Rousseau's answers, the vicar ordered that he be rebaptized, apparently
thinking that the holy water would clinch the deal: whatever the priests
hadn't taught him, the waters would. With that, Rousseau later wrote,
"They advised me to live as a good Christian and be faithful to grace; they
wished me good luck, they closed the door on me, and everyone disappeared." He was alone, he was Catholic, and he was almost broke. But he
was thrilled to be out of the hospice, and the priests were possibly even
more delighted that another Protestant had seen the true light of the pa-

pacy, and that the waters of baptism had thoroughly and conclusively done their job.[16]

More important than the stagecraft of a baptism is how it affects people. The currents of baptism are deep and unpredictable, with baptism at birth sometimes making a surprisingly significant dent on our souls. Louis IX of France, for instance, relished the baptism that he could not even remember above all else. "I think more of the place where I was baptized," rhapsodized Louis IX, "than I do of the Cathedral of Rheims where I was crowned the king. It is a greater thing to be a child of God than to be the ruler of a kingdom. The latter I shall lose at death; the former will be my passport to everlasting glory."

Louis was so devout that he never signed himself as "Louis, King," but as "Louis of Poissy," after the town south of Paris where he'd been baptized in 1214. Tutored in Latin and the arts of war and government, Louis was raised by his mother, Queen Blanche, to be above all in awe of anything related to religion. "I love you, my dear son," she often said as he was growing up, "but I would rather see you dead at my feet than that you should commit a mortal sin." (Affection in the royal household was apparently confused with a surfeit of piety.) Throughout his reign, Louis made his mother proud, protecting vassals from oppression by their lords, reforming the legal system so every citizen had a better chance of receiving justice, and founding a hospital for poor blind men and a home for reformed prostitutes. Beggars were fed from the king's table, and Louis ate their leftovers and washed their feet. He was probably the only king in Europe who heard two masses daily and traveled with priests who chanted the hours.[17]

This was no ordinary monarch, and it's hard to know what other kings thought of him, besides simply noting that his reputation was so impeccable that foreign rulers regularly approached him to arbitrate their disputes. Louis's zeal, in fact, may have encouraged Baudoin II, the emperor of Constantinople, to approach him about buying relics associated with the Passion of Christ. (The bankrupt emperor was happier to part with his holy possessions than risk the embarrassment of going belly up.) In 1241 Louis paid the equivalent of $200,000 for Christ's crown of thorns, a nail from the Cross, and actual fragments from the Cross itself—the holiest pieces of lumber in history. They were transferred to Paris, where Louis began constructing a shrine worthy of them—the Sainte Chapelle. One hundred feet long and fifty-five feet wide, the chapel was placed in the courtyard of the royal palace, which was then on the Ile de la Cité. The chapel, a bejeweled reliquary for the greatest treasures in all Christendom, was a fitting gift to the followers of Jesus from a king whose entire life had changed as he was dipped into a baptismal font in Poissy.[18]

Unfortunately, most of the chapel's relics have disappeared. During the French Revolution, mobs grabbed them—selling some, trashing others, losing most. The few that survived—a nail from the Cross and a piece of the Cross itself—were eventually housed at Notre Dame Cathedral, where they can be seen today.

Six centuries later, a New England poet was dismayed that her parents and their Congregationalist minister had tried to determine her fate by baptizing her when she was a baby: "I've stopped being theirs," Emily Dickinson wrote when she was thirty-two,

The name they dropped upon my face,
With water in the country church . . .
Baptized, before, without the choice.

Dickinson decided to live by *her* design, pursuing salvation on her terms and not yielding to what her elders deemed best. A weaver of rhythms and words, she was wresting her life (and her destiny) from the font where she'd been baptized. For her, Jesus was life and always would be. But the "original sin" which had been "washed away" in Amherst's Congregational church was balderdash. Baptism wouldn't save her, she figured, because these waters were dammed up by narrow minds and constricted imaginations. Only she could save herself, and that she would do, as she wrote in another poem, by "dwell[ing] in possibility . . . to gather Paradise."[19]

But delaying baptism by a few years does not necessarily guarantee that it will be any more warmly embraced than it was by Emily Dickinson. In August 1973, for instance, a nine-year-old girl who would never have the wealth of Louis IX or the fame of Emily Dickinson was "absolutely frightened" at her baptism in Knoxville, Tennessee. Luckily, her fear was abated by sharing the stage with "my three good friends—Suzanne, Christy, and Lisa. We wore white robes that tied around our waists. When our turn came, we walked the five steps into the baptismal font, which was about eight by eight feet. The preacher—*never* a woman in the wealthy Southern Baptist church—covered my mouth and nose with a handkerchief, and I tried to keep my feet down and bend my knees, because that's what I'd been told to do. He said those magic words as I held my breath, and he dunked me backward into the water. I wanted to smile at my mother, whom I saw just out of the corner of my eye. But I caught her mouthing, 'Don't smile.' The preacher pulled me back up and said some more words, which I couldn't hear because water was in my ears. Suddenly, I was free to go. I walked up the five stairs on the other side of the font, where my mother dried me off with a towel. Not long after that, we went home for a reception, mostly cake and coffee, something, really, more for the grownups than for me or my friends."[20]

In a slightly faded color photo taken at the reception back home, Michelle Duvall is standing behind a folding bridge table. Everything around her is bare—no tablecloth, no pictures on the wall a few feet behind her, no furniture in the tightly cropped picture relieve the surreal spookiness of seeing her almost suspended in time and space, captive to what her parents wanted and to what she had acquiesced. The brown on the wall, on the table, on the few inches of carpet caught by the lens is relieved by her white dress trimmed with yellow; by two white candleholders, each holding a lit yellow candle; by a yellow doily under a white platter which is holding, of course, a brown cake—a chocolate cake. Also, she is positively beaming, although in later years she would measure the day with a more biting, more acerbic calculation that the entire production had been waged more for her mother and for appearances than for her own soul. "I'm not sure that *anyone* in my immediate family knew what it meant to take Jesus as your personal savior," she said in 2005. "All I did know was that baptism made sure I wouldn't go to Hell. Being at the church almost every single day affected me more than the baptism. I went there Sunday morning for Bible class and services, and Sunday evening for advanced Bible class, and Wednesday evening for services, and several nights a week for teen club and puppet club and clown club. Around seventh grade, I began realizing that this wasn't working for me. I couldn't understand how there could be a 'forgiving' God *and* a Hell. I couldn't stomach that too many people were either avoiding my questions or giving me cant.

"My mother says I'm a Christian because I received Jesus at my baptism. 'Once saved, always saved.' It didn't bring me closer to God. If I'd been baptized when I was in fifteen or sixteen, at least I would have been more conscious of it. But that doesn't mean it would have meant any more to me."[21]

By the time she was nineteen, a full decade after her baptism, Michelle could not wait to leave her faith and her region. Nothing of endurance had come from church, baptism, or mother. Ready for what lay beyond these borders, she would not settle for a world with a church that never spoke to her, a baptism that hadn't moved her, and a mother who, she sadly realized, had never heard her.

Surprisingly, anyone can perform a baptism: Christians, pagans, heretics, atheists, even people from other faiths. All that's required is the right intention; the words "I baptize thee in the name of the Father and the Son and the Holy Spirit"; and almost any kind of water—salt water, marsh water, mineral water, dew, melted snow, melted hail. In a pinch, soda water will do.[22]

Letting anyone say that prayer, summon that intent, and sprinkle that water has produced all kinds of mischief. I know an eighty-year-old woman in Brooklyn—a devout Catholic who has never missed a Sunday service or a weekly confession, even as her husband was giving more hours to the racetrack than to church. His wife, knowing he would never consent to having their five kids baptized, carried each one, within days after their birth, into the bathroom, closed the door, sprinkled some tap water on them, and whispered, "I baptize thee in the name of the Father and the Son and the Holy Ghost." Years later, her husband learned what she had done and stormed out of the house. Soon his betting—and his losses— increased. The only possible benefit was that he was remembering the name of the Lord more often; unfortunately, that was usually as a curse every time one of his horses came in last.

One notorious case of baptism gone awry involved Edgardo Mortara— a six-year-old Jewish boy in Italy whose family's servant girl claimed she had secretly baptized him when he was a baby. He was very ill, she said later, and she was worried that if he died, he would go to Hell. In 1858, hearing about the baptism, Catholic authorities kidnapped the boy. This was in accord with the papal law which ruled that part of Italy: the baptism had made him Christian, and Jews were forbidden from raising Christians, even their own children. Jews were especially alarmed about Edgardo's kidnapping, not just because their own children were now in constant danger, but, as David Kertzer writes in *The Kidnapping of Edgardo Mortara,* "Having endured centuries of forced sermons . . . and having been brought up on cautionary tales of fanatic converts torching Talmuds and baptizing hapless Jewish children, . . . [the Jews] knew just what kind of devil Edgardo . . . could turn into."[23]

Throughout Europe, Protestants demonstrated and diplomats protested. Thinly veiled plays based on Edgardo's kidnapping were produced in Paris, Milan, and New York, with the American performance pandering to the anti-Catholic tide sweeping the United States: a mad pope screams for inquisitors to "imprison every Jew" and Edgardo's father's fingers are dislocated and hot oil is poured on his arms. Worse is threatened for little Edgardo: "to rack thy son and burn his eyeballs out, to flay his feet and make him walk on sand, to roast his flesh and lay him on crushed glass." In all these plays, Edgardo is part victim, part villain, with the Jews in particular fearing that the boy will grow into an unwitting weapon in the campaign to convert them to Christ, and everyone but Catholics deeming Edgardo's "rescue" as nothing more than a glorified kidnapping.[24]

Also in Manhattan, two thousand people swarmed to a rally, where the pope was denounced as the "Prince of Darkness" and a Jewish humorist cleverly asked the crowd, "What would happen if a band of Jews sneaked into the Vatican, . . . seized the Pope, held him down and circumcised him? Surely, that would not make a Pope a Jew, any more than the sprinkling of water made a child of a Jew a Christian."[25]

Edgardo stayed with the pope, living in various Catholic boarding schools and sometimes in the Vatican itself, always under the protection of the Holy Father, who thundered that he "couldn't care less what the world thinks." Eventually, Edgardo became a priest. Confirming Jews' initial fears that he would become one of the Vatican's more insidious weapons against them, he specialized in missionizing to the Jews. He was formidable as a propagandist for the church, evidence that at least one Jew who had seen the light was basking in it. But not every Catholic endorsed Edgardo's efforts to brings Jews to the church. When he came to New York in 1897 to evangelize among the city's Jews, the local archbishop blocked his efforts, saying they embarrassed the church.[26]

Edgardo died in a monastery in Belgium in 1940, an eighty-eight-year-old man who'd been happily devoted to his "second father"—Pius IX; who'd preached fervently about the power, love, and compassion of Jesus Christ; and who had been "saved" by an illiterate servant girl who'd sprinkled water on him when no one was looking, taking upon herself the authority, indeed the privilege, of salvaging his young, impressionable, and otherwise doomed soul.

Protestants cringe at transubstantiation—the Catholic belief that communion *is* Christ. For Protestants, communion is a symbol, an image, a rough and never-quite-sufficient apprehension of their Lord: for them it was sufficient that Jesus had come to earth. *That* was the miracle. Having Jesus return in mass after mass, communion after communion, would cheapen that miracle. It would also cheapen the faith of anyone taking communion: you don't need Jesus' body or blood to accept the Resurrection. That's so empirical that it's almost in another category from faith.

But whether as a symbol or real blood and real flesh, taking communion for the first time, usually when you're seven or eight, can be a moving experience, even if youngsters really don't understand what they are doing. For years, they watched everyone else in church take communion. Now it's their turn to enter the mystery, which they do with excitement and anticipation and, if they're Catholic, some apprehension. It's one thing to pray to God. It's another to absorb Him.

For many families, first communion is a chance to explain to your child—and yourself—what you believe and why, something impossible at an infant baptism. And it can help you reassess why you belong to a church or why you don't. When it was time, for instance, for their daughter to have her first communion, the Leonards of Long Island balked. For years they had skirted around organized religion, and now that Annie was seven, it was time to make some type of commitment. "If we ever wanted Annie to know what it meant to be Catholic," Joan Leonard said, "we couldn't skip her first communion."[27]

They shopped around for churches in their part of Long Island, settled on St. Anthony's, and enrolled Annie in the twelve sessions of instruction that would qualify her for communion. Annie hated it. Few of her friends were Catholic, and none of them went to St. Anthony's. She only perked up in her classes at St. Anthony's when she got to color the saints in the prayer book. She was bored, and everyone knew it. "What'd you learn today, Annie?" her father would ask when she got home. "Um, forgiveness," Annie would mutter. "Can I go roller-blading now?" So much for a theological discussion.

Unexpectedly, Annie's classes brought her mother back to religion. Going to the church so often reminded her of "the artifacts of my childhood— the fonts, the missals, the scapulars, the rosaries." One day, Joan spotted a small statue of her patron saint on a high shelf in the church gift shop— St. Joan, "tall and fierce in her green pants and royal blue tunic. . . . Despite my long struggle with my own faith, the belief that someone or something should protect us . . . from all the harm in the world beckoned to me." Joan paid $57 and returned home with the Maid of Orleans.

When her communion day finally arrived, Annie wore a lovely white dress and a veil and everyone gushed over her. Annie ate it up—until they got to the church and she ripped off the veil. "I'm not wearing it," she announced. "It itches. None of my friends have to do this. Nobody on our block is here. I'm the only one here."

Joan prayed, then quietly said, "You're not the only one here, honey. Take a look at these." She pulled three photos out of her purse. There was Annie's great-grandmother, young and somber in high-button shoes; and Annie's grandmother, serene and poised, except for the veil that had slid down to her eyebrows; and Annie's mother, a 1950s tomboy forcing a smile for the camera. Each photo had been taken at first communion.

Looking at the pictures, Annie asked, "So all the girls in our family made their first communion?" When her mother nodded, Annie said, "Then I'll be the fourth. At least my veil isn't as bad as Grandma's."

Joan secured Annie's veil, and a few minutes later, she and her husband walked Annie down the aisle as the priest recited, "Let us proclaim the mystery of the faith."

Annie's communion brought Joan's family back to church. This time, they stayed. All of them. "We rediscovered," Joan said, "a Catholicism that was more about love than guilt or fear. I guess St. Joan is still watching over us."

And then there's confirmation, the final ritual, in many Christian denominations, for coming of age. For centuries, confirmation meant accepting the catechism—fully and faithfully and unquestioningly and unswervingly. This was the stuff of truth and doctrine, a compilation of questions and answers—anywhere from a few hundred to two thousand (the record was set in 1891 by the Baltimore Catechism)—that cover the practical ("At prayer, the most becoming position of the body is kneeling upright"), the theological (Adam's sin "darkened our understanding, weakened our will, and left in us a strong inclination to evil"), and the cautionary ("we must accept . . . [the Catholic Church's] teaching as our infallible rule of faith"). Youngsters were terrified that at their confirmation, the bishop would ask—in front of the entire congregation—*any* question from the catechism, and that the only acceptable response was the one they'd memorized word-for-word in class.[28]

Archbishop William H. Cardinal Keeler of Baltimore, who was confirmed in 1939 while in second grade at St. Matthias School in Bala Cynwyd, a suburb of Philadelphia, still remembers some of the questions and answers more than half a century after the event. The entire confirmation, in fact, still lives in Keeler's memory, although he is now in his late sixties: "The sister who prepared us for it did it with a lot of enthusiasm. We were told we were going to receive a special gift of the Holy Spirit to strengthen us, to make us a 'soldier of Christ.' This military terminology was from the Baltimore Catechism, which had been prescribed by the plenary of Baltimore in 1884. I didn't know that at the time, of course.

"For the confirmation, we were dressed in our school uniforms—the boys in white shirts and blue ties and the girls in white shirts and pleated skirts—and we filled up the front pews in the church, the boys on one side of the aisle and the girls on the other. The organ music was uplifting, and everybody was singing, and the prayers were in Latin, and when we said, 'Amen,' we could feel that the Lord was near. The bishop made a sign with the holy chrism, or oil, on our foreheads, followed by a slap—a ceremonial slap—to remind us that we should be willing to suffer for our faith. People would later say, 'Oh, my! A slap!' It was a gentle slap, although it was electrifying because we knew what the symbolism meant: that we should be ready to suffer.

"It made a tremendous impact on us. I don't think I would have said to someone, 'You can't do that because you were just confirmed.' But I did say to myself, 'I better do what Mother or Dad tells me to do because that's one way to show that I'm following through on my confirmation.' Now being a 'soldier for Christ' meant we had to do the right thing as almost a public person now, not just a private person."[29]

These days, churches care more about understanding catechism than memorizing it, and bishops rarely grill the youngsters who are being confirmed. The entire confirmation, in fact, is more relaxed. Catholics, for instance, are no longer called "soldiers of Christ," a slogan that sounded as if they should be ready to slip on a suit of armor and head off to the latest crusade. Rather, the slogan meant that they should be ready to do battle with their "spiritual enemies"—soul against soul and heart against heart. In the 1980s the phrase was dropped as too shrill, too strident: an image from another era. The loss was not much lamented.

It's the rare youngster who has the strength and willpower *not* to be confirmed. Going against the grain is not quite heresy, but it's not blessed, either. Over a decade ago, Brittany Kirsch was about as good a Catholic girl as you could find on the Caribbean island of St. Thomas. Always bright—she entered first grade when she was four and would enter college when she was sixteen—she attended parochial school and thrived there. The services every Sunday in Cathedral of St. Peter and St. Thomas were "illuminated," she recalls, "with extraordinary stained glass windows." In sixth grade, Kirsch spent weekends with the nuns who were her teachers, sleeping at their convent and assisting them at a shelter for battered women, taking this so much to heart that she seriously deliberated spending her life as her nun friends did: devoted to God, "married" to Jesus, teaching kids like herself, and spreading joy and virtue among the poor and abused. The nuns handled this newfound ambition "appropriately," Kirsch says, "neither encouraging nor discouraging me or my best friend who was also doing this. They answered our questions honestly, and let us know it was something we would decide for ourselves when we were older. We had mass in the convent, just my friend and me and three or four nuns. It was odd to celebrate mass in such a small group. We also played board games and made meals and hung out. It was like a slumber party with a religious undertone."[30]

As Kirsch got older, her devotion gave way to doubt. While traveling with her family in the late 1970s, she attended church in Europe and North America, and a disturbing discrepancy emerged. "I understood that the pulpit in my church wasn't used as a bully pulpit. The homily was never about social issues. Rather, it was always about how to be a good Christian. This was almost in the abstract and had little to do with the world around us. In other countries, I heard homilies that were calls to social action," which mirrored her own progressive politics—women's equality in the church, gay rights, abortion rights. She yearned for a church that mustered the courage to speak truth to power and Gospel to poverty and inequality.

"I quickly understood," she says, "what it meant to be one of billions in a wider church, to belong to a church so heavily dominated by the pope. Before, I'd had a narrow appreciation of the church. Now, I began to believe that it was the church that was narrow."

When Kirsch was about fourteen, her church announced that catechism class would soon begin for teenagers intending to be confirmed. "Very consciously," she says, she decided to abstain. "There wasn't much discussion about this in my house." And there also wasn't much social cost: "My friends were curious about my decision, but I wasn't ostracized." From her vantage point, there wasn't much religious cost, either. Convinced that her relationship to God superseded her relationship to the church, she was certain that her connection to God would not change. She didn't necessarily need the church. She needed what the church promised, and she could find that herself.

Kirsch attended her friends' confirmation, the one she would have participated in had she followed church doctrine. "It was joyous," she recalls, "although I wanted to shake them and ask if they knew what they were doing. The bishop said the Holy Spirit was empowering them. The Spirit was in me, too. There's enough Spirit for everyone."

Sixteen years later, Kirsch is a medical researcher in a midsized city in New England. She attends a fairly liberal Catholic church that discusses—openly, sometimes fervently—such issues as gay rights and abolishing the death penalty. She does not regret missing her confirmation: her heart is firmly with God. But in some ways, the church, with its politics and rigid bureaucracy, intrudes on her intimacy with God, complicating an already inexplicable relationship, since communing with the divine is hard to attain and even harder to explain. She sometimes wonders why she continues her churchgoing. Habit? Perhaps. A link to her family and her youth and her ancestors? Possibly. The tendrils of faith have their own logic, impenetrable to outsiders and often almost as inexplicable to those who express that faith.

Kirsch may have mellowed since balking at being confirmed when she was a teenager. Now, she says, she would rethink having a confirmation, but only if her family made it clear that this was immensely important to them or if she was "seriously" dating a Catholic, since confirmation is required for a wedding in the church.

The one thing Kirsch regrets is that her decision hurt her godparents. "They feel like they failed," she said. "One of their 'duties' was to make sure I was confirmed. But I've told them many times that they were wonderful and that they gave me the best possible gift: they taught me how to think."

Maybe Kirsch did have a confirmation: a confirmation of knowledge, of taking on personal responsibility. Perhaps she was confirmed in the task of being herself, which is no light chore. And yet, if she had considered leaving Catholicism, the Quakers most likely would have opened their arms to her. While other Christians were arguing about the timing of baptisms and whether a few drops of water in the right hands can actually save souls, Quakers were content in having no outward baptisms, no confirmations, and *no* communion. In fact Friends, convinced that outer religious practices pale beside the inner light with which God communicates to us, have *no* rites and *no* sacraments.

This smacks of religious minimalism: less is more. Bauhaus meets God. It sounds Spartan, maybe severe, a rude rejection of how 99 percent of Christians celebrate their Lord and are waiting, patiently, for His return. But as Deborah Suess, a Quaker minister in Greensboro, North Carolina, explains, Quakers are not quite as plain as they appear. They do have rites. These are just more circumspect, more personal, more quiet than they are in other Christian denominations.

"Whenever anyone asks 'Do you have communion or baptism?'" explains Suess, "I always say, 'Yes, but it's an inward experience. It is our hope that communion takes place whenever we take a bite of anything or take a breath of air.' And Quaker meeting also provides a palpable sense of communion."[31]

Quakers, then, exalt in the ordinariness of the everyday: eating, breathing, walking, talking. In simple, modest gestures. In the grand hush of the light, which you enter with gratitude.

And yet, some Quaker meetings have events that resemble rites of passage. As teenagers approach the age of eligibility for the armed forces, their minister or a meeting elder may ask them to write a statement explaining their understanding of pacifism, a key belief among Friends. The ministers do this not only to help younger Quakers clarify their thoughts about the military, but also as a "matter of witness"—a carefully reasoned rejection of war and violence, refuted with a calm quiet that's as fierce and determined as any soldier in the thick of combat.

Some Quaker meetings ask teens who have been in the church for several years if they want to become members. If they respond "Maybe, but not now," the offer still stands. If they respond "No," then, says Suess, "We tell them we love them and that they can always worship with us." If they respond "Yes," they write a letter to the governing body of their local meeting explaining why they want to join. Two elders meet with them, probing their faith and gauging whether the Friends are a good fit for them. If the candidates progress beyond this point, they are officially welcomed as Friends at a Sunday meeting. It's all very simple. It's all very plain. No Holy Sprit descends. No wafers turn into the body of Christ. No wine magically transforms into the blood of Christ. No one is purged of sin and born anew. Sometimes a little quiet, a little light, and a lot of concentration can be as powerful as a cathedral full of bishops and cardinals or streams and rivers lined with people eager to be baptized. The Lord truly does move in mysterious ways.[32]

And then there are the Mormons—often misunderstood or misrepresented as a cult; or as non-Christian, even anti-Christian; or as a haven for polygamists. Members of the Church of Latter-Day Saints—not those who have been excommunicated for aberrations and heresies, for living on the wrong side of the law and the wrong side of God—have what's tantamount to several initiations. First there are a baptism and a confirmation. Mormons trace these back into uncharted, primeval history, with baptisms originating with God (not with Jesus or John the Baptist, as other Christians say) and with Adam, the first person, they say, to receive the sacrament. A decade or so after Mormons are baptized and confirmed, there is a demanding test of their commitment to the faith and of their understanding of it: a lengthy mission (twenty-four months for men, eighteen for women), often to another country and always away from home. The purpose is to spread the Word and gain converts. And finally, Mormons have an official induction—called "the endowment"—into the church itself. An endowment usually occurs before they embark on a mission or before they get married, whichever comes first. Receiving your endowment and, especially, baptism and confirmation is church doctrine—indispensable to salvation; being a missionary is fundamental to character building and faith testing.

Mormon males are "commanded" to go on missions, although that does not make them mandatory. "How could they be?" notes Kathryn Summers, a Mormon living in northern Maryland. "There's no enforcement of any commandment. We are also commanded to pay tithing, to avoid alcohol and tobacco, to attend church weekly, to be honest in all our interactions with others, to turn the other cheek, and so much more. The degree to which we obey God's commandments varies from person to person and from moment to moment."[33]

Men can go on missions after they turn nineteen. Women are eligible when they turn twenty-one, which is when Summers left her family's home in Silver Spring, Maryland, for Portugal—"an amazing, foundational experience," she states emphatically. Most of the time she was stationed in Lisbon, but for a few months she was located in two villages north of the city. No matter where she was, she lived and breathed Mormonism around the clock. Being a missionary is almost like being in a semi-cloistered monastery that lets you venture into the world: Summers rose at 6:30 in the morning and studied Scripture for two hours, then knocked on doors or introduced herself to people on the street, telling them about the church. Overall, she explained the basics of Latter-Day doctrine with these lessons, culminating in invitations to attend church, read the Book of Mormon, avoid harmful substances, and finally to be baptized and formally join the church.[34]

Summers worked nine to ten hours a day, with no TV and no movies and no dating, and had only a half-day off a week away to buy food and take care of laundry. Her focus was constantly on the church, on its teachings, on saving souls, on learning and knowing what she believed and why she believed it, and on "seeing," she said, "the choices that you make and that other people make and gaining a far deeper appreciation of human nature." Seventy-six people she taught came into the church, although she also vividly recalls discussions with one man that helped reconnect him with his own (non-Mormon) church. To her, the experience was less about swelling the ranks of the Saints than "about loving people. It was really, really hard work, and I was really exhausted. But I felt that people's happiness depended on what I did."[35]

The young man whom Summers would marry soon after returning from Portugal—John Friese—had spent his two years as a missionary in a locale far less exotic than Portugal: Charlotte, North Carolina. A convert to the church only two years before, he had the zealotry of a newcomer. "To me, this was a lifeboat, and people were sinking," he told me. "All I wanted to do was get people into the boat. I wanted them to have the same happiness that I had."[36]

Whether you're in Lisbon or North Carolina, missionaries have a baptism by fire: you're plunged into another world, an almost exclusively non-Mormon one. And you keep the faith. If all goes right, non-Mormons feel its heat and its balm and its strength. Confirmation and baptism are what cleanse and prepare you for this adventure. They make you worthy and pure and strong. With baptism, the sins *you* created—not inherited— are washed away, since Mormons don't subscribe to the notion of original sin. You're also now accountable for *all* your actions and mistakes and glories and accomplishments. And since the Latter-Day Saints have priests galore, many males have numerous opportunities to baptize someone, often a close relative, sometime during their life. Boys become deacons when they are twelve, preachers at fourteen, priests at sixteen, and elders at nineteen or older. Since a priest—any priest—can perform a baptism, it is not uncommon for fathers to baptize their own children and, sometimes, even for newly ordained sixteen-year-old priests to baptize their own siblings. That's what happened when Kathryn Summers's brother Michael, ordained for only a few months, baptized his eight-year-old sister, Lisa. This was the first baptism he performed and was a turning point for both him and Lisa. But since a priest who performs a baptism often feels a certain responsibility for shaping the character of the person he's initiated as well as for that person's safety, Michael—to this day—looks out for Lisa's well-being. Brother and sister, already joined by blood and by faith, are now knitted together, ever more tightly, by duty.[37]

Confirmation—essentially laying on of hands and receiving the gift of the Holy Ghost—is usually done immediately after baptism. If baptism is performed on a Saturday, then confirmation invariably takes place the next day during the congregational meeting. Only a priest who is in the highest category of Latter-Day Saints religious leaders—the Melchizedek priesthood—can officiate at a confirmation. Here, as in many aspects of doctrine, Mormons veer from traditional Christian teachings. In Genesis (14:18–20), Melchizedek appears to Abraham and is identified as "a priest of God Most High"; and five Psalms (110–14) name Melchizedek as a representative of the priestly line through which the future king of Israel's Davidic line was ordained; and since the New Testament (Hebrews 7:3) calls Melchizedek a king "without father or mother or genealogy," some Christians take this to mean that Melchizedek is truly an angel, not a mortal. Some even say that he is actually Jesus.[38]

With all this "heresy" arrayed against Mormons, most Christians reject Mormon confirmations and baptisms as null and void. Confirmations, because they are conducted by fraudulent priests who have usurped Jesus; baptisms, because, while the Mormon invocation at a baptism is virtually identical to what more mainstream Christians say, "I baptize you in the name of the Father, of the Son, and of the Holy Spirit," Mormons are not referring to the usual concept of the trinity. For other Christians, the trinity is three entities who comprise different qualities of *one* divinity; for Mormons, the trinity is three *separate* gods who come together, in effect, as one cooperative divinity. Realizing that, in 2001 the Vatican ruled that the Mormon trinity was so odd that "one cannot even consider this doctrine to be a heresy arising from a false understanding of Christian doctrine."[39]

The Vatican's ruling was especially severe since it reversed over a century of recognizing Mormon baptisms. Generally, the church, according to *L'osservatore Romano*, "had the tendency" to overlook incorrect intentions of the person officiating at a baptism precisely because baptism was so indispensable for salvation. But growing doubts about the Mormons' creed spurred Rome to make a wholesale reexamination of the Saints and to find them wanting.[40]

None of this fazes Kathryn Summers. Forty years old and thin, with a curly halo of frizzy red hair, she was sure when baptized in 1974 that her sins had been so thoroughly washed away, that she was so clean, so pure that, after changing into dry clothes for the rest of the service, she "just remained in [her] seat [at a Mormon chapel in Maryland], not wanting to do anything that might be a sin." One false move, one slip of the tongue, one wayward thought, and she would be sullied and soiled, as sinful as if there had been no baptism. As she recalls, most likely her repose was broken by her mother "insisting that I come do something, probably talk to someone. Naturally," Summers said with a smile, "she wouldn't have known why I was sitting there. At home, I tried sitting in my room again, this time for maybe twenty minutes or so until my mom called to me. I was then the oldest of four (soon to be five) children, so she would have needed help with something. I was pretty dismayed. It wasn't until years later that someone explained to me that the purpose of taking the sacrament every week was to renew the covenant of baptism. It would have greatly helped my eight-year-old self to have understood that particular doctrine."[41]

The next day, there was again disappointment. At her confirmation, Summers "didn't feel anything clear or definite when I received the gift of the Holy Ghost." Again officiating, as he had at her baptism, was her father; assisting him were other Melchizedek priests, all gathered in a circle around Summers, with their right hands on her head and their left hands on the shoulder of the next man. Meanwhile, her father put both of his hands on Summers's head and blessed her: "Kathryn Summers, by the authority of the Melchizedek priesthood which we hold, I confirm you a member of the Church of Jesus Christ of Latter-Day Saints and say unto you: 'Receive the Holy Ghost.'" He then added a more personal blessing based, Summers said, "on what he felt prompted to say by the Spirit." With that, she said, it became her duty "to receive the Spirit, to learn how to recognize it and follow its guidance, and to live so that I can be worthy of the constant companionship of the Spirit."[42]

That day, she says, "[I] tried hard to see if I did, in fact, feel different, but I just didn't. So then I felt like I was probably lacking in faith, that I wasn't worthy of the Holy Ghost." The Spirit may have eluded her then, but she believes that she felt its "influence many times while growing up." But she didn't consciously realize she was feeling its power until her first year in college: "I was in my dorm room reading a passage in the Book of Mormon about the physical resurrection. Suddenly I had an extremely powerful witness that this was the truth about why we were alive, that I had specifically been sent to earth to learn and to grow and to choose, and that the stuff I was reading in the Book of Mormon was, in fact, the truth that I needed to guide me back to God.

"For me, the influence of the Holy Ghost is a powerful feeling of peaceful, stabilizing, precious truth. It puts the whirling sense of self and world to rest. I feel loved, and I feel hope and strength, even when the particular message from God might be that I have erred and need to do better. Nothing in mortality compares to those moments. I have a brush with eternity, and I feel the power of God. The Spirit stands ready to visit me at all times. I only have to turn toward him or seek him."[43]

It took several years for Kathryn Summers to know that what she felt was the Holy Spirit. It took Sarah Fisher, who was a few years older than Summers when she had her confirmation—a Catholic confirmation—an instant to know she'd been touched by the Spirit of the Lord. A year after the confirmation—now sixteen years old and as spiritually invigorated as at the confirmation itself—she was still fending off "friends" offering her marijuana and other illicit temptations and spurning pubescent suitors who wanted her to do what she was not ready to do. The Holy Spirit had sustained Sarah for a full twelve months, which is far more than the few seconds that most people—if they're lucky—say they sense its presence and its vigor and its penetrating, illuminating buoyancy. Sarah was confident that this was no fleeting relationship with the Spirit, a close encounter of the very brief kind.

"As I see it," she said with a wisdom beyond her teen years, "these sacraments are like a ladder. Each takes you another step closer to Heaven. Each fulfills you, and each takes you higher and higher until you know Jesus and you're walking with Jesus and you get to spend the rest of your life— all eternity—with Jesus. I couldn't think of anything better."

2 · *Bob Abernethy*

NO FUNDAMENTAL,
LIFE-CHANGING EXPERIENCE

In 1994 a bear of a man came back from five years in Russia with a
bear of an idea. Bob Abernethy, wrapping up a half-decade assign-
ment in Moscow with NBC, had just figured out how to spend the
rest of his life: he'd anchor a half-hour news show about religion.
"Even from five thousand miles away," Abernethy recalls, "it was clear
that there was a lot of . . . attention in the U.S. to the national media
ignoring religion." When NBC, Abernethy's home for four decades,
didn't cotton to the idea, he peddled it at PBS, which has happily been
broadcasting *Religion and Ethics Newsweekly* since 1997.

God may not see it this way, but putting Him on TV is actually
a dangerous idea: the medium likes to play it safe, and not much is
more intimate and personal and potentially incendiary than religion.
In a sense, *Religion and Ethics Newsweekly* was anti-TV, a light among
the vacant bimbos and dopey reality shows that have hijacked television. At first, some viewers mistook the show for televangelism,
not journalism. After all, about the only religion they'd seen on their
home screens was hectoring from high-octane preachers, all rich as
Croesus. But soon, as the show began addressing everything from
atheism to Scientology to an African American on his first hajj, it
attracted awards, praise, and an audience drawn to its tone of learned

curiosity and to Abernethy's stately demeanor. If nothing else, the show dislodged viewers from assuming that religion on TV was always Bible thumping interrupted by commercials for snake oil.

Most of Abernethy's resume doesn't mark him as the right guy for this gig. Covering Washington, Los Angeles, Moscow, and London made him an expert on the world—not on religion. But in 1984 Abernethy took a year's leave from NBC to study theology and social ethics at Yale Divinity School. "I went because I could: my wife had died and I felt I could afford to take a year off. And it seemed like unfinished business. I'd been encouraged to do this right after college, but I never felt a call to the ministry. I also thought the material we'd study would be interesting. I was right. It was a great year. I remember most, and with the greatest gratitude, not the substance of what I read, but the kindness of the people I studied with, especially a theologian named David Kelsey. All those with whom I worked seemed to practice what they preached, and I was much affected by that.

"I don't think the year in New Haven made much difference in getting the idea for the program, but it has given me a little more standing as one who cares about religious life."

Aside from those twelve months at Yale, what made Abernethy ideal as *Religion and Ethics* anchor was that he'd led a bit of a double life. He didn't need those twelve months in New Haven to draw him toward God. His entire childhood had been immersed in faith, liturgy, prayer, church. Through a series of sad circumstances, he had lived with his grandparents in Washington, D.C., where his grandfather preached at a prominent church. "My boyhood home was a parsonage," he told me over lunch at a Washington restaurant around the corner from his TV studio, his ruddy complexion offset by a gray herringbone tweed jacket and a ready-for-prime-time blue tie. "My grandfather was the pastor of a big downtown church, just a few blocks from here. Essentially, I grew up a preacher's kid."

Some journalists grow up reading newspapers and can't wait to get their first byline. Some get the bug from their parents, who might be journalists or at least informed citizens. Some model their lives after the comic strip character Brenda Starr or on Carl Bernstein and Bob Woodward, the *Washington Post* reporters who brought down Richard Nixon's crooked White House. But Abernethy grew up reading the

Bible, hearing about the Bible, discussing the Bible. He was surrounded by God talk every day. "The effect of all that religiosity," he
said, "made me comfortable in a religious environment. It made it easy
for me to say 'God' on television." Abernethy's grandfather may have
died long before his grandson took the helm of a TV show on religion,
but he would have been pleased that young Bob had learned from his
Sunday preaching that he could utter God's name to a national audience and never blush or stammer or inject just the slightest note of
sophisticated, world-weary irony.

Perhaps the most distinguished connection that my grandfather's church
had with power—temporal power—was that, while president, Warren
Harding was a member. And he could be seen occasionally raising his eyes
to the balcony, where his mistress sat.

Another influential member was Charles Evans Hughes, then the chief
justice of the Supreme Court. He sat in the pew right in front of ours.
Sunday after Sunday after Sunday, I would watch my grandfather preach,
looking past the full, white, very well-trimmed beard of "the Chief."

But other than that, Calvary Baptist was a large, middle-class, really
thriving congregation—an old, red brick building, right on the edge of
Chinatown. Maybe half the people worked for the government. The rest
were businessmen and merchants and doctors.

My grandfather—William Shaddock Abernethy, he was my father's
father—was a sweet man, and there was never any doubt in his mind about
what was true and what he was preaching. His community very much
looked up to him. It's different now. I don't think pastors—well, most of
them—have the status that they used to. He was a big man, with a big
head and enormous farmer's hands. He'd had a paper route as a boy in
Minnesota, and had also played some baseball. He loved sports and good
stories, and was a wonderful preacher, informal in his manner. He'd lean
on the pulpit with his left elbow, and one day—preaching at another
church—he leaned so hard he broke the pulpit. His conversational, and
very effective, preaching style was especially remarkable because, as a young
man, he had stammered terribly. It must have taken a lot of faith, which
he certainly had, to go to divinity school (the University of Chicago) with
such a handicap. A professor of homiletics there befriended him and got

him to relax. Gradually, he became able to speak, and went on to a greatly respected career. I never once heard him stutter.

My grandfather and grandmother took my mother and me in in the early 1930s. I'd been born in Geneva in 1927, where my father was a secretary for the international YMCA, editing a magazine called *The World's Youth*. He was part of a generation that gathered in Geneva after World War I, hoping that the promises of the war to end all wars might come true, and that they might help it come true.

Ten months after I was born, my mother brought me to the United States to see her father and show me off. She got tuberculosis and spent a year in Lake Saranac, New York. We forget how little pharmaceutical power doctors had in those days. They didn't have sulfur. They didn't have penicillin. They didn't have anything. Then my father came back and got a job as a teacher. His parents were taking care of me while my mother was sick. The three of us were briefly together until my father died. I was two. His parents took in Mother and me.

The house was about six miles north of the church, at 1349 Iris Street, past what's now the Walter Reed Medical Center. It was brick, and small by today's standards, but completely adequate for my grandfather and grandmother, my mother and me. Every morning, we'd have breakfast together, and when we were finished, my grandfather would get out the Bible and read aloud from it. Then he prayed aloud. I learned to read in his lap, reading the Bible.

On Sundays, there was Sunday school at nine, then the 11:00 A.M. service, then my grandfather would greet everybody who wanted to say hello to him and tell him about their troubles. Finally, maybe around 1:15 P.M., we'd drive home and have lunch. But it was never called "lunch." It was "dinner"—the main meal of the day with the best silverware and china. Because of the government, Washington in the 1930s was somewhat insulated from the worst effects of the Depression. So we had roasts and Swiss steak and chicken. It was all very elaborate.

That's the way the world was. I just accepted it. No one questioned whether I enjoyed it. You went to Sunday school. You listened to someone talk to you about the Bible. You heard it every morning. You read from it. And that was that. The effect of all that religiosity was an inoculation more than an inspiration. It may have prevented any real engagement along the way with the fundamentals: Is this true, or no? Or quite simply, What do I think about certain things? What do I think about the Incarnation? What do I think about the Resurrection? I just kind of sailed along, comfortable in my little church. I love the hymns and I love the stories, and I feel very much at home. But I've never had what it took—a crisis or intellectual rigor—to be as intentional about my faith and my practice as I think a lot of people are. I probably should be.

When he preached, my grandfather wore a cutaway coat, striped trousers, and a wing collar. Some Baptist preachers wore a gown or robes. Not in *his* church, which was pretty upscale. For baptizing people, he had a pair of hip boots, which he would put on over his black trousers before wading into the baptistery, and the people who were being baptized would come in and he'd take them down and bring them back up, sputtering. The immersion lasted just a few seconds—down and up and preceded by an exchange between you and the pastor which the congregation was supposed to hear: "Do you accept Jesus Christ as your personal savior?" "I do."

When I was thirteen, I was among the boys in white trousers and white shirts who came into the baptistery, which was behind the pulpit. The boys entered from one direction. The girls from the other. The idea of *not* doing this never occurred to me. In some vague way, I was aware that this was a declaration of my free choice that Jesus Christ was my savior. But it felt more like I was being dutiful. My grandfather wanted it. My grandmother wanted it. My mother wanted it. So I did it.

There was no fundamental, life-changing, worldview-changing experience. It probably would have been good for me to have been more affected by my baptism, but I pretty much just accepted it as something I was expected to do. Most things about Calvary were familiar and comfortable for me, and wading into the water toward my grandfather, in his morning coat and hip boots, was in keeping with that. Besides, I could swim, and there was no need to panic.

This may be why I envy the Jewish coming-of-age tradition. A bar mitzvah seems very explicit: there's the biblical preparation and then the speech that the bar mitzvah boy makes and it's the celebration of an *individual* boy coming of age. Baptisms, traditionally, are group affairs. I don't see how the two ceremonies—baptism and bar mitzvah—could be blended, but maybe it would be good for a Baptist boy if more was expected of him. As it is now, a baptism is not an occasion for feeling that you have become something that you weren't before, in terms of your faith or your place in the world.

And yet I never felt the baptism ceremony was pro forma. It was a big deal, and it may affect lots of kids spiritually. I hope so. Among Baptists, of course, it's a time when the youngster decides he or she is ready to give his or her life to Christ. It's a religious commitment more than a rite of passage based on the time when one becomes a man. I guess what I want somewhere in my tradition is a ceremony that honors the maturity and responsibility of the boy, as well as his decision to accept Jesus as his personal savior.

I think Jews have it right. When my first wife died, it was very interesting how my Jewish friends knew instinctively what to do, and my Christian friends seemed less sure. Do you bring food? Yes, everybody knows that. But I was so moved when [veteran NBC newsman] Herb Kaplow and his wife [both Jews] came over to the house one night. They just sat. It wasn't necessary to talk or entertain or offer food. They just came. And I loved that.

Many of us who come from a more stoical tradition are not comfortable just coming and sitting. We don't know quite what to do. Yet on almost any occasion, Judaism has guidelines. Maybe the older religions have the best traditions. If your own tradition pretty much started in the sixteenth century, you still have a way to go.

I have two daughters—one, Jane, from my first marriage, lives in Chicago; the other, Elizabeth, from my second marriage, is a junior at Princeton. Neither was baptized. When Jane was thirteen or so, we were attending a Presbyterian church in California and we felt kind of temporary and my wife and I were not of that particular tradition. So it just slipped by. With Elizabeth, my younger daughter, we had been living in Moscow and then came home. Again, we were sort of transient and it was easy to let it slip.

Is anything lacking in their life? Yes, in the sense that these events are a symbol of a religious upbringing, and missing the event was part of missing a whole lot of things that we did not pass on. Well, that's a little harsh. My older daughter is very much a cultural Christian. She loves the music. She's familiar with the Scriptures, much more than my younger daughter. Part of the reality for the younger one is that, since my wife is Russian Orthodox, she only occasionally would go with me when I went to our church, and I occasionally went to her church. Again, we were betwixt and between, and the one who suffered from that did not have the details of religious instruction or practice.

In my experience, it's all interwoven—not so much the specific ceremony of baptism as everything: that ceremony and Sunday school and the Sunday dinners and Christmas and the wonderful cake that my grandmother would make for Easter, something like a sponge cake in the shape of a flower, filled with whipped cream and decorated with an orange to resemble a lily. It's all a wonderful tapestry that defines who you are and how you live. It's part of being around people who are religious and who love you and try to do something with their lives that they think will be a way to follow Jesus. It's all completely intertwined, and it's beyond definition. If I don't go to church on Sunday, I'm conscious of feeling not so much guilty as incomplete. That's the tapestry at work.

Many Christians talk about a "journey." It's perfectly normal and understandable that people's interests change as they age and have more experience. I find myself loving the old hymns and the memories of the kind of worship that I grew up in. And for a long time, I've been much more interested in social action, in the importance of the social gospel, in taking the message out into the world to the poor and the sick. And I'm increasingly interested in the spiritual part of all this—the formless, wordless effort to have direct contact with God. At the same time, I'm interested in a more rigorous liturgy. I'm also interested in the bones on which to attach that experience. But I'm kind of lazy, and I don't do much about it, and I can't exactly say that I'm church shopping. But whatever I do will be strongly influenced in more ways than I'll be conscious of by my early years at Calvary Baptist, the church of my grandfather.

3 · *Chinua Achebe*

WHAT MAKES SOMEONE
GIVE UP THEIR RELIGION?

It was raining, I was wet, and the dirt road was no help. All it did was get me wetter and muddier and send a slight shiver through my already damp bones. Rain in January is not good, especially in upstate New York. Then I spotted the lights from a small house, and I knew there wasn't much farther to go.

I jumped onto the twenty-five-foot wooden ramp that extended from the house to the ground, delighted to step on something that didn't squish. I knocked on the door at the end of the ramp's slight incline. It was apparent that a handicapped person lived here, maybe someone who used a cane or a walker or suffered from a really bad limp. Then the door opened. A gracious man with short, salt-and-pepper hair gave me a beaming smile, and I was face-to-face with Chinua Achebe.

Well, not quite face-to-face: he was in a wheelchair, where he's been since he was paralyzed in a car accident in England in 1990. But there was nothing diminutive about him, nothing that put him at less than eye level. Yes, physically, I had to look downward. But Achebe was right there with me. And I had the feeling that even if he could stand and was taller than me, he would be no higher. Metaphysically, that is. Rather, wheelchair or not, he met me right where I was—an impressive quality in a man who knew exactly who he was and did not veer from that, despite his circumstances.

Achebe and I sat across from each other for almost two hours, his gray cardigan lending him a slight grandfatherly air and his hoarse, African-accented voice giving him elegance and warmth and informality, all at the same time. He'd had several lifetimes before ending up at this rather simple house tucked away in a corner of the sprawling campus of Bard College in New York State's Hudson River Valley. He was born in 1930 into the Ibo tribe in eastern Nigeria. The Ibo, Achebe notes, are "one of the three major ethnic groups in Nigeria; one of the major ethnic groups in Africa, in fact. Fifteen to twenty million people are Ibo; they are bigger than some countries." Among the early converts to Christianity in their community, his parents were missionaries, so determined to shed their African ways that they baptized their son "Albert Chinualumogu," in tribute to England's Prince Albert. They also forbade him from attending the religious ceremonies and festivals of his non-Christian neighbors. He did this on the sly anyway.

Clearly Achebe, resisting his parents' (and British colonialists') contempt for indigenous ways, was pulled toward the traditions and history of his people at an early age. Nonetheless, he appreciated European authors and their tales of Africa that he read in high school—until realizing they'd "pulled a fast one on me! I was not on Marlowe's boat streaming up the Congo in *Heart of Darkness.* I was one of those strange beings jumping up and down on the riverbank, making horrid faces." Determined to depict his culture more realistically (and more honestly), he began writing for his college newspaper. Eventually, Achebe wrote several novels, all illuminating two irreconcilable facets of modern African life: the humiliations visited on Africa by colonialism and the utter moral worthlessness of what replaced colonial rule. Along the way, Achebe directed the Voice of Nigeria and was a diplomat for the short-lived nation of Biafra during Nigeria's civil war.

Achebe's writing is plain and sparse, void of technical tricks and dedicated to the narrative. He is so wedded to the story, in fact, that he says it "owns and directs us. The story is our escort; without it, we are blind."

His work, led by *Things Fall Apart*, his best-known novel, has been translated into fifty-three languages. More impressive than this number is what propels him as a writer: "to help my society regain belief in itself and to put away the complexes of the years of denigration and self-abasement." How do you save national and cultural identity from the blending of different cultures? That, Achebe wants to know. And how do you affirm that identity while adapting to the new and the alien? That, too, Achebe wants to know. "The world is big," he said. "Some people are unable to comprehend that simple fact. They want the world on their own terms. . . . But this is a foolish and blind wish. Diversity is not an abnormality, but the very reality of our planet."

Achebe grew up in Ogidi—population: around ten thousand. There were two major markets and several smaller ones, but no running water, only two springs and a stream. His family lived in a seven-room house with a corrugated tin roof and whitewashed earthen walls. A few chickens and goats wandered around the yard, and an occasional pet dog scrambled near the house. Almost every day, Achebe saw the consequences of the myopia of the English and the capitulations of the Nigerians. Now, Chinua Achebe wants to honor tradition without ignoring change. Indeed, things do fall apart, but they are never static. The same holds for him. A practicing Christian, Achebe longs for what his parents would not give him: a connection to his past, to the long chain of ancestors that came before him. From that small home at the end of a muddy road in Dutchess County, his heart belongs to Africa, his soul reaches for the traditions he hardly knew . . . and his writing belongs to us.

My sons had what I didn't. When they were about twelve and fourteen they were initiated into the secret Masquerade Society on the same day in our village in Nigeria. I had sent them to the elders in my family. I didn't want to be present because this was not my initiation. That was the way I wanted it to be.

This was in the early 1980s. Children should be given an opportunity to feel that they are owners of their culture, and my sons had reached the age to be able to handle this in a *manly* way. It's also important for society itself to say that there were things we threw away that we shouldn't have, even if it is simply to salute this in passing.

The boys had gone to primary school in Nigeria; then I was so very tired from the very bloody civil war in Nigeria that I decided to travel. It was the first time I left my village to live abroad for a while. I taught at the University of Massachusetts, so for three years they went to school in America; then we went back to Nigeria, where they attended secondary schools. And then to university. The oldest boy began in the University of Nigeria and ended up with his brother at the University of Kent in England.

Like me, they were raised as Christians. But with that ceremony into the Masquerade Society, which is called *ikpu-ani,* my sons have secret information that I don't. I hope that they, and the Ibos, make use of it to salvage a civilization that has been damaged. These are not things you can necessarily fix, but we can make these gestures and the gestures are important. This was also a way for me to pay my homage, belatedly.

During the initiation, the old men of the village take eleven-, twelve-, and thirteen-year-old boys for one night to some secret place in the woods. The boys are scared, although this experience is obviously very profound to them. You know it's profound because, at that age, being able to keep a secret from your friends who have not gone through this is quite a challenge. And, of course, no girls are a part of this. Keeping the secret of the mask from women is one way that the males dominate the society.

The Ibo people are told that the masks are our ancestors coming out of the ground, which is where they live. They exit through tiny holes made by ants. It's all very magical and elaborate. The masks cover the face and the head of the elders who wear them; the rest of their bodies are covered with raffia or cloth.

The masks are our link with tradition and perform different functions. They appear at a number of festivals. The major festival in my village, Nwa-afo, was celebrated every August or September: a four-day holiday that is less a religious festival than a week of joyfulness. It may have started as a celebration of dry weather after the season of heavy rains. Men in these masks go up and down the village, ending in a procession, which is quite a sight, up a hill. And there were half a dozen smaller festivals, different kinds. One was for the new yam. [The yam is the king of crops among the Ibo.] In *Things Fall Apart,* for instance, there's a scene in which a number of masks preside over a case of a man beating his wife. They act as the supreme court. There are masks that dance or entertain the community. It's a great offense to dishonor the mask. Whoever uncovers the man who is wearing it, especially to the profane gaze of women, is punished. In the past, that would be a capital offense.

The night the boys are being initiated, the bullroarer is howling away. This is the name for weird sounds that indicate the presence of spirits. I'm only guessing, because I didn't go through this, but during the ceremony, somebody wears a mask and then uncovers himself for the boys to see, to behold, and think, "That's somebody I know!"

The morning after the initiation, the boys are back in the village. They look very, very self-assured. Before the initiation, the boys ran away from the masks; now, they can accompany them through the village during festivals or ceremonies.

If I had one of these initiations, perhaps I would have been stronger in some ways, but not necessarily in others. Because, you see, the strength I need for the kind of life I've chosen, a life of witness, is not necessarily what some people call strength. I believe that what we call weakness is sometimes more valuable than strength. The fact that I did not have a certain experience has made me into the kind of person who makes sure his sons have that experience.

I call myself a Christian, but I do not have the complete faith that my parents had. I find the notion that you must accept Christ as the beginning, the middle, and the end very difficult. To accept that, then all humanity that existed before Christ lacks salvation, and that is very uncharitable. And people in other countries, the Ibo, for instance, or the Chinese or the Indians who did not get to hear Christ are all treated harshly. This seems to be a quite primitive way of thinking.

I don't really know why my parents converted to Christianity. What would make someone give up their religion and faith and culture and pick up something totally new and carry on with it? The easiest explanation would be, "Well, they were traitors to their culture." But I know they were not traitors. Something deeper than that was at work. And it's then not just my parents. It becomes a whole culture, because this is what Africa was engulfed in.

So what happened? What was in my father's society that he found so unsatisfying, so inadequate, that he had to leave it? We don't do that kind of thing for nothing. I think I have the rough edges for why this happened. The society had disintegrated. A lot happened to their society over four or five hundred years—the slave trade and colonization—and they were no longer sure *what* their culture was.

When something like this happens, especially to a people who are not literate, the memory of their story is lost. Something like that, I think, happened to the Ibo people that made them no longer champions of their culture, made them ready to accept something that was given them.

Their culture had become so bad that they were not willing to fight or die for it. Clearly, my father's generation no longer saw their culture as good, if not better, than that of the Europeans when missionaries came in the nineteenth century.

Strangely, my great-grandfather, who had raised my father, did not object to his conversion. He used to be violently opposed to any new thing. He didn't agree to the conversion. He just said, "Good luck!" Which says something about the Ibo culture: it is not a fighting culture, a culture that goes out to convert others. In fact, neighbors in our village were a wandering people who had come from somewhere. There was plenty of land, so when you weren't happy where you were, you moved somewhere else. One couple asked if they could live next door to us, and our people said, "Yes." Then they said, "Can you give us your gods to worship?" and our people asked, "Why? What's wrong with your gods?" Our people thought about it and said, "Well, they must have very good reasons for asking for our gods. Let's not press them too much with questions. Let's give them our gods." Next door were people asking to be converted and the Ibo had problems with *that*. Obviously, we are not evangelicals by nature.

I had certain Ibo ceremonies and certain Christian ceremonies. The first rite that a child goes through is birth itself, when the child comes with a name. The name is not conferred by parents. Or by anybody. The reason is that you are born on a particular day, and every day has a name. There are only four days in the Ibo week: Nkwo, Eke, Oye, and Afo. A child born on Eke day is called "the child of Eke." That's your *chi* name, because it is the name that your creator gave you by bringing you on that day.

Chi is a very complex deity. It's as if God sends a part of Himself when we come into the world. Each individual has his or her own Chi, and everybody's is unique. I don't know any other culture that goes quite that far. In fact, Chi makes a bargain with you before you come to this world. Everyone chooses what they are going to do, what they are going to be, what's going to happen to them. All this is agreed to and signed. This is called "assigning of gifts," which is why we all have different talents. Some of us are singers, some are dancers, some are painters, and so on. All these constitute our humanity, and we are not victims, since we negotiated who we would be.

In this world, Chi is our supporter as long as we are what we are supposed to be. When you begin to forget—and, in fact, we forget completely, which is why we don't know we ever signed this "contract"—Chi withdraws from us. Chi will not be a party to reneging. If, on the other hand, you discover that you want a slight change with the contract you made—it can't be a very big change because an agreement is an agreement—then it is possible to negotiate that, if you put forth a lot of effort.

My Chi name was Nwa Nkwo, since the day on which I was born was Nkwo and *nwa* means "child." On the eighth day after birth, an Ibo child is circumcised, and on the twenty-eighth day, seven Ibo weeks, the parents or older relations, maybe a grandfather or a grandmother, name the child. I had a baptism, not an Ibo naming ceremony. My dad gave me the name "Albert." I also had a sister named "Victoria." I dropped Albert when I went to college, although my mother kept it to the bitter end.

When I was about fifteen, I had a confirmation. Almost immediately, I became a godfather to one of my classmates because he didn't have Christian parents. He was being baptized and he asked me to be his godfather. This was not that unusual in this weird, topsy-turvy world of our lives. Fortunately, it helps if you see humor in it.

I don't remember my confirmation having any world-shaking consequence, although it must have meant something for me to go through with it. Some of it, I think, was simply: "Okay, we're Christians, and *this* is what we do." You go through the things you're supposed to unless there is a good reason not to. It didn't seem to do any harm. But on the other hand, I'm not going to become a worshipper of any of the Ibo gods—the gods of the river or the gods of the trees or the supreme god whom the Ibo call Chukwu. Chukwu created everything. He is up there somewhere. The sun is his eye, and when he sees something he doesn't like, he lets us know.

My parents taught me to feel superior to my friends who weren't Christian, but I still tried to talk with my friends about their secret initiations. I had a natural curiosity about things, and why things happened and how.

I couldn't put that away. I knew, theoretically, that we Christians were right and we were going to Heaven, yet I still wanted to be present where certain things were going on. I was just curious.

We Christians were doing better economically, educationally. We were the lucky ones. At that stage in life, you know, being lucky didn't seem like "being lucky." It just seemed like "being right." We were the right ones. So I didn't, therefore, waste too much sympathy on the village, or on the people in the village who were not Christian and who were going to be initiated. But I was jealous of them up to a point—they got to do something that I did not.

At this point in my life, I don't know that I wish I had an Ibo initiation. I'm really quite superstitious. I think that anything that happens to me has a value in itself, whether it's for good or bad. You are given something less than you need and you do something with it. A small amount goes a long way. That's how I see my life. The writing I do, in fact, is a consequence of all these bizarre historical conjunctions. I didn't plan this. It just happened, and it could have happened any other way. People say, "If it had happened differently, would you have been a writer?" I don't know. I certainly hope that I would have tried to be a writer, writing about a different situation that I did get.

My children are perfectly comfortable with what they want to take from our culture. For them, it works. Unless you want to lead a kind of purist life, many aspects of our Ibo culture indicate that things can coexist. Anni, the earth goddess, is, in some ways, the most effective divinity around. Because Anni is so close to us, she's more likely to really give us hell. Once in a while, the Ibo people build a place to honor Anni: they make images molded from earth and paint them black and white. Anni is usually in the center, with many divinities alongside of her and behind her. She's carrying a sword and is a fearful personage. And in one instance created by the Ibo people, she's wearing a cross. She simply thinks it looks nice. The idea of mixing faiths can seem bizarre, but this story shows that it's possible to pay respects to more than one deity. Which leads to a belief that we've not dreamt of enough philosophies.

I've looked at such basic questions as, Who made me? If God did, then, well, who made God? We have no equipment for certainty in that line of thinking. There are many things we must accept that we will not know, and we must settle for that. In my view, religion doesn't stand in the way of any of that. My religion is not as certain and authoritative as my parents', which is why I leave room for my children to figure things out. Some are very religious and some are like me. I don't need to go around saying, "There is *no* God" or "There *is* a God." Because after all this time, I still don't know.

4 · *Huston Smith*

RELIGION SATURATED THE HOUSE

Only one person has done hatha yoga daily and prayed five times
a day in Arabic while facing Mecca, all while still calling himself a
Methodist. Huston Smith has meditated with Zen masters in Japan,
prayed with Buddhist monks in Burma, danced with Sufi dervishes
in Iran, practiced tai chi with Taoist masters in China, observed
Shabbat with his daughter and her Jewish husband, and taken peyote
with Indians in Mexico and psychedelics with Timothy Leary and
Richard Alpert (soon to be Baba Ram Dass) while they were still
teaching psychology at Harvard.

   This insatiable appetite for religious experience, for getting into
the skin, and into the souls, of people who practice other faiths, is
what makes Smith the grand old man of religious scholarship. Armed
with curiosity and humility, he haunts faith after faith, extracting
wisdom from every religion he explores.

   Luckily, there is nothing of the religious voyeur about him. That
would corrode his journey, tainting it as spiritual adventurism or
anthropological curiosity seeking. His quest is redeemed by its purity.
He never proselytizes, never missionizes, rarely hectors or scolds.
He ventures out to hear and see and understand, to stand witness—
qualities that made such an impact on Bill Moyers that he devoted a
five-hour PBS special (*The Wisdom of Faith*) to Smith, impressed that
"what Huston Smith has learned, he has applied to life."

Now eighty-six years old and living in Northern California, Smith remains in good health but has lost most of his hearing, a development he takes with aplomb and good humor. In 1999, while attending the World Parliament of Religions in Cape Town, South Africa, a friend tried to whisper the comments of the keynote speaker—Nelson Mandela—into his ear. When it was apparent that that wasn't working, Smith signaled for his friend to stop, whispering, "It is enough for me to be within Mr. Mandela's *darshan*," a Hindu word for being in the presence of a revered person. Glancing at Smith out of the corner of his eye, the friend was struck by the "utter raptness of Huston's attention, the dignity of his bearing." Then he recalled a passage in Smith's classic book, *The World's Religions*: "All we can do is try to listen carefully and with full attention to each voice in turn as it addresses the divine." With most of his hearing gone, Smith was still listening. What he heard went beyond the words.

Religion has been Smith's life. The middle child between two brothers, he was born in China, where his parents were Methodist missionaries. Surrounded by Buddhists and practitioners of Chinese folk religion, he was aware of differences between Western and Eastern religions at an early age. He was perfectly content with Christianity until he was in his twenties and discovered the Vedanta, the philosophical aspects of Hinduism. Here he found "a profundity of worldview that made my Christianity seem like third grade." For ten years, he perfunctorily attended a Methodist church while finding his spiritual center with a Hindu group, where the discussions and lectures fed his soul. Then, he found the same truths in Christianity—in Meister Eckhart and St. Augustine and others. No one, not even his professors in graduate school, had told him about these authors. Next, he learned about Buddhism, and "another tidal wave broke over me. In none of these moves did I have any sense that I was saying goodbye to anything. I was just moving into a new idiom for expressing the same basic truths."

With all his exploring, Smith is unfailingly appreciative of his origins: "The faith I was born into formed me." He is also unfailingly critical of those who expect to find redemption in Eastern religions or in the hodgepodge of New Age faiths and disciplines. "The notion that Western religions are more rigid than those of Asia is overdrawn.

Ours is the most tolerant society that history has ever known. Almost the only thing that is forbidden now is to forbid, and Asian teachers and their progeny play up to this propensity by soft-pedaling the rules in Hinduism and Buddhism and Sufism, which make the Ten Commandments and the Rules of St. Benedict look flabby in comparison.

"The New Age movement is optimistic and enthusiastic, but needs to distinguish between belief and credulity. Has it come to terms with radical evil? How much social conscience is there? Has it produced a Mother Teresa or a Dalai Lama? Not that I can see. At its worst, it can be a kind of private escapism to titillate oneself."

For more than eight decades, Smith has not "escaped." Rather, he has plunged into the varieties of religious experience, a truth seeker among the confused, always asking, "How can we hold our truth to be the Truth when others see the truth so differently?"

And he has always remembered that he is a Methodist.

I was born in 1919 in a Chinese village—Changshu, about seventy miles northwest of Shanghai. Maybe fifty thousand people lived here. There was a wall around the city, maybe a mile in diameter. Throughout the city, there were lanes that were so narrow you could spread out your arms and reach the buildings on both sides. About 80 percent of the people were illiterate and practiced folk religions. The rest practiced Confucianism and Taoism and Buddhism—the religions of the literati.

The folk religions were mainly directed to warding off evil spirits. Over the doors of their houses, which were wall-to-wall and had no yards, were bottles, with their necks pointing upward. Evil spirits may be mean, but they're very dumb. The bottles were intended to fool them into thinking they would get hurt if they ventured inside these homes. Also, evil spirits cannot turn corners. So the lanes in the city twisted and turned so the evil spirits could not roam around.

I was totally bilingual while growing up. At home, we spoke English, but all our friends and acquaintances and church members were Chinese, and we spoke Chinese with them. They were our life. They were our community.

There were five of us in our family, although my oldest brother died of cholera at the age of two. This was on Christmas Eve. He died in my father's arms. China, in those days, was not an easy land to live in. Epidemics and illnesses were frequent. When my father arrived, there was a dinner for him in Shanghai. The next morning, one of the guests at that dinner was dead. Also of cholera.

We were a very functional family, a loving family. Their Christian faith was their life. Religion saturated the house. After breakfast, we would go to the living room, and the cook and the servant would join us and we'd have morning prayers. And my mother would lead us in singing a hymn—all this in Chinese, of course. Then the adults would take turns reading verses in a Bible passage. And then, we would stand up, face our chairs, kneel, and place our faces in our hands. In the evening, when we went to bed at night, we would all kneel by our beds and say our nightly prayers.

My mother was actually a second-generation missionary. Her father, Terrance, had gone there in the nineteenth century. She was born there and came back to the United States to study music at Knox College in Illinois. She wanted to teach young women to play the piano so they could accompany hymns. She met my father, Wesley Moreland Smith Jr., while she was in the States. He was working on a bachelor of divinity from Vanderbilt. They were not fundamentalists, and they were very well educated. They got married and returned to China, where my mother, a music major, taught women to play hymns for the church service. My parents also found that there was no education for women. So the first thing they did was to found a school for women, even before they built a church. There were no other churches in town, so the church was simply called "the church," or *chao dong* in Chinese. This was a simple building, made of brick, maybe seventy-five by thirty-five feet. Inside were rows of wooden benches, each with one board behind them as a backrest. An aisle down the middle of the church separated male seating from female seating. A plain wooden stand served as the pulpit.

I was baptized when I was about a week old, and, of course, I don't remember that. But my confirmation when I was twelve was very simple. It was held in the church. We didn't adopt the Christian dress. I wore a tie and a white shirt, and I was asked some questions about believing in God and accepting Jesus Christ as my savior. I also pledged to read the Bible and adhere to its directives. It was traditionally Christian, but I was a little disappointed in it. I don't know really what I expected. Maybe that the heavens would open and I would feel the Holy Spirit descending on me. I was disappointed because I really didn't feel any different.

You know, these events *can* be important. They are the points at which you know your life is different, that you have certain responsibilities. All religions make a great point of this. The point is to drill home, "Okay, you've been playing around and people been taking care of you. But now you are an adult and that carries all kinds of responsibility." That is a real rite of passage with *power* in it.

Hinduism, for example, has four stages of life, with rites of passage that mark them all. The first is the student stage, when your responsibility is to learn. The second is the householder stage—you get married and assume a vocation. The third goes by the name of "forest dweller," when, traditionally and ideally, you go off into the forest and meditate so that, before your life is over, you understand what it's all about. The fourth is *sinnyahsin,* when you come back into society having discovered who you are.

You need to break the ties of home and vocation. If you stay around, the demands will all be there on you. You have to make a geographic break. And when you understand life's purpose and what it's about, geography becomes irrelevant and you can come back into society and maybe even to your own hometown. Maybe before you were a member of the city council and you were very respected—a pillar of society—now you may turn up at your friends' backdoor with a begging bowl and beg for a handout. Hinduism has taken rites of passage further than any tradition I know of.

But we Protestants are not very good at rituals, partly as a revolt against thinking that conforming to sacrament will save us. I'm going to sound pessimistic now, but deep down I'm not. There was a sharp divide in the West in the sixteenth and seventeenth centuries when we discovered the scientific process. Who among our grandparents could imagine people walking on the moon or communicating instantly, orally and visually, around the world? But it also changed our worldview. And that has been a tragedy because all traditional societies have what you might call a "two-story" view of the world. There's this everyday world and then there's another world which exceeds it by every criterion you can imagine and which is more powerful. All traditional societies aspire to accommodate their lives to the demands of the world that envelops them. We've lost that, and that's the problem with secular society.

The good news is that, after three hundred years, this is changing. We are finally coming to see that, while science can give us all kinds of physical benefits, these are limited. No one has ever seen a "thought." No one has ever seen a "feeling." Yet *that's* where our lives are lived.

So, for three centuries, we have been trying to live completely and fully in an incomplete world, in a "one-story" universe. In Plato's famous allegory of the cave, this is like the shadows on the wall, whereas outside the cave there is a beautiful, Technicolor, three-dimensional world, one that we've lost. But we're coming to see our mistakes.

It's a serious detriment to modern Western society that we have become such a secular culture. Of course, religion is all over the map still, but it has become privatized, and often the closest we have to a rite of passage is getting your driver's license. Of lesser importance at that age is being able to vote. Such events are very secular and don't have an effect on the character of the individual, although I must say that my daughter, who converted to Judaism and married a Jew, a very learned grandson of one of the last rabbis in Poland, had a rite of passage when it was her turn to go up to the podium in synagogue and read the Torah portion for the day as fluently as if she were reading English. It was truly thrilling, for her and for us. Afterward at the social hour, everybody at the congregation congratulated us. And I asked, "How was her pronunciation?" The unanimous verdict was "Perfect, just perfect." And at her son's bar mitzvah in Santa Rosa, California, in 1998, his reading from the Torah was thrilling, too. He stumbled about more than she did and probably rehearsed more. But to see him up there with the prayer shawl and the yarmulke with the rabbi and other elders of his, giving the morning's reading in Hebrew, and with the entire congregation involved, there was a tremendous, almost palpable sense that he was moving into a different stage of life, more than at many Christian rites of passage I've attended.

I've studied many faiths, and I've practiced their teachings and rituals, but I've always kept my Christian heritage. I never converted to another faith. Christianity has always been my main meal, but I'm a very strong believer in "vitamin supplements." But I'm so sad that in our secular society, we've lost so much of these rites that would really make an impact on people's character. We've gotten too modernized and we're seeing the ill effects of this. Even the Boy Scouts have lost their real effectiveness. A society that does not have effective rites of passage for adolescents ends up with bizarre things like gangs to show that you are a "man." Getting a driver's license is not enough of a rite of passage. We need something that connects us to our roots and traditions, something that connects us to ourselves.

How can we make these events more effective? How can we restore them? The only honest answer is that I do not know. Once we see the mistakes of thinking that matter is the fundamental reality, it will open the way to recovering a deeper sense of reality, a sense of the total nature of things. And that would give us a different stage on which to work out dramas of passage.

5 · *Julia Sweeney*

THAT SOLDIER-OF-CHRIST, SLAP-ACROSS-THE-FACE STUFF IS SICK

Revelation often comes at the oddest moments and from the least expected people. For Julia Sweeney, revelation came when two "cute, young" Mormon missionaries knocked on her door, announcing, "We have a message for you from God." After being ushered into her living room, they asked, "Do you feel loved by God?"

"Did I believe, with all my heart, that God loves me?" Sweeney, an actor and comedian, began asking herself, unintentionally embarking on the sort of spiritual journey from which no one returns unchanged, a journey that only the people who knew Sweeney best would have anticipated. (She'd become famous for portraying the androgynous "Pat" character on *Saturday Night Live*, not a shtick that instilled confidence that this was a person who took life seriously.)

Sweeney began sorting out how she'd been raised amid four siblings by her attorney father and homemaker mother. And what priests and nuns had instructed her in parochial school. And how she'd related to a poster of a really hunky Jesus that she'd thumbtacked to the wall of her bedroom in Spokane. (This was roughly the same time that she was discovering boys, and Sweeney kept hoping she'd find someone as dreamy as her matinee-idol Prince of Peace.) Reading the Old Testament, she was disturbed by all the blood and guts and sexual depravity and by a God who was tough as nails and mean as hell; reading the New Testament, she discovered a Jesus who was haughty and cruel and lashed out at disciples when they couldn't comprehend his oblique parables and who refused to see his mother when she came to visit, claiming that the apostles were his new family. "Family values" this Messiah did not have.

Sweeney joined a church, but the priest's counseling came down to faith, and Sweeney's kept shrinking. She read the *Iliad* and the *Odyssey*, perplexed why these were "myths" and the Bible was "true." She trekked through Nepal and Bhutan and was appalled at Buddhists impressing seven year olds into monasteries. After reading Darwin, she sailed to the Galapagos and saw birds pecking out the brains of their weaker siblings. "God is not nature," she recoiled. "Nature is cruel." Almost as a last-ditch effort, Sweeney devoured shelves of books by New Age gurus such as Deepak Chopra, who, she concluded, was full of hooey—"so arrogant, so clueless."

Tenacious and insistent, Sweeney kept searching. "I need God," she said, "because we have a whole history together." In the end, reluctantly yet conclusively, she "changed the wallpaper of [her] mind," casting God into the wastebasket of "faith": "It's because I take You so seriously that I don't believe in You."

Sweeney's father wouldn't talk to her for weeks. For him, confessing that she was gay would have been more socially acceptable than being an atheist. Her mother hoped that Sweeney's four-year-old daughter, Mulan, would be the instrument of God's revenge by eventually becoming a nun.

Sweeney felt a burden lifted: no longer a prisoner of cant or faith, she saw the world with fresh eyes. No less moral or ethical than before, she (and all of us) was now responsible for making the world good and sane and whole. Not God. We were our own inspiration, our own fulfillment. We all had our own answers to life's persistent questions. God had had a long run. We were on our own now.

Sweeney's depth and honesty inform the one-woman shows she's performed (and written) since leaving *Saturday Night Live: God Said Ha!*, an improbably funny account of the battles waged against cancer by her and her brother concurrently; *In the Family Way*, the story of the travails—and joys—of a single, divorced woman (Sweeney) adopting a baby from China; and *Letting Go of God,* a public confession of her loss of faith.

The morning I pulled up to Sweeney's modest bungalow in Los Angeles, she was securing Mulan into the backseat of a slightly battered first-generation Toyota Prius. Waving me over, she invited me to tag along as she took Mulan to daycare. When we returned to her house, Sweeney—freckle faced and T-shirted—sat in the living room on a wingback chair that had seen better days. I sat on the couch. An exercise treadmill took up the majority of space to our right, shelves packed with kids' games (Chutes and Ladders, Candyland) and adult books *(War and Peace, How to Know God)* were behind us, and a kiddie-sized table ablaze with a glorious painting of the sun was between us. ("This is where Mulan and I eat most of the time.")

Sweeney seems to intuit the power—and the variety—of rites of passage. In April 2003, two months before her father died, in a bravely sweet letter she sent him about their life together, she recalled asking when she was a kid, "what was so great" about *The New Yorker,* of which he was a big fan. "You sat me down and showed me how it was laid out. How there was 'Talk of the Town' and then the theater and movie and art listings. And then the essays and the cartoons and the poems. Later, when I was in college and starting to get a real film education, we started making bets on how many movies each of us had seen between new and revival listings in *The New Yorker.* And you had always seen more. Then one day, when I was a senior, I won! I had seen more. You were so pleased. And I felt like I had passed over some rite of passage."

As I said, revelation has its own timing—wry and unpredictable. Coming out of nowhere, it can set things "right," like when Sweeney "won" that film competition with her father. Or it can cause endless worry and consternation, as when those "cute, young" Mormons asked Sweeney about God. But once you are past the consternation, there comes a sigh that this is the world as it is, *this* is the journey from unknowing to knowing. The destination reveals wisdom; and the journey encompasses doubt, frustration, and a capacious, maybe capricious, curiosity.

In 1967 when I was seven, I had a first confession so my soul would be clean for first communion. Parents were supposed to take their kids to St. Augustine's, our church, on a Saturday between one and three in the afternoon. And there, you had two options. In a confessional on one side of the church was Father McRand, this young, good-looking, easygoing guy; in a confessional on the other side was Monsignor Buckley, this old, angry guy.

I got there early in the afternoon. All my classmates were lining up on either side, and I got in line for Monsignor Buckley. You know, they don't announce who will hear your confession. You only find out once you're inside and you hear the voice of the priest. Also, nobody knows what their sins are when you're seven. So you make up a few things.

I went in and told Monsignor Buckley that I lied to my parents or that I had disobeyed them a few times. I don't even remember what I said. And he said, "You have to say the rosary on your knees in the church."

I thought, "I can't do that penance. That's huge! I don't even know if I can do the whole rosary." So I walked across the church and got in the line for the other priest. I went in and told him the exact same sins. And what did Father McRand, the modern priest, say? "Give your Mom a compliment today."

So I came out, went back to the other side of the church, and told everyone in the Monsignor Buckley line that I had told the *same exact* sins to both priests, and that Father McRand said to give my mom a compliment and Monsignor Buckley said to do the rosary on my knees! Everybody ran over to Father McRand's line and it caused a bit of a commotion and people had to be stopped.

That was my first confession.

Of my first communion, I mostly remember that there were about sixty kids in my class and that you had to have a white dress and a veil and that the teacher had said—or maybe I came up with this all on my own—that you could tell how religious someone was by how they clasped their hands together when they prayed. If you were like this [Sweeney clasps her hands loosely in front of her chest, fingers pointing straight ahead], you weren't very religious. But if you were like this [presses her palms together just below her chin, fingers pointing upward], God would see that you were much more religious.

So, during the whole mass, I held my hands like this [again pressing her palms together below her chin]. All of a sudden, my veil started sliding downward. I was too afraid to unclasp my hands and fix the veil, thinking, "If I do that, God will see that I am not very religious."

The veil kept sliding and sliding, until it finally covered my face. Of course, all the parents were looking at me. I know it didn't go all the way down—over my mouth—because I went up and got communion. But I do remember looking at my mom, who was mouthing, "Put your veil up! Over your head! Over your head!"

As for the communion itself and eating the "body" of Jesus, I just thought it was a piece of bread that had some magical thing happen to it and that, when I ingested it, it made me part of this community. Most people don't think, "I'm cannibalizing a person." But now I just think of how barbaric it is. It's actually more than barbaric. It's tribal. It's ancient. It's like sitting around a campfire ingesting the body of a dead leader whose essence, you think, is in their body and that will somehow enter your body if you eat part of it. But when I was a kid I didn't think about that.

In my neighborhood, the Catholic Church was really prominent. We grew up on Twenty-sixth Street. That's on the south side of Spokane. No big ostentatious houses, but cute, middle-class houses. And there was a park a few blocks away. There were about fifteen kids my age in the neighborhood. We all knew each other, and walked to school, and walked to church, which was about a mile away, but we did it often. It was a local kind of life. We knew everybody. To me, it was just Norman Rockwellian idyllic.

I adored St. Augustine's and all the rituals there. Rituals and community make you feel safe when you're a kid. I especially liked when the priest came out with the incense and sort of flung the smoke over people's heads. And I liked the bells and all the kneeling and going up for communion because people got to see what you were wearing and you got to see what everyone else was wearing. There was *everything!* A fashion show! And the Lord!

To me, the Catholic Church was very romantic and very mysterious in kind of a theatrical way. When I look back, I think, "Well, I got to see *theater* every week." People were in costumes and wine changed into blood and a wafer changed into a body. There was pomp and circumstance, and a certain smell. Everything about it felt holy and sacred and meaningful. It was the sacred meeting place for our community.

From kindergarten through eighth grade, I went to St. Augustine's Catholic School, a three-story brick building that was really old-fashioned, with ivy growing on it and little rooms with little desks and narrow hallways. My father had gone there. That was really meaningful to me then, and it still is. Next door was a convent where the nuns lived who taught in the school.

For high school, I went to Mary Cliff High School for two years, and then to Gonzaga Prep for my junior and senior years. Gonzaga was much more liberal than Mary Cliff, and I was attracted to the conservative rituals of the "old" church rather than the more relaxed attitude of the "new," post–Vatican II church. The priests who taught me at Gonzaga were almost agnostics. Very liberal. We still did the ritual of mass, of course, and everyone believed that Jesus was the Son of God. But they were very open-minded about how you define God. In fact, I wonder how many of them are still priests today.

The nuns at Mary Cliff High School lived in the most beautiful old building. Just gorgeous. Like a mansion, a manor. With big columns out front, but not garish. I went there maybe six or seven times. It all started with Sister Antonella, a really tough English teacher who was not very personable. She had really skinny legs and dark hair and dark eyes and really prominent cheekbones and kind of a harsh stare. Somehow, she liked me. I wrote a couple of essays for her my freshman year and she took me aside to say that they were really good. And then we got to Shakespeare and I *loved* it. It was all so alive to me. I went to the convent to read different parts of Shakespeare with her and she asked if I could stay for dinner. It was just so pleasant, and the nuns enjoyed having me there. This was my own "special nun relationship."

At my confirmation, I did feel the Holy Spirit. You tell kids that the Holy Spirit is descending on them and they're gonna feel it! It was vague and specific, at the same time. It was everything somebody wants it to be. And along with that came a feeling of transformation that's associated with the religious feeling.

And there was the moment when the bishop slapped your face. Well, it's not a slap. It's more of a tap. I think it's to slap the devil out of you, to make you into a "soldier" of Christ, someone who will be like those martyrs we heard about who went to their death defending Jesus. Now that

I'm older, I think of how they made it acceptable to give up your life for a completely unproven idea. That really is about control—political control. And it's about wealth. I doubt if the priests or the teachers felt that way. They felt as we did: soldiers for Christ stood by their convictions. No matter what. It didn't mean you were defending an ideology against someone else. It meant that you had integrity. Yet now I look at it in such a darker way. That slap across the face teaches people to be obedient, to follow leaders in ways that, I think, will ultimately end the world.

A couple of girls chose not to be confirmed because they didn't believe everything that you had to say [the confirmation prayers]. And I remember thinking, "Oh, how can you *not* be a part of this wonderful ritual? If you do it, you'll be an adult in the church." Sure, we had to say all this stuff, but it seemed like a small price to pay.

Looking back, I think that those girls were showing a certain amount of maturity and integrity at a young age. Maybe now they're born-again Christians or maybe they're nuns. I don't know what happened to them. But I do think, "Wow, I would be really impressed if Mulan [her daughter] had the wherewithal to not partake in a ritual that the whole community was participating in because she didn't feel comfortable saying what they asked her to say." I would be so moved if that happened to my daughter. But at the time, I just thought they were outcasts and surly and not joiners. *I* was a joiner. I was *in* the group. At the time, I didn't know what those girls disagreed with, although now of course I find *everything* offensive.

I almost think that being changed is not the point of these rituals. The point is to go through the initiation and know that you are part of the tribe, part of the culture. You've reached a certain milestone and everyone acknowledges it. It's like wedding ceremonies: what do people really *feel* in that moment about it? Who knows, but they probably feel a lot looking back on it, reminding themselves what they said. The repetition in your mind becomes the meaningful thing. Not the event itself.

You know, puberty is an important marker in just about any group, any tribe. And with acknowledging that you now seem more of an adult than a child come certain responsibilities and expectations that could be solidified by a ritual like that. I wish I had known that when I was confirmed. I wish I didn't think it was about becoming a soldier of Christ but rather about saying, "You're about to enter puberty and this is what that means:

you're now a girl. You're not one of the kids. Society looks at you differently and that brings certain advantages and certain power and certain responsibilities and certain behaviors." I wish it had been more that way. But of course, the Catholic Church doesn't even see it that way.

After the confirmation in church, there was a party in our backyard. I got a necklace that I promptly lost. I got a statue of the Virgin Mary and other religious things. I think I got an Infant of Prague statue. That's for a certain manifestation of Jesus in Prague. And he holds a big world and he wears a king's hat.

There were other rites of passage that were definitely a coming of age, like losing my virginity when I was seventeen and writing in my journal, "I'm a woman today." (These days, I wish I'd said, "No, you are *so* not a woman today!") And the boy saying, "Now we'll have to get married." And I remember thinking, "No, we *do not* have to get married! We have discovered a new thing, that's all! Things make sense now that didn't make sense yesterday."

And then there was going to college and not being able to move home. Within half an hour of my catching a plane to Seattle for the University of Washington, my brother moved into my bedroom. And I realized that there was no place to come back to and that if I did come back home again, which I only did once in the summer for a couple months, it's not like I'd come back to my bedroom. Basically, the whole family was so excited for me to leave because there was more room in the house! And that was a big transition.

Another major rite of passage was buying a Volkswagen bug, loading every single thing in it that I owned, and driving to L.A. That was in 1981. A friend came with me for the first twenty-four hours, then flew back home from San Francisco. I drove the rest of the way, terrified when I hit the freeways in L.A. I slept on the roof of a friend's house for a few months till I got a job and began getting it together. This was a very hard transition; I wanted to go back to Spokane all the time. But I stuck it out.

I guess I don't know any religious rites of passage that are good. I've never been to a bar mitzvah or bat mitzvah, but they seem to be so much about money and the party. It's exactly the wrong thing to do for someone who is thirteen. What you want to do is send them into a cave for a few months. Let them not eat for a couple of weeks! Slap them around a little bit and say, "*This* is the world," and then let them come out. Taking them to a hotel for a big party seems crazy to me. That's gotta stop!

And confirmation is horrifying. To think that they inculcate kids with this. That soldier-of-Christ, slap-across-the-face stuff is sick. If I had my way, that would be out.

My journey has been about realizing that the rituals are important and the religion isn't. And acknowledging that going through rites of passage is very important. Look, I don't want to sound like some hippie who's gonna make her kid look at the moon at certain times. But there's no reason why we can't have a ritual that all kids who enter puberty in America would go through. I wouldn't want it to be nationalistic, but we have Thanksgiving dinner every year, and we have the Fourth of July—we have all kinds of celebrations that are secular but are still holidays. Even getting your driver's license is sort of a rite of passage that the country puts on for sixteen year olds. You have to pass a test, and you have to go be with a stranger, and then you get to be part of society. Maybe there should be big parties surrounding people getting their drivers' licenses! I don't know.

I'm not going to raise my daughter in a religion. I don't know what else to do. And it makes me sad that she won't have rites of passage to go through. Yet maybe she will. Maybe she'll join the Girl Scouts and there'll be something there that will be meaningful to her.

I don't think I could be part of a church. I couldn't stand the God talk. "Belonging" is part of all this, but I already feel community: I have my theater group and Mulan and I go to museums a lot and the school is important and our tennis club is our clubhouse. But for Mulan, I'll try to supplement with nature the sacred and spiritual part of all this, although I *hate* both those words because of their religious connotations.

I really feel like I was born again when I stopped believing in God. I had to look at everything differently. It was like I had been dropped to earth from somewhere else. My eyes were opened so profoundly. I hope that Mulan can have that sense of awe and wonder and discovery and interest in the natural world and the world, and so much sooner than me.

There was a moment recently when I thought, "Oh my God, I'm coming close to praying." It was something dumb, like, "Oh, I really hope it doesn't rain." This is a habit I still have to get out of, although I don't ever feel tempted to believe there's a God. That's such a done deal for me. It's like this: you grow up thinking that there's a purple dinosaur in your garage and one day you actually look in the garage, and there's nothing there! After that, do you ever accidentally really believe that the dinosaur is in the garage? No. I'm not saying I'm free of illusion. But that particular illusion seems pretty done to me.

6 · *Jim Zogby*

THE WAL-MART-IZATION OF THE CHURCH

Jim Zogby likes his cigars, one after another after another. And his coffee black. And the service quick and familiar, because the staff knows his likes and dislikes without him having to more than nod or gesture. And all this at Zogby's version of a men's club: the Library Lounge at the St. Regis Hotel, a power room if ever there was one— two blocks north of the White House, smack on K Street, Washington's Boulevard of Lobbyists. Calvin Coolidge cut the ceremonial ribbon at the hotel's grand opening in 1926. Ever since, no American president has failed to visit the place, and a pride of kings and prime ministers have stayed there. The St. Regis likes to describe the atmosphere in Zogby's favored Library Lounge as "casual sophisticated." For once, the PR people are right on target.

"Casual" and "sophisticated" apply to Zogby as well. He blends right into his usual corner of the Lounge: sinking into the wingback chair at a small table, leather-bound books on the shelves behind him, white button-down shirt framed by a brown V-neck sweater, gold wire-rimmed glasses perched on his aquiline nose. He looks so right sitting here that the hotel could have hired him to beef up the atmosphere, sort of a rent-a-guy. Actually, the Lounge is where Zogby holds court when not in his real office: the Arab American Institute, housed on the sixth floor of a building across the street.

Zogby founded the AAI in 1985, intending it to be the political and policy research arm of the Arab American community. Since then, it has been active in voter registration, education, and mobilization, all aimed at moving Arab Americans into the U.S. political mainstream.

The job is perfect for Zogby: he's always been a political animal. In college, he was active in the civil rights and antiwar movements. Not long after graduating, he founded the Palestine Human Rights Committee, a group whose title's first three words rankled more than a few people in the United States. Next came his involvement with a raft of big-name organizations, all Arab or Middle East oriented: executive director of the American-Arab Anti-Discrimination Committee; cofounder of Save Lebanon, Inc.; and copresident of Builders for Peace, a private sector group that promoted U.S. business investment in the West Bank and Gaza after the signing of the 1993 Israeli-Palestinian peace accords. He also taught at several universities, advised Al Gore during his 2000 presidential campaign, and analyzed data for Zogby International, the high-profile public opinion polling company run by his brother, John. All this prompts many people to say, "Where's he get all the energy?"

Zogby's breathless career—nay, his breathless life—started in Utica, a small city in upstate New York with a long tradition of hospitality toward refugees and immigrants. Zogby's father, Joseph, emigrated from Lebanon when he was twenty-five. Eventually, he ran a grocery and, in 1926, proposed marriage to Cecilia Ann Zogby. (The two were not related: "Zogby" is a fairly common name in Lebanon.) Only nineteen, Cecilia turned him down. She wasn't ready for marriage. First an education. Then—maybe—marriage. She graduated from college, helped put her brother through law school, and when Joseph proposed again—she was now thirty-eight—she accepted.

Zogby's father died when Jim was fifteen; he attributes his sense of history, ethnic pride, and social justice to his mother, who spoke three languages, liberally sprinkled her conversations with colorful Arabic proverbs (always preceded with "As my mother always would say . . ."), and, while devoutly Catholic, was never parochial. She made certain her children weren't, either.

Born in a Pennsylvania coal mining town, Cecilia never forgot her

Lebanese roots. In 1927 she wrote a newspaper article encouraging Arab Americans to embrace their heritage, believing that they should not be ashamed to learn Arabic or be seen in the company of other Arab Americans. She admonished, "How . . . can we ever aspire to win the admiration and esteem of our American friends if we do not respect ourselves?"

Cecilia Zogby also respected her faith. Her children attended two churches: the local Roman Catholic church, St. Agnes, and the local Maronite Catholic church, St. Louis Gonzaga. Maronite Catholicism, alone among the Eastern Catholic churches, has always recognized the primacy of the pope and complied with most directives from Rome. Yet Syriac, not Latin, is the liturgical language, and celibacy is restricted to monks and bishops, with deacons and priests exempted. Maronites are deeply devoted to Mary, Jesus' mother, honoring her strength and fidelity by calling her Cedar of Lebanon.

Zogby's mother died in 1999. She was ninety-two years old. Today, few people doubt that Jim inherited his impulse to make this a better world from her. Or that his inability to be quiet and retiring is nourished by a conviction that Catholics, like their martyrs, are destined to carry on the good fight.

All this would make his mother proud. Maybe the one thing that wouldn't is all those cigars he smokes at the St. Regis. No doubt, they match the Lounge's celebrated mood—"casual sophistication." But just as surely, they don't comply with the advice of Zogby's personal physician. Or with his mother's wishes that Jim live a happy and long life. On the other hand, she did teach him the value of viewing life from the perspective of someone riding by on horseback, and for that he is deeply grateful.

I took the normal route for a Catholic kid. I got baptized—I don't remember it. I had my first communion—I don't remember it. I had my confirmation—I don't remember it.

For me, these were not transformative experiences. They all just sort of happened, and they happened when I was so young that they were more like the air you breathe or the water you swim in. I was barely two months old when I was baptized: too young to remember anything. I was seven when I had my first confession and communion. I have a photo of me in my communion suit that was in my mother's photo album, but about all I remember about an early confession was that a girl ahead of me went into the confessional and, all of a sudden, urine began to spill out from the bottom of the door. She was so scared, she peed in her pants. Maybe because I was a tricky Lebanese kid, confession never really bothered me. Early on, I figured that I could always say that I'd disobeyed my parents— just about everything I did fell under that rubric. But after a point, maybe after saying that eighteen times or so, the priest said, "Exactly how did you disobey your parents?" Then I was screwed and I had to go into details.

Of my confirmation, I remember absolutely nothing. Yes, I know there was a slap from the bishop that's supposed to remind you that you'll be challenged because of your faith and you'll defend it to the death. But I knew about slaps: I'd been slapped by priests before. That was no slap.

For me, these were not the transformative events, and I didn't lose anything because they didn't transform me. What did transform me in the church was being an altar boy from the age of eight until I was twenty and knowing Latin and becoming part of a tradition. Being a Catholic did not mean first communion or confirmation. It meant getting up early every morning with my father and having the same breakfast as he. *That* was a big deal! We'd have coffee and toast. Nobody else had coffee and toast at that age. Of course, I'd have a lot more milk in my coffee than he did. Then he'd drop me off at church to do the seven o'clock morning mass, and then the seven thirty mass, and then the eight o'clock, and then I'd go to school at eight thirty. I had the experience of being alone on the altar with the priest, and behind me were, at most, twelve people in this huge church that was bitter cold because the heat had not yet filled up the place. They were older Italian people, some of them sort of praying their own prayers. You could hear a woman whose false teeth didn't quite work right. Whenever she said "Jesus," she'd whistle. I knew the Latin and I'd ring the bells, and if the event warranted it, I'd light the incense burner. And just garbing myself in a cassock transported me into another place and created out of me something quite different.

One of the things impressed upon you was poise. You had to kneel a certain way and fold your hands a certain way and behave a certain way and you couldn't slouch. Doing this three times a day was never a burden. It was exciting each time. It was me and the priest and the Latin, which is quite mysterious and quite significant, and he was engaged in a transformative event that occurred every day: manifesting the body and the blood of Christ. And I was part of that. I washed his fingers before he did and washed his fingers afterward and distributed the Eucharist with him.

All this was a whole world to me. And on alternate Sundays when I wasn't serving mass or singing in the choir, I'd go to the Maronite church. This was more a function that I was in school at St. Agnes and, during the school year, a lot of my life revolved around the church and school.

Good Friday at the church was incredible. They literally took the body off the cross and wrapped it in a shroud and carried it in a procession through the church, and people brought flowers and put them on the body. Then they buried the body, singing as if they were Mary: "My son, look what they've done to you." It was just heart wrenching. Then on Easter, when Jesus rises, they took the body out and put it back up. To this day, it's so moving to me. This faith connected me with two thousand years of tradition, with monks hiding in the hills in Lebanon. You thought about the stories of these saints, and you saw their pictures in church. Or in my other church, you thought about the Latin, and about the regal church of the Middle Ages and the Holy Roman Empire.

To me, all this was the bigger event. Not the first confession or communion or confirmation. This is what brought me together with tradition. This connected me with my past. There was the sense that if you were an altar boy, you did the tough thing. Not the easy thing. What Jews do at a bar mitzvah—learn a language, learn a tradition—I did as an altar boy. Confirmation was a mass event, but I did this *every day* as an altar boy. It was *my* show.

There were so many other events that were transformative for me. Whenever I'd complain about my haircut, I'd say, "I can't go out! I don't want anybody to see me!" and my mother would use an expression which translates as, "Would it be noticed by anyone riding by on a horse?" I took that to mean, "He'd be going by so fast he wouldn't see it! So what are you complaining about?"

When my father died, my mother was a wreck and I was numb. Three or four days later, I broke down. I cried and cried and I said, "How can we go on?" And Mom said to me, "Would it be noticed by someone riding by on a horse?" I was stunned and somewhat angry. This wasn't about a haircut! But she said that wasn't what it meant. It meant that history is a continuum. It moves on, and you will look back at this event years from now and remember the good things that came before and you will have created memories that will go on after, and Dad's death will be in the middle of it. It wasn't the end of the world, because somebody riding by on a horse would see it as one event along the way of a whole lot of events.

This took me a long time to absorb, this sense of not being so self-absorbed with the tragedy of the moment that you can't see that life goes on. It was more transformative, for me, than anything that could have happened at confirmation or confession.

We grew up as part of a bigger world: We were in that neighborhood in Utica but not necessarily part of it. We had a splendid turn-of-the-century house in a working-class neighborhood. It was my father's pride and joy. The big story was always that he paid for it in cash. It was on a corner and had white posts, and, by itself, it was an important part of our sense of what Dad had done, how far he had come.

Dad was quiet and worshipped Mom and he worshipped us and he worked hard. He left the house at seven in the morning and came back at seven at night and when the first supermarket opened a few blocks away, there was a crisis atmosphere: Would it put Dad out of business? It didn't. People kept coming. He was a good guy, and they wanted to shop with him, and they liked him. I learned that business is about people liking you and trusting you.

And Mom was incredibly literate. Growing up in this immigrant community, she was the most educated person around. She spoke Arabic and English and French and translated documents for people in the neighborhood. She was a fervent Democrat and a historian, of sorts, and all my high school friends wanted to sit around our table and hang out just to talk to her because she always pressed them on politics. She was a woman of such learning that she turned down my father's first proposal by saying, "I'm not going to be in the kitchen while the men are in the living room talking politics."

She was a deeply Catholic woman and compassionate to her core. I recall coming downstairs [in June 1953] and seeing her sitting at the table, crying. I said, "What's wrong?" and she said, "Something very sad happened today," and she told me that "two people had just been killed [Ethel and Julius Rosenberg, convicted Soviet spies] and they have two boys just like you and your brother, the same ages. The government said they sold secrets to the Russians, but I think they were executed because they were Jews." That stuck with me.

We grew up knowing about things that most kids in the neighborhood had no clue about. After the Hungarian uprising in 1956, we got a refugee kid in our class. Mom knew what that meant, what we could learn from him. Other than Mom, in our neighborhood the most interesting thing that happened was who got the most home runs in a stickball game. But when we got home, the conversation was completely different.

The church I knew, and the tradition I knew, was an ornery one, in part because of Mom. But the lessons I learned that made me committed to defending value as I understood it and defending tradition as I knew it, those rites of passage came in other forms than what the church offered. There was going off to college and dealing with the war in Vietnam and the civil rights movement—those were more relevant than being confirmed when I was twelve, when you're supposed to be an adult and you're not. There was going to Lemoyne College, where Daniel Berrigan [the outspoken, often jailed priest who protested against war and poverty] left the year I arrived, but his tradition lived on. I got to know him, and *that* became my Christianity, the idea that, if you are confirmed, you do the hard thing.

It would be great if you could ritualize these experiences. I don't know if you can. I don't know if you ever could. The saints were always the exception. They were never the rule. The Berrigans were always the exception. They were never the rule. And all of us are like little guys on the stage looking at these big models, and the degree to which we feel challenged by them is the degree to which they've had an impact on us. Would that confirmation could do that to everybody. And that everybody, the minute the bishop slaps them, says, "I am going to be a defender of truth and value."

But I'm not sure it ever worked that way. And it sure doesn't now. Confirmation today is like the Walmart-ization of the church. It's like everybody goes—whatever! The fear and the mystery that were part of the ritual are gone. One of the problems is that it is done so much by rote and at too early an age: it's become a ritual hollowed out of content and is part of the broader culture of the tradition of faith rather than an epic event along the way. The notion that you got at confirmation that you would be called on to defend the faith, that you would be challenged to do what the martyrs had done, that's not there. It's not understood as a passage into that sacred circle of those who gave their lives for their faith. No one is challenged to do what the martyrs did.

On the continuum of things that I care about, I'm not going to go to the mat and say, "Don't confirm people until they're twenty" or "Don't baptize them until they're eight" or "Don't give them first communion until they're fifteen." But there is something quite remarkable about knowing that you're doing those vespers as they have been done for a thousand years, and you're participating in this ritual that goes back two thousand years. There's something quite significant about that. And that you're making it happen.

The church theologizes that "the slap" gives you the grace that you need when the moment comes for you to be ornery, to defend the good, to try not to do it the easy way. I learned this from Mom, and I learned this as an altar boy, and I learned this by being immersed over a long period of time in the culture, and I just wish there was some way to institutionalize this.

PART TWO

JUDAISM

Would Anne Frank Sing Karaoke?

When I became bar mitzvah, my grandfather, Eleazar of Amsterdam, of blessed memory, came to me one night in a vision and gave me another soul in exchange for mine. Ever since then, I have been a different person.

SHALOM OF BELZ, *Hasidic master*

Let young people . . . be sure that every deed counts, that every word has power, and that we all can do our share to redeem the world in spite of all its absurdities and frustrations and disappointments. . . . Let them remember to build a life as if it were a work of art.

ABRAHAM JOSHUA HESCHEL, *ABC interview, 1972*

WHAT, *REALLY*, IS A MAN?

It's odd that when Christians talk about rites of passage, one particular ritual often comes up, one that has set a certain standard for rites of passage in the United States; one that makes some people wince and others envious; one that's much maligned, much ridiculed, much respected—and much misunderstood: the bar mitzvah.

In the United States, bar mitzvahs (for boys) and bat mitzvahs (for girls) get more attention than first communions, baptisms, or confirmations *combined,* even though Christians outnumber Jews 590 to 1. Bar mitzvahs get all the headlines. They're the summit, the zenith, the tops when it comes to teenage rites of passage—usually for all the wrong reasons.

These days, even some Christians want a bar mitzvah! In 2003 twelve-year-old Laura Jean from Dallas told her parents that she loved bat mitzvahs: the singing was "inspiring"; the parties were exciting; the attention, no doubt, was flattering. Why couldn't *she* have one? She'd even learn Hebrew, that ancient, holy language of patriarchs and prophets who thundered and scolded against a wayward and forgetful people and of tens of thousands of stammering students who try to stay awake in tedious classes that meet in synagogues after secular school. The lengths to which Laura Jean was willing to go for her bat mitzvah were great—the only problem was that she was Methodist. In the end, that didn't stand in her way. One hundred and twenty-five friends and relatives attended her "bat mitzvah" at a snazzy country club in suburban Dallas, and Laura Jean went to bed happy that night, a sweet gentile who'd set her sights on one thing: "I wanted to be Jewish so I could have a bat mitzvah. Having the party fulfilled that."[1]

Laura Jean wasn't alone. Around the country, a lot of Christian teenagers are aping what their Jewish friends are doing. On Long Island, one "bat mitzvah" was held in a massive tent with chandeliers; in Malibu, one was held in a beachfront hotel. It had a Hawaiian theme. These affairs are such close copies of what Jews do that they have the same caterers and dancers and DJs, even the same kind of candlelighting ceremony in which, one by one, the boy or girl's parents, grandparents, close relatives, and friends are called up to light the candles on the cake.[2]

Why all this? Christian kids see their Jewish friends having bar or bat mitzvah parties with jousting matches or supermodel Claudia Schiffer blowing kisses to the guests and entertainment by Natalie Cole or the Dallas Cowboys Cheerleaders—all at the best hotels in town. Or they go to aprés bar mitzvah shindigs on the *Queen Elizabeth II* in Long Beach, California, or on Ellis Island in New York Harbor (with a six-minute, $20,000 fireworks show). Or they see $150,000 black tie receptions at Tavern on the Green in Central Park with a sixty-foot-long mural depicting the Beatles, the bat mitzvah girl's favorite band. They see all this and they feel left out. Apparently, the parents do too. As one California mother said, "The kids who had great bar mitzvah parties were elevated socially. We felt pressure to hold an event people would remember."[3]

Bar or bat mitzvahs used to mean that thirteen year olds are now responsible for their religious and moral conduct, and certainly every bar mitzvah has the same elements: on a Sabbath near his thirteenth birthday, a boy reads part of the Torah and all of the weekly section from the Prophets chapter of the Hebrew Bible; gives a talk about what he just read; and is praised by the rabbi for his compassion, humor, scholarship, and discipline. Even the Jewish sage Judah ben Tema—whom Rabbi Jeffrey Salkin calls the inventor of bar mitzvahs—would be happy with most bar mitzvah ceremonies today. In the second century C.E., ben Tema envisioned how a Jew's life should unfold: "At five, one should study Scripture; at ten, one should study Mishnah [the code of Jewish law]; at thirteen, one is ready to do mitzvoth [commandments]; at fifteen, one is ready to study Talmud; at eighteen, one is ready for the wedding canopy; at twenty, one is responsible for providing for a family."[4]

In one sentence, an entire life was structured, scripted, and directed. Yet long before ben Tema, there were intimations that thirteen was no ordinary age: at thirteen, Abraham smashed the idols in his father's house; at thirteen, Jacob and Esau, who'd been quarreling since birth, went their separate ways—Jacob worshipped God and Esau worshipped idols. Eventually, rabbis observed that, when they turned thirteen, boys were filled with the *yetzer hatov* and the *yetzer hara,* the dueling forces of good and evil. They could sit on Jewish courts, make promises that were legally binding, lead prayers in synagogues, read from the Torah, and be counted in the minyan (the ten adult Jews required for a communal religious service). These boys had entered fully into their people's society. They were "men." But not until the sixteenth century was a ceremony in place to commemorate this Jewish coming of age.

Always, it seems, there was a tendency for bar mitzvah celebrations to have a touch of the gaudy. And always, there have been efforts to tone this down. In the seventeenth century in Poland, Jewish councils ruled that bar mitzvah celebrations had to include at least one poor man. His presence would remind people that Jews should be observing *tikkun olam*— reforming the world, making it a better place, aiding the weakest among us: the "widow" and the "orphan," in the language of the Torah. In the eighteenth century in the Italian town of Ancona, a festive meal could only be given to the immediate family of the bar mitzvah boy, though coffee and sweetmeats could be served to anyone calling to offer their congratulations. Locked in their ghettos, the Jews of central Italy feared antagonizing their gentile neighbors. Life was bad enough, and ostentation wouldn't help.[5]

Luckily, some kids see beyond the glitz. In 1998 Alexis Waxman gave a talk during her bat mitzvah about Anne Frank's search for her Jewish identity. Everyone was moved; a few people cried. ("What is a Jew?" she'd asked the congregation. "A Jew is able to find the courage to deal with pain.") Then she attended the reception her parents threw in a four-star restaurant overlooking Manhattan's East River: music by the Hampton String Quartet; long tables groaning under Peking duck, a sushi bar, fried calamari, and eggplant rollatine; life-size cutout figures of the Queen of Hearts and the Mad Hatter. "I . . . I don't know what to say," Alexis tactfully murmured. "I'm amazed. Just amazed."[6]

The extravagance has not gone unnoticed. In 1992 one rabbi complained that he'd seen every theme at bar mitzvahs "except human sacrifice." Another was indignant about a reception with centerpieces depicting the bat mitzvah girl with shopping bags from expensive boutiques. That same year, Judaism's Reform movement demanded an end to this "idolatry and . . . commercial colonization of our sacred events." From then on, the only acceptable receptions celebrated "family cohesion, authentic friendship, acts of *tzdekah* [charity]." Unfortunately, Reform rabbis had passed a similar resolution in 1964. And in 1979. And all the events described above—fireworks and go-go dancers and a mini-concert by Natalie Cole and the Dallas Cowgirls struttin' their stuff—happened *after* the latest resolution. Was there no way to halt this juggernaut?[7]

Yes, and it could come from the person most affected by a bar or bat mitzvah—a thirteen-year-old kid, such as Nathaniel Graham, who in August 2005 had his bar mitzvah in Auburn, Alabama. About one hundred miles west of Atlanta and with a population of forty-six thousand, Auburn's main industry is education: Auburn University employs about seven thousand people, and from September to June its almost nineteen thousand students contribute mightily to the local economy. Nathaniel's father, in fact, is a professor of art history at Auburn; his mother teaches the same subject at the Atlanta College of Art, a long commute but, from her perspective, well worth the drive.

With that kind of pedigree—having professors for parents can be daunting as well as stimulating—it's not surprising that Nathaniel is precocious. "I'm really a humanistic Jew, an agnostic Jew," he said matter of factly, almost professorially. "I believe in science more than religion. In fact, I don't literally believe in God. For me, 'God' is a metaphor for 'kindness.'"[8]

Strong, profound words coming out of any thirteen year old, but even stronger when that same kid says it in his *d'var torah*, his commentary on his Torah reading, at his bar mitzvah, which is exactly what Nathaniel did. In Nathaniel's reading from Deuteronomy, Moses tells the Hebrew people that God refused to let him enter the Land of Israel; instead, the Lord instructed him to ascend a tall mountain and view the Promised Land from there. In this, essentially his farewell address, Moses predicted that future generations would turn away from God, worship idols, and be scattered to many lands. There, they will seek God and return to His laws. Nathaniel's reading also included a repetition of the Ten Commandments and the

Shema, which declares the fundamentals of the Jewish faith: "Hear O Israel, the Lord is our God, the Lord is One."

The Shema is the bedrock of Judaism: *This* is the God of the Jews and He is one—powerful, indivisible, indestructible, eternal. Nathaniel understood this, and in a certain manner, he accepted this. But Nathaniel's idea of God was neither as patriarchal nor as omniscient as what Jews had been embracing for thousands of years, and his ultimate act of chutzpah was not necessarily believing as he did: the more liberal strands of Judaism respect individual autonomy. Rather, his true chutzpah was to stand at the head of the sanctuary at Beth Shalom in Auburn and espouse humanism.

But one boy's chutzpah is another person's knowledge of self, and Nathaniel possessed that in spades. His family had joined Beth Shalom when he was four years old, and he'd been learning Hebrew since he was seven. Then, the shul lost its rabbi—it's hard to retain a rabbi in a synagogue with about forty Jewish families, the total Jewish population of Auburn. So members who were well informed about Judaism taught the youngsters in the temple's Hebrew school, which is how Nathaniel learned Hebrew and Jewish Scripture and history. He had a knack for this, a curiosity probably honed by being reared by academics. But as Nathaniel's bar mitzvah approached, it was apparent that he needed instruction that was not available in Auburn.

Enter Debra Kassoff, who's sort of an old-timey circuit rider rabbi. Originally from Columbia, a once-idealistic suburb snuggled between Baltimore and Washington (when designed in the 1960s, Columbia was intended to be color-blind to class and race: it hasn't quite worked out as intended), Kassoff headed to Jackson, Mississippi, after her ordination as a Reform rabbi in 2003. There, she became the Institute for Southern Life's director for rabbinic services, essentially spending two weekends every month driving around the South in her blue van, ministering in towns whose Jewish roots may go deep but whose Jewish populations have often dwindled toward nothingness. Natchez, Mississippi, for instance, once home to more than two hundred Jewish families, now has one temple with only fifteen members. Jews are so scarce in the South—more Jews (456,000) live in Brooklyn than in the entire South, excluding Florida— that 34 percent of its 334 congregations lack a full-time rabbi. The situation is so severe that, when attending a seminar on how to serve small congregations, Kassoff was stunned when "small" was defined as anything with less than two hundred members. "If that's 'small,'" she thought, "then I'm serving micro-congregations."[9]

Kassoff is such a star for Jews hungry for a "real" rabbi that people have been known to drive ninety miles to hear her read from the Torah and lead services; sometimes, as the *New York Times* noted in November 2005, "there are even more Christians in attendance than Jews." Apparently, gentiles in a rabbi-starved region of the country are as fascinated seeing a flesh-and-blood rabbi as Kassoff's own breathren.[10]

Kassoff is as much a teacher—a long-distance teacher—as a leader of services and a reader of Scripture. In the summer of 2004, she added Nathaniel Graham's temple to her rounds, and soon after, his mother asked Kassoff if she would officiate at Nathaniel's bar mitzvah: a rabbi hadn't officiated at a bar mitzvah in Auburn for years. Kassoff was delighted not just to officiate but to help Nathaniel prepare for his bar mitzvah. In the months leading up to the event, the two of them spoke on the phone at least once a week and for no less than an hour. Nathaniel sang his Torah portion, Kassoff offered guidance when he was done, and then he'd do it again. They also discussed how he would interpret his Torah portion.[11]

Initially, Nathaniel was skeptical about the arrangement—telephonic instruction for a bar mitzvah was not a time-honored Jewish tradition. But soon he got into the rhythm of the weekly phone calls; also helping was encouragement from his friends, who were being tutored by a layperson at their temple. As Nathaniel recalled, "They said that working with Rabbi Kassoff was like 'bringing in a pro.'"[12]

The bar mitzvah went swimmingly. Nathaniel dazzled the congregation with his command of Hebrew and the Torah and, not unexpectedly, with his beyond-his-years *d'var Torah* regarding his humanistic take on Judaism. And he thoroughly appreciated Rabbi Kassoff's contribution. "This was the first time I'd been to a bar mitzvah," said Nathaniel, "when someone said more than a few sentences for a *d'var Torah*. Rabbi Kassoff put God back into the bar mitzvah, rather than it just being a big birthday party."[13]

Also contributing to the quality of the day was the fairly low-key reception at the Grahams' country club—no band, no DJ, no racket. It was hushed and muted; by the usual standards for these things, it was almost somnolent. "I like quiet and I like nature," Nathaniel explained to me, and with that in mind, he had the reception that he wanted: reflective and sociable, with guests able to talk to each other and not forced to shout over a band whose decibels exceeded those of the Rolling Stones' last concert at Madison Square Garden. This was no ear-splitting endurance contest. People left pleased and relaxed, and by the end of the day, the most pleased was Nathaniel, less by the quality of the reception than by his newly shifted status in Judaism. He knew now that, whenever he walked into a temple, "it's about the people, not about God. I see my name on a plaque on the *Etz Chaim* [the Tree of Life, a sculpture on a wall in Nathaniel's temple with names added to each leaf to commemorate certain events in the lives of congregants] and I see my name inside my yarmulke [from his bar mitzvah] and I know that Judaism—and bar mitzvahs—all come down to individuals and family and community. I don't think about this all the time, of course, but it does make me feel different whenever I walk into the synagogue."[14]

Nathaniel's family makes up about one-thirtieth of the Jewish population in Auburn, a distinction which doesn't faze Nathaniel. "I feel like a minority," he said confidently, "not like an outsider." But almost a thousand miles to the west, the family of another thirteen year old held a greater distinction: the Nulls were the *only* Jews in Altus, a town of twenty thousand people in southwestern Oklahoma. Nathaniel, at least, had a synagogue in town; the synagogue nearest to the Nulls—the House of Jacob—was ninety minutes away in Wichita Falls, Texas. But the Nulls started attending the Reform temple fairly regularly in the mid-1990s, and their oldest child, Alexandra, began learning Hebrew there when she was five. Given the absence of professional teachers at the temple—all the teaching was done by congregants—Alexandra learned little more than Hebrew letters, about as rudimentary a Jewish education as you can get.[15]

All that changed when Alexandra was eleven. That's when she decided to have a bat mitzvah, partly because she'd heard so much about them from her friends from Dallas who attended the same Jewish camp that she did in Bruceville, Texas; and partly because she wanted "to keep the tradition alive," a tradition she'd inherited from her mother, who was Jewish, and not from her father, who grew up as a Methodist. In fact, according to Alexandra's mother, Lynn, until the Nulls moved to Altus from Jacksonville, Florida, in 1990, they had planned to teach Alexandra and her sister, Jacquelyn, "about both religions, and everything would be hunky-dory. Then we came here, and it was apparent that it was important to me to teach them about being Jewish."[16]

The subtle curse of the small town—the isolation; the lack of a community around the corner or just down the street; the memories, for Lynn, of another life in another world, of family and holidays and tradition, all imbued with Judaism to one degree or another—was, in a sense, a blessing. It revealed Lynn's true leanings, exposing the instincts that even she wasn't aware of. Raised in Tallahassee and then near Tulsa by two Jewish parents, Lynn "didn't have to think about being Jewish." It was natural and it was a given: part of her consciousness which she unknowingly took for granted. Altus changed that equation. It also changed her life and Alexandra's as well, a girl with no Jewish friends in town, for the simple reason that there were no Jews other than her family; a girl who first heard about bat mitzvahs from her displaced mother and then from her friends who lived in Dallas, so far away and, comparatively, so worldly.[17]

At the House of Jacob, Alexandra now began learning how to read Hebrew: she wanted to know more than mere letters. A few months later, in March 2005, she started studying with Rabbi Kassoff, who had recently included the House of Jacob on her rounds through the South. "I really liked Rabbi Kassoff," Alexandra told me, "and I thought it would be cool to have a woman rabbi officiate at my bat mitzvah." Initially, they talked on the phone—one hour a week; as the bat mitzvah drew closer, this expanded to daily conversations and lessons, mostly about Alexandra's recitation of her Torah portion (Numbers 25:10–30, a tract about women's rights of inheritance) and how she would interpret this for the congregation.[18]

Finally the bat mitzvah arrived—July 23, 2005. About one hundred twenty-five guests attended. They came from all over, especially Florida and New York—two centers of Jewish life on the East Coast. Alexandra was especially pleased that ten of her friends from Altus attended: not one of them had heard of a bat mitzvah before Alexandra began studying so hard for hers.

Alexandra's mother was moved that the thirty adults from Altus were "touched and in awe. The event was the talk of the town." The reception, held at a hotel in Wichita Falls, was a downsized version of the bat mitzvahs that Alexandra had attended in Dallas. Lavish by Oklahoma standards, this bat mitzvah was modest by the more ordinary standards for these events. Alexandra's mother had to keep reminding her out-of-town relatives, "I know this would be a very small deal in New York, but believe me, it's a very big deal for Altus."[19]

Most important, Alexandra felt "more Jewish, more responsible in the Jewish faith, closer to God. This whole learning process made me feel so much a part of Jewish tradition." That, of course, is what a bat mitzvah is all about: getting closer to God, to Judaism, to yourself. But the Hebrew tradition doesn't talk about the difficulty of being Jewish in a small town like Altus, of being isolated yet determined to have a bat mitzvah. Alexandra forthrightly addressed this during her *d'var Torah* at her bat mitzvah. "Getting to where I am today has been a journey," she acknowledged, "and I'm still heading for my destination. The question is, 'Why bother when it is such a big hassle?' I knew it was not going to be easy living in southwestern Oklahoma without a synagogue or a Jewish community nearby. Maintaining a Jewish lifestyle and being different has not always been easy. Having friends from home all being non-Jewish is hard because they're always going on cool church trips and youth activities. It is also hard for me because no one in my town is Jewish . . . so I have nobody to share my Jewish learning with."[20]

Alexandra couldn't have told the congregation who she was any better: a committed thirteen year old, someone who knows who she is and who she wants to be, who clings to her faith and her tradition and her beliefs not because it is the fashion or the expectation, at least in her town or in her social circle, but because it is her conviction, her solace, her rock: her past and her future. Alexandra had a bat mitzvah neither to satisfy peer pressure nor to reap status: there's not much status in being the odd man out. Indeed, Alexandra and her family were essentially a minority of one in Altus. In such a situation, the only choice is to summon the courage to be who you are; to muster the most private approbation that you have found the right path for yourself; and to be content that this sanction is emanating from your guts and your soul and not from a certain social milieu beyond some distant friends who share your faith or from your own family, all of whom reinforce your beliefs and your traditions but who, like you, are strangers in a strange land.

Alexandra Null in Oklahoma and Nathaniel Graham in Alabama are to be treasured. They are that wonderful rarity: they are the wise children, the children commended in the Passover Haggadah for yearning to learn and for having the talent and the smarts to know what to do with what they have learned. Unlike the other children that the Haggadah mentions—the wicked child and the simple child and the child who doesn't even know how to ask the right questions—the wise children marvel at what they have been given. Amid the atomization of their people, a fragmenting rendered by holocausts and pogroms and a multitude of diasporas, of which their own predicament in small-town America is a new variation, these wise children stand, shoulder to shoulder, with all that has gone before them and all that will come later, and especially in the case of Alexandra and Nathaniel, they spurn excess and blandishment and allurement. They may be isolates, as it were, on a virtual prairie, yet their yearning to truly come of age within Judaism emanates from a yen to be one with their God and with their people (though they may know few of them in the flesh, for that is the life of the small-town Jew). They come to bar and bat mitzvah to proclaim, in their own small voices in their own small towns, that they are no remote islands, detached from the main. Rather, they hear *the call,* the same call that went out from the burning bush to Moses and that the prophet Isaiah (55:3) told the ancient Hebrews, "Incline your ear and come unto [the Lord] and your soul shall live," the same call that spills forth from the shofar, the ram's horn, on every Rosh Hashanah and Yom Kippur, waking Jews from their stupor and their complacence, carving out a consciousness and an honesty so they are fit for repentance and forgiveness.

In fact, these wise children teach those who have taught them, and Alexandra and Nathaniel's ultimate *mitzvah* (good deed) was to hew to the spirit and the purpose of a Jewish rite of passage. To some degree, it may be harder to do this in more metropolitan areas than in diminutive hamlets where there are fewer temptations and fewer precedents. If so, then Aaron Lemle also deserves much praise. In 2003 Aaron, a New Yorker, knew exactly what kind of bar mitzvah he wanted. His vision came after attending twenty-three bar and bat mitzvahs in one year; once, he went to four on the same day, three at top tier hotels (the Plaza, the Pierre, the Waldorf) and one at the American Museum of Natural History's new Rose Planetarium, an architectural ode to the stars. These events were for the privileged and the affluent; all were remarkably alike and remarkably impersonal.[21]

Aaron wanted a bar mitzvah in *his* image: quiet, reflective, introspective. But first, he had to come to terms with actually wanting a bar mitzvah.

Aaron had been raised in a fairly freewheeling religious environment that picked and chose from faiths at will. His father, who made documentaries about spirituality, had been raised Jewish in Manhattan. By now, he was essentially Buddhist/Jewish. Aaron's mother, a Baptist from Georgia, had explored Judaism, Christianity, Buddhism, even voodoo. The family didn't belong to a temple, and when Aaron was seven and eight and nine, he'd watch his friends go off to Hebrew school several afternoons a week and think, "Wow! Lucky me! They have to go to temple and listen to someone who's overweight and probably smells bad tell them about Judaism."

When he was around eleven, Aaron began to revise his thinking. "There's gotta be a better way to get a Jewish education," he reflected. He mentioned this to a friend of his father's in 2002, and soon she was tutoring him in Hebrew and Jewish history and traditions. For both of them, this was an experiment: she'd never taught before, and he'd never heard of most of this stuff before. Twelve months later, he was reading Hebrew—and *understanding* it, a facility acquired by few boys who study in a more traditional manner for their bar mitzvah.

More impressive was that Aaron's reasons for wanting a bar mitzvah were changing. Originally, he intended to emulate his friends. They were having big parties and receiving lavish presents—why shouldn't he? But then "that kind of backfired," he told me about a year after his bar mitzvah. "I began thinking that this could be extremely meaningful to me and to everyone who attended. It would almost be my 'job' to have the best bar mitzvah I could. Not the one with the best DJ or the best music, but the one in which the kid having the bar mitzvah really put himself into it. I wrote my own speech. No one helped me. I invited only people I wanted. I planned the party. I wanted this to be *my* rite of passage."

In less than a year, Aaron had traveled from wanting a bar mitzvah to keep up with his friends to wanting a real rite of passage. "I intended," he said, "to be inducted into the faith."

Aaron's bar mitzvah was held under a large white tent in the backyard of his father's house in East Hampton, Long Island. Ninety guests came, all selected by Aaron. He read his Torah portion with panache—a section from Genesis about God creating the world. He mentioned his delight that his parents were creative people—"not just doctors or lawyers. Half the audience was doctors and lawyers. I guess I insulted them. I think they forgave me."

Probably. He's a good kid. He deserves to be cut some slack. But the adults also cried when a Holocaust survivor called Aaron's bar mitzvah an emblem of Jewish survival and resiliency—a slap at Hitler's Jew-free world. They cried again when Aaron's mother, Beth, showed the guests the *wimple* she'd made for the day. A *wimple,* the fabric that's wrapped around a Torah to keep it closed, is usually embroidered with Hebrew that states the child's name and birth date. But Beth—an artist—hadn't made a traditional *wimple.* This one had bright, almost psychedelic colors and scenes she'd appliquéd on it featuring key moments in Aaron's life: riding a wild horse in Mongolia, learning how to swim in the Atlantic, handling a sailboat for the first time. Most *wimples* were bland. This one had pizzazz—just like Aaron.

The reception afterward was fairly muted, just as Aaron wanted: a band played some quiet jazz as everyone enjoyed Aaron's favorite food, *masala dosas* with chutney, spinach, and potato. The meal—not the usual bar mitzvah fare—was catered by an Indian carryout just a few miles down the road, where Aaron and his father liked to hang out.

Aaron loved his bar mitzvah. But it didn't make him feel any different—not that day. A few days later, he realized that there had been a change, a subtle one. "I didn't feel like I was a *man,* like I could get a job in corporate America. Yet I did feel that I was moving on from my childhood, that adults would now respect me, something I'd wanted for a really long time." There was another benefit: "Now, I don't even look at most bar mitzvahs as 'Judaism.' They're just 'party time.'"

What especially galls Aaron is how much cash and glitz have distorted the reasons kids have a bar or bat mitzvah. "There's an informal competition to see who gets the most expensive gift or makes the most money," he said. "One day, I was riding the bus with a friend who'd just had his bar mitzvah. 'I made $17,000,' he told me. Thinking at first that he'd said '$1,700,' I replied that I'd received a bit more than that. Suddenly, I understood there were *three* zeroes after the 'seventeen,' and I went, 'Whoa! That's amazing.' 'Well,' my friend said, 'my grandparents gave me $10,000, and the other $7,000 came from a whole bunch of other people.' This shows how much of a 'business' bar mitzvahs have become."

Indeed, for many people, young and old, the quality of a bar or bat mitzvah can be measured in columns: one for the money, two for the show. This is not how Judah ben Tema, the father of bar mitzvahs, would have measured the day, but then, he'd never been at the Plaza and Claudia Schiffer had never blown kisses at him.

It's not unduly harsh to say that many bar and bat mitzvahs suffer from a moral vacancy, from a zeal for money making and a zest for showing off. That makes it difficult for thirteen year olds to find the spiritual DNA that can connect them to distant places and long-ago people and an eternal, forgiving, all-powerful God. They have to work hard to resuscitate meaning, to unearth the intent of all this. That means laserlike focusing and studying, and that can be difficult, weighty. Maybe tedious. Yet a certain solace awaits them. All this could be part of a plan—as usual, a divine one. As Abraham Joshua Heschel wrote, "God is hiding in the world. Our task is to let the divine emerge from our deeds." God is also hiding in bar and bat mitzvahs, and thirteen year olds can help the divine emerge. "Whoas" from sensible kids like Aaron Lemle or Alexandra Null or Nathaniel Graham can be an invaluable first step.[22]

I'M TONE-DEAF TO BELIEF

I hate to write someone's epitaph, but Leon Botstein will go to his grave as a wunderkind. No matter how old he is, or how much he's accomplished, or how solid a niche he's earned in academia and music and letters, Botstein's obit, you can bet, will prominently mention that he was the youngest president of an American university. Ever.

Which isn't bad, until you flip through Botstein's seventeen-page resume and realize that he hasn't exactly been a slouch since being appointed head of New Hampshire's now-defunct Franconia College when he was twenty-three. (That was 1970, and no one else wanted to head the place: locals were trying to run it out of town for its supposed links to left-wing terrorism.) Botstein had a bachelor's from the University of Chicago and a master's from Harvard and not much else, other than energy, curiosity, a formidable intellect, and a great determination to silence his scoffing critics. Five years later, with Franconia finally solvent and accredited (and Botstein's critics shushed), he left for Bard College in upstate New York, another campus with a far-out reputation. He discarded (some of) Bard's bohemianism, burnished its intellectual rigor, and brought it close to the top ranks of American higher education.

Not bad for a "kid" born in Zurich who settled in the Bronx with his family as a tot; who graduated from New York's tough High

School of Music and Art when he was sixteen; whose strong Bronx accent has a slight overlay from Cambridge—the one in Massachusetts, not England. He's written six books and more than one hundred seventy articles (on everything from "Hannah Arendt: The Jewish Question" for the *New Republic* to "America's Stake in the Estate Tax" for the *New York Times*). In whatever spare time he has, Botstein is also musical director of the American Symphony Orchestra, and his conducting with such groups as the London Philharmonic is available on twenty-four recordings.

Some kid! Some polymath! No slouch!

Botstein's house at Bard—roomy and cream colored, with green shutters—is clearly the home of an academic and a first-rate mind. It is a bit disheveled, with books piled where they shouldn't be; a piano, a harpsichord, and a small organ in one room; a few carpets with abstract designs scattered about; and a study at the rear for Botstein, where the books on the shelves from floor to ceiling are mostly about art or music: *Notes of Seven Decades* by Antal Dorati, *French Opera at the Fin de Siècle* by Stephen Huebner, *Marxism and Art* by Maynard Solomon, and many more.

The clutter is impressive, and it's amazing how Botstein somehow keeps track of everything. More staggering is that he keeps so many balls in the air—right in front of you. For our interview, a lengthy one, Botstein rarely removed his telephone headset. There were many distractions and calls—a daughter needed his attention; a musician needed a few pointers—yet, whenever he came to back to me and my many questions, Botstein focused exclusively upon them, issuing thoughtful, revealing answers, some with full annotations, others with subanswers and subplots of their own, all spilling nonstop and rat-a-tat-tat from his fertile, never-at-rest mind. It was a sight to behold. A bravura performance!

Botstein is scarcely an observant Jew: his is a Judaism of the intellect and less of faith, which is really nonexistent for him, a Judaism of history and literature and philosophy, of the matters of the mind and of civilization. He is also critical of the occasional narrowness of American Jews and especially disturbed by the opportunism of neoconservatives. He is a voice of the moderate, ruminative center—independent of ideology and resentful of party politics. Jews have become too successful, too "normal," he has said. After nimbly moving into the mainstream of American life, they are now "too typically complacent, lazy, and unengaged with learning and public service. . . . [They] have broken with a traditional historic alliance with the poor and the oppressed and against the entrenched interests in government and the marketplace. . . . Being Jewish represents an inspiration to assert genuine individuality, . . . to transform one's life from the ordinary to the extraordinary. That transformation depends on the life of the mind, and the cultivation of idealism. In Judaism, learning is prayer."

From his aerie at Bard, Botstein learns, which of course is his form of prayer, a mode of worship which lets him confront and satisfy his renown as a wunderkind of enormous and, possibly, unlimited promise.

I'm rigorously agnostic and have a dubious view of religion. I'm not an atheist, mind you. Atheism is another religion. I'm fascinated by theological belief, but I'm tone-deaf to the actual belief. I'm an old-time rationalist. I believe in the Enlightenment project and I take my lead from Jefferson and Adams. I am a real believer in the secular and in secular democracy; I am not a believer in religion as the source of moral values. The only route out of moral hypocrisy is emancipation from religion. I'm an old-time rationalist.

And yet, we came to this country from Switzerland when I was two. It was 1949. My parents were physicians from Eastern Europe: Poland was irretrievably anti-Semitic. My father's family had very strong Zionist roots, and my mother's great-great-great-grandfather had been chief rabbi of Moscow. I grew up with a tremendous amount of pride in our Jewish identity; it was very fascinating to me, although I grew up without any benchmarks of my parents' youth. They couldn't show me the high school they went to. They couldn't show me where they grew up. It was all behind the Iron Curtain; let alone the fact that my parents were poor and couldn't afford to travel there. They had no childhood friends here, although there were survivors from the Polish Jewish community who lived in New York. We saw them for tea in the afternoon—tea in a glass, Russian style. And everyone talked about the old country.

Being Jewish to us was not gefilte fish and not Woody Allen: those vulgarities of the American Jewish self-image are offensive. One of the things that set me apart from my fellow students at the University of Chicago was that they were embarrassed by being Jewish, and I went to synagogue on Rosh Hashanah and Yom Kippur. I did it as a matter of symbolism. I did not believe. To this day, I belong to a synagogue. I've realized that what is important to me is the emotional continuity with my ancestors and the tremendous pride I feel in the community I was born into. I didn't choose it, but I am happy that it is what it is. It's a matter of honor to be part of that community; I cannot abide people who do not acknowledge that identity and do not participate in the communal life of the people whom they were born into. Barring that, for me, attending synagogue is symbolic. I go the fewest times possible over the course of the year. I can no longer, as an adult, sit there and read stuff I can't possibly get my mind around.

Having a bar mitzvah was a foregone conclusion. It was comparable to being asked, "Do you want to have dinner?" It was not an option. This was a European environment. There was no negotiation. The one thing that was slightly negotiable was whether I would quit my formal Jewish instruction *after* bar mitzvah. The rabbi teaching it was not a favorite of my parents, and I must have said something arrogant in class. I believe I suggested that we read the New Testament. He sent me home and then called my parents. They told him that they took my side. From that point on, I was exempted from attending. My parents hated parochialism and provincialism.

Of the bar mitzvah itself, I don't remember anything of the actual event. I don't think I distinguished myself in any way. I'm sure it was a perfectly routine affair. I don't remember a line of my haftarah. The reception was at our home in Riverdale in the Bronx, and there was family and a small group of the old country people. It was no big social event and there was no band and there was no caterer. There may have been modest help in the kitchen, but we're not talking anything lavish. I visually remember my sister's bat mitzvah and I visually remember my brother's bar mitzvah. But not my own, maybe because I had a very, very low self-image: a deep, deep irrevocable and irremovable insecurity. I was left-handed and there was a failed attempt to change me to right-handedness, which was a European custom. I also stuttered all my childhood, and I was very shy and immensely clumsy and nearsighted. I spent most of my time alone: I was not very popular and didn't have a lot of friends and spent a lot of time reading. And because I was the younger brother of two very bright siblings, I was considered dumb. (When I was in sixth grade, I made family legend by writing a required autobiography. The first line was, "Until I entered the fifth grade, I was mentally retarded.") So I had no perception of myself as either bright or smart or charming or attractive.

I am an unbelievable overachiever. I am not an underachiever. I was deeply motivated by the desire to find that elusive thing which is "security," an inner security, and to find a sense of worth. I can't say I've succeeded, but I certainly have worked hard enough to transform the demons into work. In other words, I've put what might otherwise be self-destructive energy to a constructive use. I am willing to believe that going to Hebrew school and having a bar mitzvah was an important part of making that possible. But I don't remember its causal relationship. I don't remember the credit which I owe it. I did have one Hebrew school teacher who liked me. That was important. It's very important to have adults who are not your relatives take an interest in you.

People think that if they remember something, it's significant. That's not correct. One doesn't need to be Sigmund Freud to understand that if we forget something, it could have been as significant. What we tell ourselves is not the same as what actually happened. Nor is what we remember that which influences us the most. Which is why our account of our own lives is essentially unreliable, except for the externals. Yes, I'm probably a reliable witness that I graduated high school. I'm probably reliable about who taught me in some cases, certainly in college. And I certainly take responsibility for my memories in adult life. Important things had to have happened, but not every event that was important do I remember. I'm sure that my father would have remembered my bar mitzvah pretty clearly. I don't.

I think we confuse the actual bar mitzvah with its unspoken significance. And the unspoken significance, in my view, is that not only did it take, did I go through the routine of being taken seriously, but it also was a humbling event. A bar mitzvah focuses you on the complexity and the wealth of Judaic tradition and thought. It opens a door into a house of wonders. I didn't choose to go further into that house, but it framed me—it frames all of us who have these ceremonies—in terms of modesty and in terms of a lifelong trajectory of learning. You knew that this begins at the age of thirteen in earnest and that it's lifelong. I would not underestimate the powerful significance of the bar mitzvah. It may seem as trivial as getting a passport. But then you open that passport, and you see the crest of the United States, and you realize that you hold a symbol of a national tradition. It's the same thing. With a bar mitzvah, you are getting a passport into something that is vast, unending, and endlessly fascinating.

These are tremendously important events. They signal in some bizarre way the need to no longer infantilize the child. What is great about a bar mitzvah as an idea is the acknowledgment—the public acknowledgment—of the significance that a child is now an equal member, even a child who had been unseen or was considered negligible. This is an extremely important public ritual. We baby talk to children. We don't treat them with respect. We don't give them responsibilities. Any ritual that is institutionalized and forces people to listen to a thirteen year old, that's good. It may be ruined by commercialization. And it may be ruined by the vulgarity of people and the inability of rabbis to find an intelligent way to do this sometimes. But when done right, it can be terribly worthwhile.

We have a Christmas tree in December and an egg hunt at Easter. None of it has any religious significance to anyone. My children are very, very aware that they are Jewish, those Christmas trees notwithstanding: the trees are purely a commercial event. My children know that they're Jewish by their last name and by the prominence of their father's evident activity. I've written a great deal on Jewish matters; they know very well who I am and where they come from. They also know that they are part of the intermarriage community that the Reform movement has embraced and that the Conservative and Orthodox communities have not. We celebrate Hanukkah and we observe Rosh Hashanah. My children have never set foot inside a church; the mother of my last two children is not Jewish and, like me, has no religious conviction.

At her request, my oldest daughter, Sarah, had a Reform bat mitzvah. She was almost ten when my second child, Abigail, who was two years younger than her, was killed [by a car]. Sarah saw it happen. Much has to be said for her desire to focus the family on a constructive event by having a bat mitzvah. The two girls had a partly competitive relationship, but they were also very close and quite different. Sarah was more introspective, thoughtful, and shy; Abby was more of an entertainer, more outgoing. Sarah had more depth as a child. She did more questioning. I think Sarah was motivated to have a bat mitzvah by some sense, as children have, that she was responsible for the death itself. Or maybe she had a little bit of the guilt of a survivor, and she wanted to compensate, to be doubly good. Her bat mitzvah was a perfectly fine event, and I think it was very important to her.

My third child, Clara, didn't want a bat mitzvah, and the fourth, Max, didn't want a bar mitzvah either. I was very encouraging of both of them. I repeatedly said, as they became ten, eleven, twelve, "Listen, you know, keep it in mind," because they have friends doing this. And they both, without much hesitation, said no. Max has private Latin lessons; he plays the violin and the piano; he goes to martial arts. He's fully occupied by things he wants to do. A bar mitzvah is something he doesn't really want to do. But I told him, "At some point, maybe in your high school years, if you want instruction in Jewish history and a close reading of the Bible, I'll sponsor you to it and I will take you to Israel," which makes sense to me because I think the only point of bar mitzvah is learning, and that learning has to be motivated by a *need* to know, not by rote. If a year or two from now Max says he wants to systematically go through the Bible from beginning to end, I will find a young seminary student to sit with him and read it through. There's a high likelihood that that might happen before long. As for Clara, she's enrolled in a course in Jewish history at Princeton and is slowly focusing on finding out a little bit more about this heritage.

Max is now thirteen and I see him schlepping to one bar mitzvah after another, to one elegant reception after another. He's become a connoisseur of these events and he has strong opinions about them. As I do. I'm not of the school of thought that the bar mitzvah is a bad thing. I believe that there's only an upside to it. There is no downside. I don't see a bar mitzvah as negative in any sense, except that the dinner/dance/party aspect of it—the conspicuous consumption of the very wealthy in New York—can be reinforced too much. But the same can be said of weddings or birthday parties. It can be said of anything, so why shouldn't it apply to bar mitzvahs?

My children live in a different time from when I was growing up. They have witnessed the gradual illiberalism of America. As I was growing up, people thought that religion would come to an end, that superstition would be supplanted, that religions would converge. My children have lived through a revival of religious fundamentalism, of intolerance even in the Jewish community, of an enormous transformation in the Land of Israel, of an enormous transformation in the Jewish community's relation with itself as it splinters into orthodoxy and fundamentalism and fails to accommodate the role of women. My revulsion at religion has grown over time as its political role, worldwide, has become more horrifying and the darkness descends and the intolerance descends. My children have grown up watching with horror the evolution in public life. And yet, ultimately what is important to me is that they, and I, have an emotional continuity with our ancestors and have a tremendous pride in having been born into that community. I'm not displeased that two of my children have chosen not to have a bar or bat mitzvah. I would have found it a source of some awkwardness, just because the institutionalization of religion in this time leaves such a bad taste in my mouth.

I WAS LIKE A SPY. LIKE A CLOSET JEW

Roz Chast lives on a small street in a small town, just one block off of Main Street. It's a short walk to a well-endowed library and some friendly stores and a few family-owned restaurants that have resisted raising their prices to Manhattan levels. Or their coffee tab to Starbucks levels.

It all sounds very normal, and when I drove by Chast's house, it all looked very normal: a white colonial on a short street called "New." It's so small townish, so *Our Town*ish. Norman Rockwell would have been happy here. Then I saw Chast standing in the window, awaiting my arrival, and her hand flapping a little wave, and her blond hair—shoulder length, but not as glamorous as that might sound—bouncing up and down as she did a little jig, and I sensed that behind the walls of this two-story, just slightly unkempt house was a presence that could be at odds with suburban Connecticut.

Since 1978, when the *New Yorker* began running Chast's cartoons, fans have delighted in her tidy, compact compressions of the neuroses of our age. Her drawings are loose but disciplined; her tone is frustrated confusion or bewildered delight—or both; her message, if indeed there is a "message," is that life is a lark, a joy, a pain in the ass—all at the same time. How else to explain a drawing of a tombstone that reads:

ED JONES

Tuned in,
Turned on,
Dropped out,
Dropped in,
Worked out,
Saved up,
Dropped dead.

Or Chast's "Required Seventh Grade Reading List":

The Red Badge of Boredom
Death, Be Not Monotonous
The Tedious Pimpernel
Silas Yawnfest
All Humdrum on the Western Front
Ennui Pond
The Dull Man and the Sea

Or her forays into the murky waters of parenthood, like a car crammed with Pa, Ma, and their brood passing a billboard that reads, "Mom and Dad Really Lose It—¼ Mile." Or a mother saying goodbye to her daughter who's heading out on a date: "Oh, you definitely look like a cheap slut in that! Have fun! See you whenever!"

Chast's brave, unflinching, zany look at us, at our world, at herself may be what prompted David Remnick, the *New Yorker*'s editor, to call her "the magazine's only certifiable genius"—high praise from the guy who runs what may be the best magazine in the world.

Born and bred in Brooklyn, trained at the Rhode Island School of Design (in painting, not cartooning), she debuted her cartoons in the *New Yorker* when she was twenty-three. Her parents are Jewish, although she was raised with scant knowledge of Judaism. She's married to humorist Bill Franzen, who was raised Presbyterian; they have two kids (Ian, seventeen, and Nina, thirteen) and two parrots,

Marco and Eli (ages unknown). As Ian and Nina weren't home during our interview, I'd assumed we'd have quiet and solitude to concentrate on the interview. But the parrots were there, and they kept squawking "Brother" and "Hello." It was disconcerting. And entertaining.

Interviewing Chast was like walking into a Chast cartoon, with improbable, freeform associations that could only come out of her cartoony mind. Except that this "cartoon" talked and gestured and clapped and grimaced and smiled and made sound effects: a cartoon come to life! Fun, yes, although sometimes getting a straight answer out of her was a challenge. When asked her age, she said, "I'm 49.9999"—her fiftieth birthday was in two weeks. Asked if anything was missing from her teen years, she exclaimed in a snooty, WASPy accent, "Oh, Dr. Magida! Our session's up already?"

The playfulness was the cost of interviewing a cartoonist. It was also the pleasure of interviewing a cartoonist, one who was religiously marginalized as a kid. And ever since. In fact, Chast was doubly marginalized as a kid: displaced from the other Jewish kids when they were excused from public school to attend Jewish after-school programs, she was left in her classroom with the few kids who were not Jewish—each of whom belonged to a minority in which Chast had no place.

When Chast first opened her door for me, she almost resembled a suburban matron, with her black pants and red-and-black cardigan sweater. Soon I realized she was no cool, aloof matron but intelligently befuddled, honestly intrigued, and pleasurably silly: she wants to make sense of the universe and the cosmos and herself, and she seeks answers for these strange lives of ours. Maybe she's waiting to be invited to the sort of bash she parodied in a cartoon titled "The Party, after You Left." Set on a rooftop terrace in Manhattan with guests milling about, kibitzing, the cartoon features a bearded guy in the lower right-hand corner exulting, "Hey! Look who just walked in! Yo! Jesus! Buddha! Over here!" If a party like that doesn't set Chast on the road to salvation, maybe nothing will—except another flurry of great cartoons in the *New Yorker.* The pleasure they give us will do wonders for her soul, and for ours.

My school was mostly Jewish, but I was not invited to any bar or bat mitzvahs of the kids who went there. Instead, I went to *one* bar mitzvah—my cousin's. The part where he said his Torah recitation was amazing, but I didn't understand so much of the ceremony; it was so boring. No one had prepared me for it in any way.

I had a very isolated childhood in many, many, *many* ways. At 2 P.M. on Wednesdays, the Jewish kids would get out of class for religious instruction. This went on from about first or second grade all the way through sixth when I was going to P.S. 217 ["P.S." is New York City jargon for "public school"]. I was very jealous. Just about the only kids left in the classroom were the Asian kid and the black kid and the Norwegian kid and me, because this school in Brooklyn was about 99 percent Jewish. But both my parents worked and the maid would have had to pick me up and take me to a temple, and she didn't drive, and it all would have been much too complicated. And anyway, my parents weren't into religion.

Sitting in that classroom with those three or four kids, I felt like leftovers. Like an outcast. Like someone who was unclassifiable. We would stay there and color or do something unimportant because the teacher couldn't continue with her lessons with just about everybody gone.

The same thing happened every Rosh Hashanah. If the school was open, my parents would send me, and I'd sit there with the Asian kid and the black kid and the Norwegian kid. I didn't even know that I was Jewish. I didn't really get it for a long time. It's kind of weird when what you present isn't typically Jewish: I have blond hair and my last name is not particularly Jewish. It isn't "Goldberg," and I don't have black, frizzy hair or whatever it is that people from the "outside" associate with Jews. Later, when I was in college, a girl said, "I transferred from Syracuse University. Too many Jews." For me, it was like, "Huh? Excuse me?" But I kept quiet. I was like a spy. Like a closet Jew.

I felt so left out when I was a kid. For me, it wasn't [adopts a pseudo-scholarly accent], "I wish I knew more about my cultural heritage." Instead, it was [starts to whine], "But Mom, *everybody's* going and I want to go, too."

We briefly went to a synagogue on Ocean Parkway, and for a little while when I was around seven, my mother enrolled me in a Bible class. They gave me this children's book of Bible stories—a hardback with a blue cover with black-and-white illustrations in the middle of it. About all I remember is what it looked like, and my mother talking about the incompetence of the teacher. I remember nothing about the content of the class. My mother paid me a quarter to go to each class. She *bribed* me! So that was kind of cool. I went three or four times and then they took me out. Why? I don't know. Maybe it was because it was inconvenient or I wasn't learning anything. If I didn't like it and it was inconvenient, then, you know, what was the point?

That was my small brush with religious instruction, and it contributed to my weird sense of isolation. My mother was judgmental about the whole situation. Maybe other parents had a similar feeling, but maybe they really wanted to go to temple. Or maybe they liked socializing with the other parents. My parents didn't, and I think that my mother sort of felt superior to the other parents. And she didn't bond with them, maybe because she was a lot older than them. And she was a working woman, which was not that common in those days.

When I wasn't invited to all those bar and bat mitzvahs, it wasn't much more than not being invited to a birthday party, of which there were so many [bursts into mock tears and wailing]. And I don't think I could ever have a bat mitzvah of my own. First of all, [a bit wistful now] I can't say that I really *yearn* for it. It's never crossed my mind for a second. And part of my problem is that all this takes so much commitment, and I'm so fucking ambivalent about everything. It always *sounds* good, and debating those ethical lessons that are in the Talmud always seems interesting—taking a point and arguing it back and forth. That's so engaging. But then there's all that other stuff, stuff that you have to *believe!* It's soooo hard to believe.

My parents were not into religion in any way. It was a combination of lack of interest and lack of commitment to give me any kind of Jewish education. I don't think they liked anything about religion. They . . . ah . . . [long pause] associated it with a lot of things that *I* associate with it: very dogmatic, close-minded people who think they have the answers to everything. My father is deeply agnostic, and my mother is slightly less agnostic, although every once in a while she personally talks to God. Like, if she gets a good parking spot, she'll go, "Thank *you,* God!" I guess this can't hurt. It's what a friend calls the Bellhop Theory of Life: you pray to God for whatever you want, and then He delivers it. It's kind of horrendous and pretty much persuades me that it's just better not to have any religious beliefs at all.

Both my parents were in "the system," which is what people who worked for public schools in New York called it. My mother was an assistant principal at a grade school; my father taught French and Spanish at Lafayette High School. They weren't interested in becoming part of a Jewish community, or maybe they felt as if they already were, because they were in the New York City school system, which was a very Jewish community in itself. But it certainly didn't include me or anyone my age. They didn't talk about religion or spiritual beliefs, and they didn't seem very interested in mine.

They're both ninety-two now. He's kind of skinny, and when he's nervous, he kind of curls up into himself; she's very sturdy—built like a fire hydrant—and has great posture. They're both pretty anxious, but my mother is like that more on the outside. Every action for my father is determined by how anxious he is. If he was sitting here, he would go from how you could fall through these couches that, to him, too easily separate to how you wouldn't want to catch your finger on that stapler on the desk over there because it has a little bit of rust on it to the sharp edge on the table that's such a "danger." He's like a chain anxiety person.

We lived in an apartment building in a section of Brooklyn called Ditmas Park. (It was known as Flatbush until realtors decided they would do better by giving parts of it fancy names.) It was a working-class and middle-class neighborhood, with a mixture of Jews and Italians and Irish and a sprinkling of Asians. And lots of stores at the street level: a hardware store, a luncheonette, a butcher shop, a shoe store, a ladies' clothing shop. My parents were very proud that we didn't live above a store. For them, that was one step up.

Our building was one of those apartment buildings with six floors and apartments A to L on one side and M to Z on the other side, and both sides connected by a lobby that had two chairs that were padlocked so no one would steal them. It was kind of like they were runaway prisoners who needed ankle chains. The lobby also used to have a rug, but that was stolen. At one time, there were these fake flowers in the lobby that were changed seasonally. I don't know if they still do that.

My parents still live there—Apartment 2J. And they have so much stuff! There's a whole archeology of rubber bands on the doorknobs. They never throw anything away! It's amazing that their apartment hasn't totally collapsed into 1J. We rarely went to High Holiday services, and we occasionally had Passover Seders, and we did very little for Hanukkah, and, of course, we had no use for Christmas, although my mother's sister married a Roman Catholic and they had a Christmas tree. I loved its icicles and silver and tinsel. It was so beautiful. To a kid, you know, there's really nothing like a Christmas tree. A Hanukkah bush just does not cut it.

So in my childhood, my Jewish identity was very tangential. But over the years, it's sort of crept up on me. Part of it is meeting people as an adult who have more of a Jewish background than you do and you think, "Gee, I wish I knew that," although I don't think I could now really learn about religion in the same way that I could have when I was a kid. I'm pretty skeptical now.

Somehow as I get older, I feel more of a Jewish identity, even though I'm not a practicing Jew and never have been. In some really basic way, I identify as a Jew. It's what I am. It's like: I'm female; and I'm a certain age; and I'm Jewish. Although my husband would say, "You don't *practice* Judaism. You don't go to temple. How can you call yourself a Jew?" And I say, "It's not *that*. It's cultural and ethnic and genetic *and* religious. It's a *whole* thing that goes back generations and generations and generations— thousands and thousands of years.

If you're from Brooklyn, a lot of this cultural aspect of being Jewish is built into you. But not necessarily the religious aspect. It would have been nice to get out of school on Wednesday afternoons with the other Jewish kids. I would have felt a greater sense of belonging. But it's just . . . it's just too much to hope for! Do people who have happy childhoods become cartoonists? I don't know.

In some ways, I had some experiences that sort of correspond to a rite of passage: getting my own apartment at Seventy-third and Amsterdam [in Manhattan] when I was twenty-three for $250 a month rent and paying all my own bills. All that started in January 1978. And in April 1978, I sold my first cartoon to the *New Yorker*. I cooked on a hotplate and had great dinner parties—one burner for the pasta, one burner for the sauce. And salad. And wine. A *lot* of wine because on that hotplate, it took about an hour for the water to start boiling and then for the pasta to be ready. By then, we were pretty pie-faced. But it *was* a rite of passage. Just not a bat mitzvah.

My thirteen-year-old daughter goes to a lot of these events. Just a few weeks ago, she asked me to drive her down to Virginia for a friend's bat mitzvah. My daughter is a very questioning person. She thinks about a lot of these things. She's interested in Buddhism, and she's been a vegetarian since she was seven or eight. But she doesn't believe in organized religion. She's interested in people and society and ethics; she's really not interested in having to go to a certain place at a certain time and being with people whom you might not even like that much.

She may end up suffering from the same sense of "not belonging" that I did. I don't know. But the kids in her classes are not almost all Jewish, as they were in mine. Maybe she suffers from this a little already—a lot of people up here go to church and form ties from that community, and some of the Jews belong to the temple in town. However, she and I talk about "stuff" all the time. Not Judaism specifically but at least some stuff that goes beyond "dinner is on the table." Maybe I'm letting myself off the hook too easily. And anyway, it's not so bad to have a little sense of being an outsider. If you're going to be an artist, you should have some of that sense. It's worked for me.

The kids haven't expressed much interest in religion, and we haven't steered them, either. I wasn't steered toward religion as a kid. Bill *had* to go to church, and he hated it. Just hated it. He can't stand organized religion and has no desire to go to church. He sees religions as mostly fear based ("God will be mad at you if you don't go to church!") and filled with superstition and meaningless rituals that do more harm than good in the world. He doesn't consider himself an atheist, though. He loves the writings of Joseph Campbell, and he's more sure than I am that there's some kind of consciousness after this life.

You know, in a weird way, I'm sometimes jealous of Orthodox families. They're not filled with the same anxiety as "modern" families. They know they belong to this faith, and they believe in it wholeheartedly, and it works for them. And they have community. And you bring up your kids exactly as they *should* be brought up. Your life is marked out for you, and you don't have time to putter around. In some ways, that's very appealing. But *I* couldn't do it. I'd be dead in a minute.

I WANTED TO MAKE MY PARENTS PROUD

If God gave gold stars for being articulate, Harold Kushner would be first in line: ask him a question, and what follows, with barely a moment's pause, is thoughtful and challenging and parses almost better than anything in Strunk and White's classic on English usage, *Elements of Style.* Kushner has a way with words and phrases, and he makes it all seem so easy, the trait of a born teacher who can invent catchy aphorisms right on the spot: "Fun can be the dessert of our lives, but never the main course." "We can handle mortality. We cannot handle insignificance."

And if God gave a gold medal for handling adversity, Kushner would get that too. In 1977 his fourteen-year-old son, Aaron, died of progeria—rapid aging—and his parents, Harold and Suzette, suffered a deep and raw grief. As Kushner, who was then with a temple in a Boston suburb, told me, "I would much rather have been left a mediocre and insensitive preacher and have my son alive." Kushner turned his search for solace into one of the best-selling books of the past twenty years—*When Bad Things Happen to Good People.* Guiding readers through the inadequacies of the traditional answers to the problem of evil, Kushner deftly helps them accommodate pain and faith and disappointment in God. "I had to believe," Kushner explained, "that God was as outraged at these painful events as I was, that He was on my side, that He wants people to live and rejoice. I need to believe in God for the confidence that the world is secure, that life makes sense, and that there is a purpose for our being here. In the final analysis the question of why bad things happen to good people transmutes itself into some very different questions, no longer asking why something happened but asking how we will respond, what we intend to do now that it happened."

By making God a witness to rather than the cause of our woes, Kushner put Him on the same plane as us: God grieves too, because he does not want to interfere with His own creation. Otherwise, the universe is a giant plaything, a cosmic board game with one player: its inventor. God wrote the first few chapters of the Book of Life and is waiting for us to finish the rest.

Raised in Brooklyn, educated at Columbia University and the Jewish Theological Seminary in New York, Kushner was rabbi at Temple Israel in Natick, Massachusetts, for twenty-four years before deciding to spend most of his time writing books and roaming around the lecture circuit. Now rabbi laureate at Temple Israel, he still delivers sermons during High Holiday services.

The writing-est rabbi in the United States, Kushner followed *When Bad Things Happen to Good People* with a string of other best-sellers—*When All You've Ever Wanted Isn't Enough, When Children Ask about God, Who Needs God,* and more. In all these books, Kushner explores our standing with God and with ourselves. "Everything in God's world," he says, "can be holy if you realize its potential holiness."

That throws the ball right into our court: There'll be no helping hand from Heaven. We have to do the heavy lifting ourselves. We have to seek out holiness: it's hidden, it's covered, and it's concealed. Nothing in Kushner's theology is easy; nothing is God-given except life. Which may be why Kushner says that a "primary goal of religion is to teach people to like themselves and feel good about themselves. All my experience has taught me that people who feel good about themselves will be more generous, more forgiving of others, less defensive about their mistakes, more accessible to change, and better able to cope with misfortune and adversity."

Four decades as a rabbi and it all comes down to liking ourselves? Indeed. If so, there's a reasonably good chance of rising above the muck and the mire and letting religion become our compass, our

North Star to decency and compassion. For Harold Kushner, who suffered so much when his only son died, it all comes down to faith and to coping, including coping with the almost seven hundred bar and bat mitzvahs at which he's officiated, where he's seen the kids' visible relief that it's over—and their parents' visible pride in their kids.

A bar mitzvah is more for the parents than for the child. When I was a regular pulpit rabbi and would talk to the kids, trying to get to know them, asking, "How do you feel about this?" the answer that came through, 100 percent of the time, was, "It's important that my parents be proud of me."

But what does a bar or bat mitzvah mean for the parents? What makes *them* proud? That they have raised this child and successfully brought him close to independence—from now on, he will more active in choosing his own friends, in articulating his own values. It means that they have successfully passed on the sense of Jewish loyalty from generation to generation: "Whatever else this kid grows up to do, we have maintained a sense of Jewish activity while we have control over it." Which is very important. It means they have helped the child do something that was difficult and know that he is competent.

You know, they're all entering a new stage in their lives. The father may be in his late thirties if this is his first child or in his midforties if it's his third or fourth; for him, it means he's starting to feel a bit middle aged. And since nothing will age a parent faster than having a teenager—the relationship between adolescents and parents naturally is stormy—the bar mitzvah is a way of saying, "Let's get this off on a good footing. Do something that will make us proud of you and we will proclaim to the world just how proud we are."

Then, every once in a while, some thirteen-year-old boy says, "This is extremely important to my parents, but I don't give a damn about them." And you know you're in trouble then. That simply verges on the pathological.

Is anybody a "man" at thirteen? I think that once upon a time, people were. You know, the Talmudic definition of bar mitzvah is not the age of thirteen but the occurrence of pubic hair. So more or less around thirteen, you're leaving childhood behind. Now I've seen a lot of bar mitzvahs and a lot of bat mitzvahs, and some kids are more mature than others. There are some girls at thirteen who look like they are ready to get married, and there are some boys at thirteen who make me wonder if they're toilet trained. But I don't know how much later you can defer the ceremony and still not be too late to mark the transition from childhood to a sense of adolescence. That is, at what point does a child start to make decisions for himself? Thirteen is probably as good as you can get it.

My own bar mitzvah took place in April of 1948. This was in the Brooklyn Jewish Center on Eastern Parkway in Crown Heights. At the time, Crown Heights was an up-and-coming community for upwardly mobile Jewish families: my father, who'd been born and raised in a small village in Lithuania, came to the United States around age twenty or twenty-two, started a toy business a few months before the crash of October 1929, went through some very hard times, and by the time we came along (I have a younger brother) the business was making it. Eventually, it was extremely successful. And the temple was then one of the largest, most prestigious congregations in the country. It was absolutely magnificent, featuring a large dome and the gates to the *aaron khodesh* [the ark which shelters the Torah scrolls] from the Jewish exhibit at the World's Fair in the 1940s. The building was a knockout.

Every Sabbath, whether or not there was a bar mitzvah, a thousand or more people attended services. We were there pretty much every Sabbath because we had a fairly serious Conservative Jewish home. We kept kosher, we lit Sabbath candles, my father would take off for the holidays. He was also an officer at the temple and personally friendly with our rabbi, who was a houseguest and trusted my mother's kashruth.

I went to Hebrew school two afternoons a week plus Sundays and got a very intense Jewish education. The teachers cared very deeply about what kind of Jews we would become, and there was a lot of emphasis on spoken Hebrew and on Bible. Since I was a good student, learning the haftarah and the Torah were no challenge. My Torah reading was several chapters about leprosy, but that Sabbath was when you proclaim the coming of the month of Nisan, which was two weeks until Passover. So my haftarah was not about leprosy, thank goodness. It was about cleansing the temple in anticipation of Passover.

Even though I was a good Hebrew student, I had no idea what my haftarah was about. In fact, when I was the rabbi in Natick, I once told a bar mitzvah boy that he had the same haftarah that I had chanted years before, and that at the time I hadn't understood it. Later on, I said, I understood that it was about setting aside a special place—the temple precincts—for the kind of spiritual activity that could only take place there, and I hoped that the thirteen year old standing in front of me would remember this day as his entry into a very special part of the world where special things of a spiritual nature happen. How did he respond to me? I don't think he did.

I didn't give a *d'var Torah*. I memorized a standard speech, which I suspect half the congregation could have recited along with me, because either in English or in Hebrew, it was the same every single week, something like, "I come humbly before you, oh Lord, on this very special occasion which marks my passage from boyhood to manhood, and I pray that you will be with me at all times, and I pledge that the tefillin which I will henceforth place on my forehead will keep all of my thoughts directed to you and the tefillin which I place on my arm will keep all of my deeds dedicated to the well-being of the Jewish people." Or words to that effect. I could have said it in English, but my parents sort of leaned on me because it was more impressive to memorize the Hebrew. So I memorized the Hebrew speech and understood maybe half of it. The bottom line was that I wanted to make my parents *proud*.

The day could not have made me feel any more Jewish. I was heavily involved in this through study and at home and in observance. I felt I passed through a gate, that my status was different. And I felt relief: I did it. It's over with. I did okay. At some level, maybe I subliminally got the message that it was in my capacity to really take something challenging and do it and do it well. In some ways, outside of the parent/adolescent connection, that's probably the most important dimension of the bar mitzvah experience. This newfound sense of competence is a wonderful thing at a time when kids are feeling so unsure about themselves. The spotlight shines on them and they excel. It can't possibly be the same if it's a group experience.

But I clearly remember—and this is very strange, since it's fifty-seven years later—how disappointed I was that the rabbi, who was probably my inspiration for going into the rabbinate, did not take my becoming bar mitzvah more personally. I was a star student, a son of the temple officer, and yet he just gave me the same word-for-word rote charge that he gave *all* the kids. I would have liked to have been acknowledged as an outstanding student from a very active family. When I became a rabbi, I always made sure I did that.

Afterward, there was a very low-key reception at home with probably no more than fifty guests and a fairly simple catered luncheon and, for the most part, some very nondescript presents. Many bar mitzvahs, in those days, were modest, but my best friend had a kind of a throwaway service and a fairly elegant but not knock-your-socks-off reception. So it was going on, but not anything like I encountered later when I was an assistant rabbi in Great Neck, Long Island, in the early 1960s, right after I came out of the army. There was a lot more money and a lot more materialism, unfortunately. At the end of World War II, many families who had been living in New York moved to the suburbs and became more affluent. With that, the bar mitzvah experience changed and, at one level, stopped being what it was meant to be. On rare occasions, I attend a bar mitzvah in a Reform temple, and it always saddens me that it's become similar to a wedding or a birthday party with prayers, with people there by invitation only. One thing that made a bar mitzvah work was being accepted into the community. But so often, the community isn't there.

Contemporary bar and bat mitzvahs also have something to do with the sociological term "potlatch," which means, "I will show how prosperous I am by giving a lot of stuff away and virtually going into hock in the process." It's an opportunity for fathers to show off. In Great Neck, I had a sense that fathers or mothers would go to a caterer, hand him a blank check, and say, "I want this to be the social event of the year. I want you to out-do everyone else." Unfortunately, it wasn't my job to sit down with parents and say, "Why don't you tone things down just a tad?" I was only the assistant rabbi. But it was vulgar and embarrassing and I wished we weren't caught up in it.

At my temple in Natick, a middle- to upper-middle-class suburb, we were surrounded by some of the wealthiest suburbs in New England, but we never had that kind of problem. And my successor at the temple has done something really nice. He can't insist, but he strongly urges that the bar mitzvah family, instead of just sponsoring cookies and wine for Kiddush, offers a light lunch for all in attendance. That symbolizes the fact that their son or daughter has been accepted in the congregation. The synagogue in Miami where my daughter and son-in-law belong does something very similar, virtually insisting on it.

In some ways, the real bar mitzvah in today's culture is getting a driver's license. Talk about adult responsibility, freedom, independence! When

I first came to Natick with all sorts of visionary dreams about forty years ago, I tried to create a ritual for a teenager who was getting his driver's license. This would be kind of a second bar mitzvah—the *real* coming of age. The kids would acknowledge how seriously they respected life and property, and the parents would say something about how much they trusted this youngster. I think one kid opted for it. Why? Two possibilities: one is that I'm not really as smart as I thought I was and I did not conduct a meaningful ceremony. And two, one of the hardest things in the world is to create a new ritual. What makes a ritual work is that this has been going on for generations. The ceremony died a death unnoticed.

The question remains: how do we move the center of gravity at bar and bat mitzvahs closer to the service and further from the party? I don't know. Some temples have a thirteen mitzvahs program, in which you have to do several mitzvahs, several good deeds, so a bar mitzvah is not simply learning a part and performing it but accepting the responsibility of what it means to become a Jew. My successor at Temple Israel in Natick has begun inviting parents to say something to their son. Two-thirds of them do, one-third opt not to. But it brings a certain meaningfulness into the ceremony. And something else which is probably the most helpful but is not in our power, as rabbis, to control is the economic limitations of a lot of families. They can't afford a big bash, and we often have the option to make the service special and more personalized. But the trouble is that a lot of parents are uncomfortable in the service; they know how to throw a party, but they don't know how to attend a Sabbath service. We keep telling them to come: why don't you spend as much time learning to be comfortable at the service as you're putting into planning the party? This takes with some people, and not with many others.

And yet, I've never been comfortable with my colleagues who want to make radical changes in how the bar mitzvah is structured because, darn it!, this is the only thing that we, as Jews, have that works. Why would you tinker with it? In the 1960s Leonard Fein [then the editor of *Moment* magazine] wrote a very interesting piece about why synagogues didn't die off to be replaced by Jewish Community Centers when the JCCs seemed to better capture the values of the average Jewish family. Essentially, he said, they have survived because of what's represented by the bar mitzvah. No matter what synagogues do on a week-in and week-out basis, there is something in the Jewish soul that says there is a religious, spiritual dimension to a child's coming of age, to a wedding, to a funeral. You can't do what the Russians tried to do with weddings [in the former Soviet Union]: sign the register [in a certain government office, usually city hall] and leave with the woman called by the husband's last name. Even people who are not religious recognize that something profound goes on in a synagogue, and that holds true for the bar mitzvah as well.

I was an army chaplain at Fort Sill, Oklahoma, when I officiated at a bar mitzvah for my first time. There was a career military family on post whose son turned thirteen; with much difficulty, we prepared him to do a little bit of something. Given the nature of the military population, most of the attendees were not Jewish, and the bar mitzvah boy's mother was overheard saying to a Christian friend of hers, "It's just like when you go mass. The guy is up there mumbling and you don't understand a word of it."

But one of the highlights of my career was officiating at the bar mitzvah of my son, Aaron. He died a year after his bar mitzvah. His progeria kept him very small, very strange looking, almost like E.T. He was also very bright. The best thing we ever did for him was put him in the Solomon Schechter School in Boston, where his intelligence was an asset and his inability to play football and basketball was overlooked. We never knew whether he would live to age thirteen. The performance part of the bar mitzvah was assumed. He learned his haftarah over a weekend and did extensive Torah reading. The only limitation was his physical stamina. We had to build a little stepladder for him to climb so he could reach the lectern. He was not more than three feet tall and never weighed much more than twenty-five to twenty-eight pounds, even as an adolescent. Of course, I had a different perspective than the average bar mitzvah father: I looked out at the congregation the whole time and sensed that everybody there was there to share the moment with us, that the entire congregation knew they were witnessing something really remarkable.

Our daughter's bat mitzvah was three years later. This was 1979. Until then, girls would become bat mitzvah on the Friday night of the Shabbat service and boys on Saturday morning; we had just changed the rules so girls would become bat mitzvah on Saturday also. I didn't want Ariel to be the first girl on a Saturday morning; I didn't want people to think I had changed the rules for her. So I made sure there was at least one other Saturday morning bat mitzvah before hers. And in defiance of all laws of genetics, she has a beautiful voice and was able to do a lot with that.

With Aaron, there was such gratitude that he had lived long enough to do this, and that he did so remarkably well. With Ariel, there was the sense that she, too, had done well, but also that she had transmitted the family heritage and brought it to the point where we, her parents, could no longer insist on it but only hope that she'd done it well enough that it will last. But we just don't know.

11 · *Letty and Abigail Pogrebin, Mother and Daughter*

"YOU ARE A WOMAN" MEANT "YOU DO THE DISHES"

Letty Cottin Pogrebin had a bat mitzvah when she was thirteen—right on schedule. Abigail Pogrebin had her bat mitzvah when she was forty, only twenty-seven years "off schedule."

Mother and daughter. Letty—pioneering feminist, a founder of *Ms. Magazine*, author of several books—worked on everything from *Free to Be You and Me*, that seventies paean to gender equality, to *Deborah, Golda, and Me*, her sometimes brutally honest memoir. And Abigail—a former producer at *60 Minutes* and a writer herself—has freelanced for *New York* and *Harper's* and is the author of the best-seller *Stars of David*, in which celebrities (Stephen Spielberg, Ruth Bader Ginsberg, Mike Nichols, Dustin Hoffman, and more) discuss what being Jewish means to them.

Clearly, this family has talent. And woes. Over the past six decades, Letty has been embedded in Judaism, strayed from Judaism, returned to Judaism. In some ways, she's still coming to terms with Judaism. And Abigail, who never received a Jewish education as a kid or a bat mitzvah, has been making up for lost time.

In 1953 Letty's father prepared her for her bat mitzvah—"his finest hour." When the day came, she was in her element, "ecstatic" while chanting the haftarah before her congregation in Jamaica, Long

Island, "conscious" that this was her "farewell address to childhood." More than her first sexual experience, more than going away to college, bat mitzvah was her "most intoxicating rite of passage." The intoxication lasted two years. In 1955 Letty's mother died of cancer. When the minyan for the mourners' kaddish gathered in her home, only nine males were present. Assuming that her bat mitzvah had conferred full Jewish privileges on her, Letty begged her father to include her in the quorum, which was traditionally reserved for men. Refusing, he called their synagogue and asked for a tenth man. With that, Letty turned her back on Judaism, not returning until Judaism was more inclusive of women, fifteen years later.

Half in/half out about Judaism—the disillusionment was hard to shake—she offered her three children (Abigail, Robin, and David) the opportunity to go to Hebrew school, but even she admits that the invitation was "desultory and lackluster, like a casual, 'Let's have lunch one of these days.'" The kids turned down the offer: "Giving up a day in the spotlight and a party with lots of presents was easier than electing years of Hebrew study."

The kids knew they were they Jewish: They watched Letty light Shabbat candles, and they attended services at the informal congregation that sprang up, more or less spontaneously, on Fire Island, where they had a summer place. But they only felt Jewish. "We all took the easy way out," Letty rues, "and they missed their official initiation into Jewish life."

This was the midseventies, and a nascent, slightly strident feminism contributed to Letty's resistance to Jewish ways. Another factor was her father, who personified Judaism for her, who needed a "Jewish world controlled by Jewish men." He was a man who had used his power to exclude her when her mother died, who had very reluctantly told her he'd been married before—and that he'd essentially abandoned the child from that marriage. This syllogism—Judaism is a patriarchy, patriarchies are bad, Judaism is bad—satisfied Letty during an early stage of her feminism. Eventually, she realized that faith and gender can enrich each other, that they are not necessarily polar opposites. (But she still can't resist quoting a sign in a Hasidic community in upstate New York: "Talmud Class Is for Everyone! Men Only!")

By the 1990s Letty was reconciled to her son having no bar mitzvah: "At least he can say he followed his father's example because Bert also missed out. But my daughters have the sad distinction of having been denied by their mother what she had herself. . . . I can only hope that when they are parents, they will revert to the tradition of giving their children what they did not have themselves."

Letty's daughter, Abigail, has children—young ones. And she intends to give them what her mother never gave her. But she wasn't willing to let the bat mitzvah experience leap over her, from grandmother to grandchildren, as she remained untouched (and maybe unmoved) in the middle. So in May 2005 Abigail had a bat mitzvah. She was forty years old, twenty-seven years past when she would have had a bat mitzvah if the Pogrebins had adhered to the usual timetable. It was her idea, which thrilled her mother.

Woody Allen would have loved the Pogrebin women, not so much for their Jewishness, with which he has enough problems, but for their apartments, which are perfect for his cinematic idealizations of Manhattan. Letty's, a quarter block from Central Park, has a living room two floors high, with wooden beams stretching across the ceiling and light streaming through tall, narrow, leaded windows. Bookcases are crammed with titles by intellectuals like Susan Sontag and artists like Annie Leibovitz; tables are jammed with photos of Letty with glitterati like Bill Clinton and Gloria Steinem; and the furniture is as comfy as any in a Ralph Lauren ad. Abigail's apartment is in the legendary Ansonia, a massive twenty-five-hundred-room building between Seventy-third and Seventy-fourth Streets on Broadway. Built as a hotel in the early twentieth century, it originally boasted a grand ballroom, a tea room, the world's largest indoor swimming pool, and a lobby fountain with live seals. An heir to a copper fortune once kept farm animals on the roof, and the walls are so massive that you could shoot yourself, as one fellow did in 1910, without the sound even reaching the next room. There's less excitement now that the Ansonia is a mere apartment building, but the high-style fin de siècle Parisian architecture still floats over Broadway, its turrets and towers a dream from another day, "a baroque palace," as Saul Bellow wrote in *Seize the Day*, "from Prague or Munich enlarged a hundred times."

It's taken a while for the Pogrebins—mother and daughter—to come to terms with their Judaism and their bat mitzvahs, and their journey has been laden with many family issues: resentments and confusion and a certain paternal arrogance, with three generations approaching Judaism in ways healthy or borderline sociopathic, with feeling accepted, betrayed, marginalized, and accepted again, on their own terms and in their own way. In the end, with much thought and great determination, each Pogrebin ended up at a very happy destination.

LETTY POGREBIN

My first bat mitzvah was a sham, though it was a highlight of my childhood. There was no such thing as being empowered back then. It was nice that they said that I was a "daughter of the commandment" [the translation of "bat mitzvah"]. But it didn't mean anything because, as we can see, I didn't count. In those days, when you became bat mitzvah, you stuck it on the shelf like a diploma you could never use.

That bat mitzvah occurred when I was slightly more than twelve and a half years old. I turned thirteen in June, but my bat mitzvah was in February. I don't really know why. Maybe because the Conservative movement was not quite sure how much to take from Orthodoxy, and in Orthodoxy, a girl becomes a woman upon puberty, which is considered to be the age of twelve. So they put me close to the middle, between twelve and thirteen.

I remember looking out at people and not being afraid and not being nervous. I didn't shake and my voice didn't shake. In fact, I'm never nervous speaking. And I remember the rabbi raising his tallit [prayer shawl] over me for the priestly blessing, and that he talked in a way that made me feel extremely important. "Now you are a woman," he said. "You are a member of the community. You are a full-fledged Jew."

I took it seriously. Why wouldn't I? That was what a student was, and I was a good student: somebody who took seriously what she was taught. I really believed this. "Well, now," I thought, "I'm entitled to my opinions."

But back then, "Now you are a woman" meant "Now you do the dishes." It meant you were entering an era of waiting—waiting for the right guy to come along. In those years, women and girls were so secondary in the eyes of men. But also, one of the motivating forces in my life has been not being abandoned. Because I had learned that my father could leave one daughter [from his previous marriage] and never see her again, I also realized that he could leave another daughter. So I was always, in a way, trying to make myself indispensable and lovable and unabandonable. I was a really pious little kid, and I loved bringing home A's and doing my haftarah with my father. It was very important to me to gain his respect. If you were really smart, then he engaged with you. He would take time with you, but always in a pedantic mode.

My second bat mitzvah began around 1970 on Fire Island [forty-five miles east of New York City]. A group of men were sitting around on the beach one day when one of them said, "Wouldn't it be great if we could have High Holy Day services here and not have to leave?" They were all "once-a-year" Jews. I was a once-a-year Jew myself, at that point. The rest of us said, "Sure! We'll do it on someone's deck." We asked a local synagogue for extra yarmulkes, and the one store on the island donated sponge cake and Manishevitz. It was all going perfectly. We put a sign-up sheet at the ferry dock and at the playground for anyone who wanted to come, and we were expecting about thirty adults and fifteen children.

Then somebody said, "Who's going to run it?" None of these men knew how to do it. They hadn't had the type of the childhood that I had had. They had all been bar mitzvah but were never seen again in temple. After hearing them say they could barely read Hebrew, I said, "I'll do it. I'll do it."

You have to realize how early 1970 was. This was before women were ordained in Reform or Conservative Judaism. There was no *Ms. Magazine*. There was no nothin'. But necessity is the mother of nonconformity, and they needed me. I became the *chazanette* [Pogrebin's female version of *chazan*, or cantor]. I chanted the Hebrew parts. A stockbroker was the "rabbi" and read the English parts.

That was my first step back to Judaism in the sense that I was saying, "This is mine. *I* can do it. I *can* do it. I can *do* it. I can do *it*." All those emphases worked for me. I remember one thing very clearly. During Yom Kippur, I chanted the Kol Nidrei, which gives me the chills. Emotionally, it's a big prayer for me. I stood there and I, an unbeliever, said to God, "If this is a bad thing, just send me a sign. If this is a bad thing, I won't do it." I stood on the bema and started to chant, and, I swear, I felt as if a mantle came upon me, saying, "This is okay. You have a right to do this." And I did.

A few years later, we got so big that services were held at the Episcopal church on the island. That was thirty-four years ago. I did it for thirteen years. That second bat mitzvah was my first step toward belonging to Judaism in my head and in my heart.

I was born in the Fifth Avenue Flower Hospital [in midtown Manhattan], and soon after that, we moved to a semi-attached house in Queens, which I thought was a palace. It was in Jamaica Estates, which was sort of a Jewish enclave with Tudor-type houses. Now I realize it had only six rooms, and small ones. But there was marble around the fireplace and terrazzo tiles on the little hearth section and modern furniture. It was so different from my grandparents' house and my aunts and uncles' houses. We really looked American. (My mother was born in Hungary and came here when she was seven or eight; my father was born in New Haven, Connecticut. He was native born but barely: his mother was pregnant while coming over on the boat from Russia.) There were gates on the dining room doors—wrought iron gates with scrollwork that you could see through. And a breakfast bar in the kitchen and a backyard and a Dodge. (We always had Dodges.) All this was the mark of really making it in the suburbs.

My father was president of our shul, the Jamaica Jewish Center in Queens, for six years. He was also the head of the county command of the Jewish War Veterans. My mother was president of the sisterhood, the local Hadassah, the local National Council of Jewish Women. We were a very Jewish, Zionist, hyperconscious-of-our-obligations-to-the-community type family.

My father was a bit of a Talmud scholar. Jewishly, he was well read and well educated and quite committed, although he cheated in terms of observance. On Shabbat, he smoked. He drove to synagogue. Eventually, Conservative Judaism decided that you could drive on Shabbat, only to or from synagogue. But he did it long before that.

Anyway, it became important to my father to educate me. I guess I was his last chance, which is how I ended up being bat mitzvah. I attended afternoon Hebrew school at our synagogue for ten years, starting when I was three, and two years in the Yeshiva of Central Queens. I didn't like that and switched to the Hebrew high school at our shul, which I graduated from when I was fifteen.

My life revolved around our synagogue. I went there after school pretty much every day because the synagogue was kind of like a Jewish Community Center before there were JCCs. It had a bowling alley and a swimming pool and a gym. It was several stories high. There were enough Jews around to justify that sort of physical plant. During services, we always sat in the first pew or my father was up on the bema. He always got an *aliyah* [the honor of reciting a blessing over a Torah reading] or it was his job to give them out. I felt like a princess in a royal family because my family was so prominent.

Outside, the synagogue had a Jerusalem stone kind of feeling, almost pinkish yellow. Wide steps led up to the front doors, which were big and heavy. Then you went upstairs to the second floor which opened onto the sanctuary. It was gorgeous, with a maroon and royal blue motif.

I was so impressed with being bat mitzvah: I was maybe the first in our synagogue. People paid special attention to it and made much of it, saying things like "We're doing this because . . ." and "We're proud to be among those who are breaking new ground." It was a moment of high consciousness for the whole community, not just for me, and I think they were still feeling their way through it.

My father was my teacher, although there was somebody at the synagogue who would have taught me—the rabbi or the cantor. But my father had tutored bar mitzvah boys while he was going through law school—twenty dollars a bar mitzvah boy, which was a very handsome fee in those years. So it was kind of natural for him to be the one who did it.

In those days, you couldn't read from the Torah if you were a girl. So it was kind of a circumscribed ceremony, and I just read a portion from the haftarah. But the opportunity to study with my father and gain his respect was very important to me. It was also important to recite my haftarah without an error. And finally it was important, and this was not incidental, because I was allowed to wear a black velvet dress. That dress stands out in my mind so much. It had a little white lace trim. In my family, which was half-scholarly (from my father's side) and half-superstitious (from my mother's side), you didn't wear black when you were a child.

That was the color of mourning. But I saw this dress, fell in love with it, and somehow my mother let me get it because I had worked so hard for my bat mitzvah. God knows what she thought was going to crash in on our heads.

Two years later, my father would not include me in the minyan for my mother. I *knew* that you don't count women in the minyan, but this was such cognitive dissonance. How can you *not* count me if I'm a "daughter of the commandments"? Torah was for men, not for me! Why stay in a system that doesn't want you?

I couldn't parse it. It was so cruel. I was in a rage. At that moment, I was aware that I was alone in the world. Knowing that is very big, knowing that nobody is going to take care of you and that your decisions are basically your own. I was fifteen, and I really felt that my father was not going to parent me.

I really adored my father until I figured out how many things he did that were really awful. He was never abusive. He never put a hand on me. He never shouted. But the fact that he had left one child, and that he lived a lie, that he really wasn't available to me, that I knew that his own life, his organizations, and the state of Israel meant more to him than I did. It's very hard to love a parent when you come so far down on the list. And then when he remarried, he chose a loathsome, cold, imperious woman, and I understood him better. He was fifty-something and still "in the prime of life." But when I came home after my first year at Brandeis at the age of sixteen, he had sold the house, married her, and I had no room. I slept in the hall. So little by little, his image unraveled before my eyes. My mother was gone, and I suddenly realized everything I'd thought of as "my family" was really her doing. My father just dropped in. He dropped in to sit at the head of the table at Shabbat. He dropped in to do the Seder. He dropped in at family gatherings and at weddings and he came home for dinner and then he left every night for organizational meetings.

Being the *chazanette* at our little Fire Island synagogue was one of the ways that I worked my way back into Jewish life. I ran services for more than two hundred people, and my father never came out to hear me. Somehow, it never interested him. I began thinking that maybe he really didn't care that much about having a Jewishly educated daughter; maybe I invented his pride in me because I needed to believe he felt it.

In all those years before that Fire Island experience and then during the thirteen years I led those services, and in my struggle to find a synagogue and in getting involved in Jewish feminism and struggling to get women ordained at [the Conservative movement's] Jewish Theological Seminary, there was still a tremendous amount of anger, a feeling like, Why should anybody have to go through this? Why should anybody have to fight for the right to be counted? I was determined to give my children the Judaism that I value, but I was very much in process in the years when Abigail and Robin [who are twins] would have had their bat mitzvahs or when David would have had his bar mitzvah. Feminism had become my religion. I was worshipping at the altar of women's freedom. Also, I didn't belong to a synagogue [in Manhattan]. There was no synagogue for me, no Hebrew school for the kids, and my husband, Bert, a red diaper baby, had been raised with no religion. He knows Marx and Engels and theory of surplus volume, but he doesn't know anything about Rashi [an outstanding biblical commentator of the Middle Ages]. But I kept going to High Holiday services. I went to different synagogues all over the city, buying a ticket for the overflow service or sitting in the basement with the student rabbi.

If I had to do it over again, I would have offered my kids a different kind of Judaism, one with more ethical and intellectual relevance to today's world, a more open Judaism that honors diverse modes of spiritual expression. And we would have all studied as a family. It would have been wonderful

Just the other night, my son and husband said they wanted a bar mitzvah. They feel they missed out on something important, a bonding experience with Jewish history and the Jewish people.

If I could redesign bar and bat mitzvahs, I would throw down the gauntlet and say, "*We're* the reason we're losing Jewish children. Because we don't know how to tell them about Judaism." We need to tell them about Judaism in ways that connect with their lives, in ways that sell Jewish thoughts to their souls. Maybe start with something like, "If you find a wallet or a bike while walking through Central Park and no one's around, do you take it?" Or, "If your dog is drowning and someone you don't know is drowning, who do you save?" Ask children questions that touch on their experience, their value system. Challenge them: "How do you make these decisions? How does anyone decide how to live a life?" and then fill it in with the pieces of Judaism that have to do with what the patriarchs and matriarchs did and why they're flawed and how we learn from biblical stories. Not just what happened, but *why* it happened and what shouldn't have happened or why God wanted it to turn out that way.

Then you've really got something. I think it's still very hard for a young person to get a good Hebrew school education. I've gone to children's services all over the city, and they're awful. There's no understanding of the kids' attention span or the kind of activities that would engage these age groups. You should have a child development person in there, not someone who just got out of the seminary.

When I came back to Judaism, I had something to build on. I could be part of a service. Stupidly, I didn't educate my children because I was in the throes of my feminist rage, angry at sexism in all institutions, particularly religious institutions and *most* particularly the patriarchal, exclusionary Judaism in which I was raised. My children were the casualties of my 1970s rebellion. I'm deeply regretful about this, as if by not equipping them with a basic Jewish education, I failed them as a parent. At the same time, it would have been hypocritical to count myself (and my family) into a faith that refused to count me as a full and legitimate Jew simply because I was a woman.

When Abigail had her bat mitzvah, three days before she turned forty, I felt elated and overcome with pride. As I watched her assiduously studying Torah for two years, then preparing her Torah portion, her haftarah, and her *d'var Torah,* it occurred to me that forty might be the best time for every Jew to undertake this ritual. She was far more motivated and focused, more mindfully engaged in the process, and more grateful for the wisdom in the text than she would have been at twelve or thirteen. It was truly a profound and meaningful rite of passage for her and for all of us who witnessed her journey.

ABIGAIL POGREBIN

My bat mitzvah was almost an out-of-body experience. It was terrific, extraordinary. It went beyond what I thought it would be. There's almost no "un-clichéd" way to describe how I felt. It was really a high. Unlike my wedding, which was really a blur, I felt more grounded, calmer, and my personality is not destined for me to be calm.

There was something heavenly about the day. It was wonderful to have all those people there; and my husband spoke at the lunch afterward about what it was like to watch me take this on, how I hadn't insisted that he make the same spiritual leap, but that the service was, for him, Judaism at its best. At the start of the ceremony, my father gave me his tallit, which my mother had given him when they got married over forty years ago. He'd never used it. The weather was perfect, a sunny spring day, no humidity; and the restaurant where we had the reception was down the street from where we held the service. The windows were open, and people were spilling into the street.

There was a fullness to the experience, and I wasn't the only one who felt it. So many people told me that the day deeply affected them. I think it made them look at the time they do (or do not) put into ritual, and how they are raising their children, and how their own childhood may have connected them to tradition. Or not.

If I learned anything overall from the experience, it's that exhilarating moments don't come about without a lot of work. The meaning, the substance, and the engagement didn't just happen. It took a certain kind of intellectual exertion. It took time. But I also didn't want to make my own "awakening" prescriptive for anyone listening. When I was writing my *d'var Torah,* it was important to remember what my rabbi, Jennifer Krause, emphasized: "Speak for yourself. Don't say that *this* is the way to be Jewish. That *this* is the way to find your door to Judaism." This was only *my* experience. It was rewarding for *me.*

From my perspective, the most memorable part was the *d'var Torah.* I'd wanted people to hook into what I'd discovered without telling them to drink the Kool-Aid, and I think that happened. My parashah [Torah portion] was from Leviticus—a hyperdetailed section about which cattle can mate with each other, and where to smear the blood of the bull you slaughtered, and what measures to take if you come into contract with stray semen. But one passage jumped out at me:

When you reap the harvest of your land,
You shall not reap all the way to the edges of your field,

Or gather the gleanings of your harvest:
You shall leave them for the poor and the stranger.

So many times we hear about "Jewish values." But until I started studying Torah, I was hard-pressed to say what, exactly, those values were and where they could be found, specifically, in the Bible. Even now that I've read the whole thing through, I still wouldn't say that the five books of Moses are dotted with maxims and morals about right and wrong. Except for the Ten Commandments and a few places in Deuteronomy, the lessons of how to live kindly and unselfishly have to be gleaned from some of our ancestors' most unkind, selfish behavior. Ethics emerge in the twists of the narrative, not necessarily in God's commands. But with this passage, God was telling us explicitly, "Don't hoard it all for yourself. You are compelled to share. You are compelled to think of those who have less than you." And "the stranger" was not necessarily another Jew. God commands us to help others survive not because they're "*our* people," but just because they're people. Humanity is holy, no matter the recipient.

I also said during my *d'var Torah* that I'd been acutely aware, over the years, of my mother's regret that she didn't give me or my siblings a Jewish education. But she *did* give us a warm, vibrant Jewish life. We had *shabbos* blessings, and holidays that we cherish to this day, and a Hanukkah we wouldn't have traded for anyone's Christmas. She made us proud to be Jewish. But she didn't teach us Judaism.

I see now that my mother has long worried that we would suffer *karet,* the ancient penalty of being cut off from your own people, a penalty which my Torah portion talks about—where it's not the disobedient Jew who is excommunicated but his or her children. I could feel my mother's worry, not that *she* would be the one cut off, but that my siblings and I would be. And yet, here I was standing at the bema and becoming bat mitzvah. That told me not that my mother had done anything *right* by not sending us to Hebrew school, but that she hadn't done anything *wrong.* I had to get there, just as Dorothy discovered on her way back to Kansas, all by myself.

I needed to figure this out, however long it took. Which might illustrate that ultimately parents don't connect their children to tradition or to faith. We connect ourselves.

Mom was really wonderfully supportive during this whole bat mitzvah endeavor. So often she's the expert, the teacher in a situation like this. This time, she was just my mom. She was very supportive and didn't push or ask too many questions. She insisted on buying the flowers, telling me, "Think of all the money you saved me when you were twelve." So a brilliant flower designer friend of hers—Bella Meyer, a granddaughter of Marc Chagall—turned the temple into something ethereal and otherworldly.

Once my mother wrote about not giving us a Jewish education, "My daughters have a sad sanction of having been denied by their mother." *She* was calling it sad. *We* didn't consider it sad. This was *her* sadness, not ours. It's been hard for me to separate out what I know in my bones *she* wants and what *I* want, although I do wonder if I would have gotten here earlier if she hadn't wanted it so much.

What set me on this path? Dating a non-Jewish guy, an Irish Catholic, for two years was sort of a touchstone. I'd been heading in the direction of maybe marrying him and was trying to figure out if I could build a life with someone who wasn't Jewish. My mother had a very difficult time with that relationship, and it was hard for me to separate her disapproval from my own real questions about it. I eventually broke up with him, but the religious differences stayed with me in a way that was deeper than I realized at the time. And then three years later, I did marry a Jewish man. I wasn't knowingly seeking out a Jewish husband, but it felt so much more natural and effortless, aside from the fact that he was a wonderful person. Once we had children and a *bris* for my son and a baby naming for my daughter and a rabbi at both occasions, it was all pretty intense for me, the idea that *they* were Jews and were continuing something. Suddenly, I was acutely aware that, if they were going to be Jews, I wanted to be able to tell them what that meant. And I knew that I wasn't equipped to do that.

What I realized was that I wanted Judaism to be part of my children's lives in a way that didn't feel so conscious and so effortful as it was for me. I wanted it to be integrated into their childhoods.

Then I started writing *Stars of David,* which involved interviewing prominent Americans about being Jewish. I didn't want to go into these interviews at a disadvantage. I wanted to at least have the vocabulary of Judaism. As it turned out, most of the people I talked to were pretty unreligious or irreligious, and I didn't need the "advanced degree." But I did start studying every week with Rabbi Krause. These were wonderful sessions. We read Torah, which I had never done before, and we'd discuss the portion of the week, and I'd ask any questions I wished. It was a very safe place to feel stupid. I'd taken one class at a synagogue before and dropped out because it felt like people were showing off what they knew rather than asking questions in a genuine, unpretentious way. I don't blame them. They *did* know more. But I didn't want to be in a situation where it was about who knows how much. I really felt that I was starting from a place with a lot of question marks.

In the beginning, I told Rabbi Krause how many of my contemporaries see synagogue as an onerous obligation. They don't get anything from the prayer book or feel connected to the text and the traditions. "It does take effort," she said. "You can't expect meaning to land in your lap. You have to engage the tradition before it gives you something back."

That was a wake-up call. I realized I'd *never* really investigated it. I would just sit back in synagogue and say, "Ugh, I don't feel anything." So I started by reading Torah. I didn't come at Judaism through prayer so much as text. I know that sounds ridiculously high-minded. But somehow, that fired in my head and translated into a feeling of spirituality. It wasn't really about prayer or about God. God is in there, yes, but it was really about this enduring, very rich tradition and the fact that *everyone* is entitled to it, and as soon as you start engaging it, you have a say.

What I loved most was the discussion and the argument and the debate, the idea that it's not something that's just spoon-fed and accepted. What you inherit is the right to take it on, to challenge all of it, which is a very different message than what my mother gave me. She never presented Judaism that way. When she had her return to Judaism, she then wanted to make up for lost time, to teach us what she knew. But she presented it as a menu rather than as a conversation to join. She didn't just open the door and let us walk through it ourselves; she didn't emphasize that being Jewish is about questioning everything. It's not about dogma. I don't think my mother thinks that it is, but somehow in the way she presented it, it was. It was presented as something finished.

At some point, Rabbi Krause said, "You should become bat mitzvah." I thought carefully about it. So much of this is about the guide, and Rabbi Krause was the perfect guide—so unaffected, with no overintensity. I think my Judaism was taking shape in a way that was very unplanned. It felt more organic and, for me, very true. We decided to have the bat mitzvah in an old synagogue on the Lower East Side that no longer operates as a full-time temple but is rented out for events. And the reception was down the block at an Italian café because that was the closest good restaurant to the temple and Katz's Deli, which was also nearby, wanted too much money. There were only about fifty people, and we had no rock band, no face painting, no karaoke, no caricatures. It was not an extravaganza, and that's what we hope to avoid for our kids. But I think everyone sort of falls into that trap. As long as you're living in New York, there are not a lot of ways to do it differently for a twelve year old. When you're forty, it can be more low-key.

While I was growing up, I really didn't have a religious education, but we always celebrated the religious holidays. There were incredibly elaborate Hanukkah parties, with lots of latkes and other traditional foods. We lit the menorah every night and opened a present every night and I truly felt sorry for my friends who didn't have eight nights to celebrate. That was Mom's way of overcompensating to the point that we felt privileged.

We always had two Passover Seders with my aunts and uncles, and when I was twelve, I started going to the feminist Seder which was created around that time. My sister and mother and I went to that. Just the three of us. So for a while, we went to three Seders every year.

Judaism, for me, was very wrapped up in family. It was very sensory. I remember foods and smells and voices. There was tremendous warmth around all this. When Mom "returned" to Judaism, it got a little complicated because she tried to make up for all the things we didn't have. At that point, we were in our late teens or early twenties and not so receptive to her suddenly being a teacher at these events as opposed to the more freewheeling way they used to be. Maybe we'd have been more open to the instruction if it had come from someone else.

Growing up, I didn't feel a lack of Jewish knowledge, except for certain moments when I would see someone who knew so much more, like a boyfriend in college who was raised to speak fluent Hebrew. When I went to his Seder, I envied his family. They knew all the prayers and songs, and their traditions were clearly rooted in the text. And when we started going to synagogue, I wished I could follow along in the prayer book. In college, I took Hebrew in my senior year. That was probably my first stab at compensating and catching up

One thing I've learned from all this is that the religious connection has to be *yours*. It took me twenty-eight years to get there, but it probably meant more than it would have as a child. While writing *Stars of David*, a number of people said, "I'm leaving the decision as to whether to have a bar or bat mitzvah up to my child. He or she can choose." But I don't think that a child can choose without having the door opened for them so that they see what's there and what it means. I'm hoping that I'm able to show my kids this landscape and that they're intrigued by it, but I also don't want them to feel that I'm prescribing one kind of Judaism to them. That just backfires.

But I'm not going to give them a choice about having a bar or bat mitzvah. That is definitely new. That rite of passage has always been a landmark in the Jewish tradition. It's one that I missed, and I don't want my children to miss it. I finally crossed that threshold at what felt like the right time for me. Maybe, in some way, I was heading toward that moment for a long time without realizing it. I wanted to fill in the blanks in my life. I wanted to officially join the conversation. I wanted to commit myself to something larger than myself. My ignorance is still enormous. That hasn't changed. But now I have the vocabulary, the basics. And that feels like the beginning of something.

I'd like to keep studying. The connection for me starts with the learning. I'd felt, until now, that I hadn't earned the right to come to the table. Now I have. I'm still the novice—the private with one crummy stripe. But I'm there. My bat mitzvah was my nascent, obviously belated way of saying to God, "Count me in."

MUSHROOMS GAVE ME WHAT
I COULD HAVE HAD AT MY BAR MITZVAH

If anyone has been at the epicenter of America's spiritual searchings for the past three decades, it is Ram Dass: seeker, teacher, eloquent guide, and agile translator of Eastern thought into American practice. Since the 1960s, Ram Dass has helped shape Americans' attitudes toward consciousness, faith, drugs, religion, and mysticism, giving them perspective and relevance, a distinctly Western relevance. Now in his early seventies, he still lectures around the country, presenting himself as a cautionary tale about the glories—and the pitfalls—of seeking God. When not on the road, he enjoys the quiet of his rented house in Maui, if only as a balance to all the jabbering when he's at the podium. When you're a teacher to the masses, repose comes when it does and where it does, and where better than Maui?

Ram Dass has lived one of the great spiritual sagas of our time. He grew up as Richard Alpert in Boston, where his father ran the New York, New Haven, and Hartford Railroad. Young Richard—overweight, insecure—was not quite certain what his family gained from being Jewish. It seemed so hollow, so vague, just more wheeling and dealing by his high-powered father. As president of his Conservative temple, George Alpert had the power to hire and fire rabbis. To his son this was tantamount to being the Almighty Himself.

Yet it seemed that Richard was destined for great things: earning a Ph.D. from Stanford, he became the youngest person to secure tenure at Harvard, where he taught in two departments before he was thirty. Then, disaster. Sort of. In 1963 Harvard dismissed Alpert and his pal Timothy Leary for experimenting with psychedelics. Professorial higher-ups do not wink at bestowing LSD on undergraduates, even for the sake of science. For Leary, mind-altering substances were the holy grail. For Alpert, psychedelics pointed the way—with reservations. Salvation suggested permanence, eternity, deliverance. Psychotropics kept opening a door for Alpert, but the door kept slamming shut on him: he was always coming down from his ecstasies. Gloom followed bliss, expulsion followed paradise: the depressions and the disappointments were inversely proportional to the splendor of the elations, and this was not healthy.

In 1967 Alpert traveled to India, met his spiritual teacher, and became Baba Ram Dass. Returning to the United States, he wrote *Be Here Now,* a spiritual guide full of perky aphorisms promising that God was only a yoga posture away: "Here we are. Here and now. That's all there is." "As soon as you give it up, you can have it all." "Only when I know who I am will I know what is possible."

The book, plus Ram Dass's winning personality and tapes of his early talks, turned him into the most durable star on the spiritual circuit. He was everyone's favorite scout from the frontlines of consciousness. In a sense, he transformed a generation. "I listened to a Ram Dass tape while I was supposed to be writing my master's thesis," a friend of mine in Vermont recalls. "His story was a revelation to me. Life, the universe, and all that changed." In fact, Ram Dass's own life became his greatest lesson: a cosmic template for aging hippies, tie-dyed teens, and lost theology students.

Then in 1997 a stroke paralyzed his left side and slurred much of his speech. His remarkable recovery has allowed him to again charm audiences with his humorous revelations about his neuroses, his depressions, his setbacks—and his delight that, somehow, he could still find God and himself.

In fact, humor is one of Ram Dass's greatest gifts to American spirituality, which can suffer from a leaden sobriety. A few days after his stroke, a doctor in Northern California gave Ram Dass a fairly rudimentary test to determine his cognitive functioning. Holding up his pen, the doctor asked, "What is this?" "Pen," said Ram Dass. The doctor pointed to his wristwatch, and Ram Dass said, "Watch." The doctor held out his necktie, and Ram Dass said, *"Shmatta"* (Yiddish for "rag"). Hearing that, Ram Dass's two friends who were in the room knew he'd be fine: he still had his sense of humor. Without that, he wouldn't be Ram Dass.

I interviewed Ram Dass at the Omega Institute in Rhinebeck, New York, about two hours north of Manhattan. It was midafternoon on a Friday in the early fall. The air was cool and fresh, and everyone was smiling: Omega is one of the premier holistic centers on the East Coast. If these people, many of them temporary refugees from the five boroughs to the south, couldn't relax there, maybe they couldn't relax anywhere. After walking across the extensive campus, I finally found Ram Dass's room. He was lying on his bed, talking with two friends. A weeklong retreat he'd led had ended just a few hours before. He was in a good mood, although a bit tired, and he needed a slight reminder about the purpose of the interview. As soon as I mentioned "rites of passage," he perked up.

"Oh, yes," he said with a smile. "For me, it was mushrooms. I was thirty years old."

"Yes, I know. I know," I said, almost wearily. "We'll get to that. But first, let's go all the way back to your bar mitzvah."

And so we did.

The Torah meant nothing to me. It was just words. Just this scroll that you read these Hebrew words out of. I can't even remember the Torah portion that I read at my bar mitzvah. That's how significant it was. And I can barely remember how to read Hebrew. All I remember are the letters of the alphabet, and I can't remember most of them.

What I mostly remember about my bar mitzvah was that it was an empty ritual. It was flat. Absolutely flat. There was a disappointing hollowness to the moment. There was nothing, nothing, nothing in it for my heart. And I had no idea it could be otherwise. It seemed like everybody was getting the same treatment. All the initiations for my friends, no matter what religion they were in, they all seemed to be flat. These events were what you were supposed to do. None of us had the courage, the chutzpah, to question it. You did it, and you got a fountain pen and a dictionary and a party, and that was it. I had no sense that it "made me a man." I had two brothers: William, eight years older than me, was a star athlete in all the schools he attended; Leonard, five years older than me, was an artist. I was a "child"—the youngest—and I remained a child until I went to college. So my bar mitzvah was no demarcation of childhood. It was just something I did.

And yet, when the rabbi opened the ark and then opened the Torah scroll, there was a little twinge in me, like I was being let into a secret. Briefly, I felt a glimmer of history, and briefly, I felt one with the generations. But again, it was just a twinge. Other than that, it was all so empty.

The temple, Oheb Shalom in Newton [Massachusetts] was cavernous and dusty and smelled funny. It had a massive dome and lovely stained glass windows. Except for the High Holy Days, it was underused. Hardly anyone came there for services. It was like a shell of something that had once been there. On my bar mitzvah day, a Saturday morning, I remember a lot of women wearing fur coats and everyone saying that I was sweet and cute. It was very important, also, that I wear a new gray flannel suit and a red tie. And new shoes, too! Oh boy! New shoes! In wartime! It was 1944. We got them at Filene's Basement. I also remember that I did well. That is, they all said I did well, so I probably did. I'll take their word for it.

After the ceremony, there was a party in the basement of the temple with gefilte fish and tzimmes and lots of other traditional food. Most of my parents' friends were there and all of mine. It was fun and fairly low-key compared to the reception at today's bar mitzvahs. But again: none of this changed me in any way.

Thirteen years before, I'd been born in Roxbury [a section of Boston, then solidly Jewish and Catholic, with a smattering of blacks]. A year later we moved to Newton, a Boston suburb. My family was moving up, so we moved out.

My father had been raised in tenements in the north end of Boston. His father had died in an accident—his truck was hit on a railroad crossing—and my father was now supporting his brothers and sisters and mother. He became a senior partner in his firm; he was even a judge for a while. There was so much music in the house. Mother played the piano, Dad played the fiddle (and had a quartet), Leonard played the organ. When I was ten, I started playing the cello and studied with the second cellist in the Boston Symphony. He spit cigar juice all over me. Now *that* was an initiation!

My elementary school in Newton was all Jews, and one of them, a girl who lived across the street, was my sweetheart. When we were eight, we smoked cigarettes in the back of the garage. That was also an initiation! About that time, my family bought a farm in New Hampshire. I had a girlfriend up there—Janet—and we kissed in the attic. Much later, I went to her graduation from college. And right after that, she became a nun.

Junior high was so different from elementary school. There were a lot of Irish, and because I was Jewish, they chased me and beat me up and pulled my pants down. That, too, was an initiation!

I really developed in prep school—Williston Academy in Easthampton, Massachusetts [about ninety miles west of Boston]. I wrote a play. I was in the drama club. I was the editor of the school paper. I had good friends on the faculty and I was settled in my homosexuality, although I wasn't public about it. That secrecy was a form of initiation. I was very good at shrouding this side of myself.

In college—Tufts University—I was a Quaker for about two years. The Quakers' social conscience, coupled with their understanding that the Spirit of God dwells in each person, drew me to them. They're as much concerned with social righteousness as with piety; George Fox, the founder, was the first in a long line of social reformers. They oppose what they call "a hireling ministry" and instead promote relief work and a peace fellowship. In 1917 they formed the American Friends Service Committee for war relief and reconstruction and, ever since, have brought hospitals and orphanages where they were needed and set up volunteer work camps to develop local self-help projects. For them, the Bible is secondary to the Spirit, and they see the light of Christ in every man.

That was my spiritual exploration. I was looking for some kind of answers to the fundamental questions. The funny thing is that I was the only Quaker in a Jewish fraternity, which had just these stupid individuals. No one was looking for answers, and no one seemed to care.

My real initiation—the one that showed me what my spirit was, what my soul was—came with mushrooms. I saw all my social roles fall away, one by one: Richard, the dutiful son; Richard, the high-achieving professor; Richard, the pilot, the motorcyclist, the sports car aficionado. Yet an

"I" remained, an "I" that was solid and permanent. Until then, I had looked at everyone else, especially my parents, to determine the rightness of my actions. Now I resisted my parents. And I turned inward, judging my own actions.

That's what an initiation should be, although after the mushrooms, not many people immediately noticed the difference with me. My colleagues didn't. My boss didn't. My family probably didn't. I was very careful to hide it from my students. I was pretty good at masking it. I was a closet homosexual and that meant I had a lot of double lives going on at once. Therefore, I was constantly *acting* for everybody.

So I was thirtysomething for my "bar mitzvah." But unless you are raised in a very religious family, you're not ready for a bar mitzvah experience when you're thirteen. A few years ago, a friend—a rabbi—took me into the Orthodox community in Jerusalem and I was blown away. In one home, a mother really brought the spirit into the house when she lit the *shabbos* candles. And the father blessed the children, who were very attentive and loving and deeply moved. Those family scenes were just beautiful. I was so jealous.

For all the rest of us, having a bar mitzvah when you're thirteen is dumb because the rituals have lost so much of their potency. And the presents and the party and all that stuff just fills your head with the wrong ideas and the wrong messages, and you're too young to resist it all. Having it at a fixed age—thirteen, in this case—could be wonderful, and I don't doubt that it is wonderful. Keeping it at thirteen means that there's anticipation, and that has value. But I do wish it was carried out more spiritually, and that people stopped associating bar mitzvah with manhood. That's crap! Bar mitzvahs can be initiations for coming into the service, for having a role in the spiritual community. If these events were really significant, they would be truly wonderful. For now, their potential to be transforming is hardly realized, and that depends largely on the rabbi and how he prepares people. It also depends on how much he got out of his own bar mitzvah. If he got nothing, then what's being passed down is an empty ritual.

That's so different from my first meeting with my guru, Neem Karoli Baba, at a small Hanuman temple in Bhumiadar, a small village in northern India near Naini Tal in Uttar Pradesh. [Hanuman, the Hindu monkey god, personifies devotion, courage, hope, knowledge, and intellect.] The immediate effect was that it changed my plans to soon return to America. The spiritual effect was that I hardly knew what mind-space I was in. This man read my mind; he knew my secrets. As I say in *Be Here Now*, "I felt an extremely violent pain in my chest and a tremendous, wrenching feeling and I started to cry. And I cried and I cried and I cried. And I wasn't happy and I wasn't sad. It was not like that kind of crying. The only thing I could say was that it felt like I was home. Like the journey was over. Like I had finished."

Maharajii [Ram Dass's guru] placed me in the home of a longtime disciple, K. K., who lived in Naini Tal. I spent some days there with his family. After that, Maharajii instructed me to move to the temple at Kainchi, where I spent the rest of the winter of 1967–68, returning to the United States around February of 1968. During that period, I did intensive Ashtanga yoga practices under the tutelage of Baba Hari Das. [Ashtanga, an ancient yogic system, focuses first on behavioral ethics, then on disciplining the body and the mind.]

My bar mitzvah was meaningless because of my family's lack of religious spirit. They had a "social Judaism," which indeed has a certain value. By contrast, all the people around Maharajii were spiritual. They all had such faith in him. The deep spirituality of this *satsang* [a religious community] was alien in my temple in Boston.

If I had taken mushrooms a few weeks before my bar mitzvah, I don't think it would have changed anything. I was stuck so deeply in my own suffering, my own neurosis, my own yugh! But a few weeks ago, I attended a psychedelic initiation for three kids. They were twelve, fourteen, and seventeen. Their parents had invited me to help administer hashish to them. They wanted the kids to have drugs in a safe atmosphere, with their parents and other caring people present, and not in a car or at a party. The parents didn't take any, only the kids, who had a wonderful time because it was so safe. That could be what a bar mitzvah experience could be— safe and transformative.

We teachers of Eastern stuff look around and see all but a few Jews at classes and retreats. And we wonder whether our Judaism led us here, or if a lack of Judaism led us here. Luckily, through psychedelics I began to see the lack of spirit in my life, and that first mushroom trip gave me the experience that I could have had when I was thirteen.

ISRAEL AND I CAME OF AGE TOGETHER

A rabbi who never had a bar mitzvah? A *shanda*, as they say in Yiddish, a scandal! Yet Jeffrey Salkin, a rabbi for more than two decades, didn't just skip his bar mitzvah. He later wrote a definitive book about reclaiming the spiritual meaning of a bar mitzvah, *Putting God on the Guest List*, a plea to parents and kids "to feel the spiritual promise of the event, the pull of the divine and the knowledge that they are participating in an event that has meaning both in the ancient past and in the very immediate present."

Was Salkin overreaching? Overcompensating? Only if you deem a bar or bat mitzvah indispensable to Jewish adulthood, which it is not. For Jews, thirteen is the age of spiritual, moral, and legal maturity, whether or not you have a public ceremony denoting this. If restoring meaning to a venerable ceremony is overcompensating, then we should all be overcompensators. Alas, we are not. Thank God, Salkin is.

In *Putting God on the Guest List*, Salkin calls for Jews to be awake, to be engaged, to care about the entire bar and bat mitzvah process, start to finish: "These celebrations are more than a glitzy theme party, more than a moment of ethnic nostalgia. They are a glorious moment in the life of the family, the synagogue, and the Jewish people. And yet, bar and bat mitzvah have too often become a banal event, a confused event, a ridiculed event."

When a bar or bat mitzvah really works, he said, "there is a reunion between the living and the dead. . . . For that reason, bar and bat mitzvah are far more 'crowded' than anyone can imagine. The visible and the invisible generations are present, just as they were present for the sealing of the covenant at Mount Sinai approximately three thousand years ago."

Obviously, this insight didn't come from Salkin's reading of the Torah before his family's congregation when he was thirteen. Even precocious thirteen year olds don't think in those terms. Rather, the "crowd" at life cycles was revealed to Salkin while officiating at these events, over four hundred by now. Witnessing them in this manner, in fact, may be the best way to gain some lasting perspective on them: if you're having a rite of passage, you're too close to it, too enmeshed in it, to gauge its merit and power over other people. You're also too absorbed with your own anxiety or pride or hope that you won't make a fool out of yourself to gauge its power to transform you.

But being a part-witness/part-participant in bar mitzvahs week after week, as Salkin has been at The Temple in Atlanta (and before that at two temples on Long Island), can make you a reluctant expert on why so many of these ceremonies miss the mark. This may be an odd specialty for someone whose resume does not list a bar mitzvah. Yet strangely, that omission may be in Salkin's favor: because he had no a bar mitzvah, he has no personal grudge against a rabbi who worked him too hard when he was a kid or against parents who skimped on a reception, serving pot roast when he really craved filet mignon. Rather than operating from postjuvenile resentment, Salkin is aggravated by parents' and kids' delight with the hullabaloo—the caterers, the receptions, the presents—as they ignore bar and bat mitzvahs' capacity to elevate and inspire.

For Salkin, bar and bat mitzvah "is about ritual maturity. It is about growing up as a Jew." True. But he's also urging American Jews to grow up, to dampen their fascination with affluence and showmanship, and to find, instead, their true life and calling, in all its glory and frustration.

In person, Salkin—fifty years old—is tall, gangly, and enthusiastic, eager to embrace ideas and even more ready to embrace people. He doesn't stand on ceremony. This attitude is slightly deceptive, as he is deadly serious about his craft—his rabbinic craft. In the end, a Salkin success—saving bar and bat mitzvah from Jews' own worst instincts—may show that it takes an outsider, someone who never had this storied rite of passage, to save a village, the communal village of American Judaism.

My parents were fairly apathetic about my having a bar mitzvah. My father grew up in a home where there was essentially lip service to Judaism, and my mother's family was antireligious. Judaism wasn't really part of their script, although I have fond memories of Passover Seder with my extended family and of going to synagogue with my father on the High Holy Days. But I lacked the standard *Bubbe* and *Zeyde* [grandmother and grandfather] who would have given me warm Jewish memories, even of Yiddish being spoken around the house. They were sort of distant people.

In some ways, while my parents cared a lot about Judaism—my brother and I were raised with a great awareness of the Holocaust—they were just very slow in getting their act together and joining a synagogue. When they finally did join, around 1967, I was ten or eleven, and I had never learned Hebrew. I was enrolled in Hebrew school at our Reform temple, and one day, I talked with the rabbi about getting some quickie tutoring. This was at my parents' urging. It was their way of saying, "Well, we've now fulfilled our effort to make this situation better."

The rabbi was a shy man and a lifelong bachelor and not a particularly gifted religious leader. He said, "We could push you through but I just don't know how. And it would mean several days of schooling a week." It was all very passive-aggressive. Essentially, he was saying, "This is gonna be a *lot* of work." His cautionary remarks were enough for me to say, "I don't think I really want to do this."

Part of the desire to have a bar mitzvah came from seeing all my friends and cousins having these major events. But I can't say I ever had a real sense that there was something Jewishly important here. It just seemed like a suburban rite of passage that you did, something neither good nor bad.

And yet, I used to love going to bar and bat mitzvahs. In those days, they were low-key affairs. Very pleasant and without much glitz. I won't deny that I envied all the attention and the presents that my friends or cousins were getting. But for me, they were a great way to meet girls.

We lived in Bethpage, Long Island, in a modest, three-bedroom house in a typical middle-middle-class neighborhood. Our development had formerly been farmland. It was built in 1958, and we were the first people to live there. My parents were extremely modest people. My mother was a schoolteacher; and my father, for many years, was a professional photographer before he taught commercial photography in high school. The neighborhood was ethnically mixed—Jews, Irish, Italians, Poles. Working-class people. But we lived on the better end of the community.

My school was largely Catholic and ethnically Polish, Italian, Irish, with a sizeable minority of Jews, who constituted a hefty percentage of the people who were the top students. The anti-Semitism was subtle. Some of it was sociological: a Jew was a "hippie." Some of it was religious, as in, "The Jews killed God." Some of it was just plain vulgar. On the playground at school, anti-Semites beat me up and teased me. One day, they took my bike while I was on my paper route and hid it in the woods.

I fought back once or twice, but these kids were bigger than me and stronger than me; I was scrawny and thin and wore glasses and braces, and these guys were what we used to call "hoods." My parents wanted me to fight back: no one wanted a wuss for a son after the Six Days' War [in 1967]. This was a time for flexing Jews' muscles.

I find it funny that the same summer that Jews were flexing their muscles was the summer that I turned thirteen. I've always thought that Israel and I came of age together, even if I didn't have a bar mitzvah. That war, for the first time, made me feel vulnerable as a Jew. It also made me feel heroic as a Jew. And part of a larger community, which led to my becoming more of an activist and going, for the first time, to a rally for Soviet Jews at Dag Hammarskjold Plaza outside the United Nations in 1969. That struck me deeply with a sense of nationhood.

And there were the summers that I went to the Reform movement's Eisner Camp in Great Barrington, Massachusetts, when I was sixteen and seventeen and I heard a student rabbi talk about Martin Buber and Mordechai Kaplan [the founder of the Jewish Reconstructionist movement]. It was the first time that I ever experienced someone "cool" and charismatic taking Judaism seriously, and it persuaded me to become a rabbi.

The camp especially sent me on a process of Jewish becoming. I taught myself about one hundred Hebrew songs, not even knowing Hebrew but figuring out how to transliterate these songs. Leading songs became my major social outlet. At school I was a nerd, but at summer camp and at Reform youth groups the rest of the year, I had a slightly different profile, an important profile.

All these—organizing for Soviet Jewry, hearing that student rabbi at camp, leading songs—were my "bar mitzvah" ceremony: each was a way for me to connect to the larger Jewish world. Lacking a bar mitzvah never hindered me in any way. Maybe because this was the atmosphere of the sixties and I was reading more into this than I should have. But by missing what could have been a very typical bourgeois experience, I did something else, something that may have been more meaningful to me. And maybe because of the resentments against me in high school—I read poetry and played guitar and wasn't involved in sports and stuff like that—I realized that the gates of coolness would be forever closed to me. So I built other ways to be cool, Jewish ways to be cool.

I've been a rabbi for more than two decades, and I've officiated at more than four hundred bar and bat mitzvahs. I've seen that the beauty of these events is what the families and their kids bring to them. If they are Jewishly connected, and if they consider the synagogue to be more than simply a bar mitzvah "factory," then there is a genuine sense of spirituality and accomplishment and sacred purpose. Yet some of the smartest, most spiritual kids I know actually refuse to become bar and bat mitzvah. They believe the event has become an idol, hollow and empty and lifeless. Just as when Abraham was thirteen when he broke his father's idols, these kids are idol smashers. So paradoxically in some ways, their refusal may make them "more Jewish," and their identity as Jews may be more secure than those kids who do have bar or bat mitzvahs.

I've always had the fantasy that we could move the whole experience to an older age, maybe seventeen or eighteen, because in America, that's the age that people really become mature. Not at thirteen. People would then be old enough to understand that they have a responsibility for altruism and community. Thirteen may have been an appropriate age at some point in our history, but no more. Ideally, a bar or bat mitzvah imparts a sense of religious citizenship: you're now past your childhood and you're ready to take on new responsibilities within the community. In large measure, that statement is incoherent in liberal Judaism because there are few places where it matters that you're now a mature Jew. To say to someone that you can now form a minyan [the ten Jewish males required for a worship service] is laughable, because I *wish* that worship were more central in our lives. But it's not. So we're using a very traditional definition in a society that is far from traditional.

When I was thirteen and didn't have a bar mitzvah, one cousin said, "You'll never be a man unless you have a bar mitzvah." That hurt, but I didn't really believe it. And I don't believe it now. That cliché—"Today, I am a man"—has been overstated so much! In traditional Judaism, that was probably the case legally: at thirteen, you could be involved in certain legal transactions. But I'm not sure if that ever really happened. And while bar and bat mitzvah may occur around the same time as puberty, most boys are a little embarrassed by puberty. Girls less so. I've never heard a girl say, "This is when I become a woman." But all the time, I hear boys say, "It's when I become a man." If it were up to me, all kids would have their own personal mentor, their own personal rebbe, or guru, or sensei, who would help coach them in the art of life. At thirteen, they're too young to understand a lot, but not too young to understand what it *could* mean to have a connection to Judaism, to "own" a piece of Judaism.

I'd also like this to be more of a holistic experience in people's lives instead of being *the* Jewish experience in someone's life. In other words, it tends to be wrenched out of its larger Jewish context and then has little connection to what happens before or after.

What is encouraging is that families often want to tie this to something deeper and higher than the party and the expense. Kids volunteer at soup kitchens, for clothing drives, in nursing homes, or at shelters for the homeless. They raise money for the Jewish Hunger Fund, and girls grow their hair for Locks of Love, which provides hairpieces to financially disadvantaged children suffering from long-term medical hair loss. I wouldn't call any of these "low-impact" *mitzvot* [good deeds], but certainly they aren't strenuous. What's important is that these are expressions of values.

Every generation has a new opportunity to correct the flaws and the faults of the previous one. A lot of the overspending for bar mitzvahs comes whenever a new generation of Jews has "made it." So we have to start with families when they're very, very young and start educating every member about what a bar mitzvah can be. Families are a wonderful resource, and we're not using them to our best advantage. We have to breed a new generation of Jewish parents who care about going beyond the social and the showy. And we have to stop the hemorrhaging of Jewish kids from Jewish education. About 50 percent of Jewish kids drop out of Jewish schools after their bar or bat mitzvah. I want to know why they even have one. I bet they'd say something like, "Because it's a tradition" or "Because I'm supposed to." To that, I'd say, "Do you always do what you're supposed to do?" Rabbis and educators have to improve the depth and the quality of our religious programs. That will give people the fewest reasons to drop out.

I hate to say this, as someone who has written about bar mitzvahs, but they are *not* necessary for being Jewish. Jewish *education* is necessary for being Jewish. Whether or not that includes a bar mitzvah ceremony may be less than relevant. I know people who have become bar mitzvah feel that it's an important part of their being Jewish, but as an outsider I can honestly say that as someone that's learned Jewishly, has become active Jewishly, going through that particular ceremony may or may not be the smoking gun. I wouldn't say avoid a bar mitzvah. But as long as you are learning, participating, and growing, that particular ceremony is not a deal breaker. Or, for that matter, a deal maker. I've seen too many kids go through it and drop out.

For serious Jews, a bar or bat mitzvah *can* make a difference. But a lot of things would make a difference. For some kids, it's Jewish youth groups or Jewish camps. For some, I dare say, it's a relationship with a rabbi or a role model. Just the other night, I attended a youth service at our temple. As I walked in, a girl who's very active in the youth group—a really lovely kid—said, "Oh, Rabbi Salkin, you've come to observe our service." "No," I said, with a twinkle in my eye, "actually I've come to participate. Some Jews are observant and some Jews are observing. I'd rather be observant." Later, the youth director told me, "Whatever you said to that kid just blew her away. You really had a major affect on how she looks at the Jewish world."

So, you just never know what will make a difference in someone's life, what will bring them closer to their faith.

My oldest son, Sam, had a bar mitzvah in September 1999. It was the Shabbat just before Rosh Hashanah, and he was deeply moved by it. For me, this was much more emotional than if he had been another child. At the ceremony, I told him that the Torah now comes into his hands and that he is doing what his grandparents and great-grandparents had done, people who had lived in Vilna and Muncasz and Prague and Antopol. Since the bar mitzvah, he's acting more responsibly in a Jewish sense. He participates more in services and wears his tallith at services. Is he a zaddik, a holy man? Absolutely not. But he does do more—and that's important.

And in seven months, my other son, Gabriel, will have his bar mitzvah, although just last night, he ranted that it's stupid and it's too much work and he's already overloaded with schoolwork. Essentially we said to him, "You have no choice in the matter. There are some things you do because you *gotta* do them. Your grandparents are getting older. We hope they'll have full and good lives, but there's no predicting anything. We want you to have this in your life, so that they can have it in theirs as well." When saying this, I don't believe I was speaking to my younger self because his family situation is so different than mine was at that age. My grandparents didn't lobby for me having a bar mitzvah. To them, it was of little consequence.

Since he's "the rabbi's son," if he does not have a bar mitzvah some people in my temple may see it, sadly, as treason. And some kids would say, "If the rabbi's kid doesn't have to do this, why do I?" That would be hard for parents to respond to.

There are other reasons for Gabe to have a bar mitzvah: these rites of passage are the poetry that make up life. They save it from being mundane and boring. I can't imagine *any* culture without such events. They acknowledge that things are happening in our lives, that we don't want to live our lives in chaos, that we want to live our lives as if things matter. They underscore that our lives have meaning. That's very powerful. I would never want to give it up.

I AM NOT GOD'S POLICEMAN

Elie Wiesel is the voice of the Holocaust, the ghostly whisper of the Six Million. He survived, and they didn't, and his task, his fate, his duty is to speak their tale and tell of their death and recount their pain, a pain which we can never come close to understanding. A storm of ashes whirled about these millions: the ashes of aunts and uncles and cousins and mothers and fathers and sisters and brothers, of rabbis and wise men and tailors and lawyers and doctors who healed and musicians who played like angels. All these gentle people were singled out at the *selektion*—"To the right. To the left," they were told, as if they were newcomers in town getting driving directions. "Turn here. Turn there. Go straight, straight into the flames." Just about everyone else was worked to their deaths, falling into mud, piss, and shit, falling into history, falling into oblivion. Falling. Forever lost. Wiesel's job is to resurrect these lives by saving their memories. "Not to transmit an experience is to betray it," Wiesel has written. Wiesel is not a betrayer.

Elie Wiesel entered the death camps in the spring of 1944. He was fifteen. His parents and a younger sister died there. In 1945 the camps were liberated, Wiesel was liberated, and he was at a loss. "My only experience in the secular world," he later said, "was Auschwitz." He'd been raised a religious Jew—a very religious Jew—in the Romanian town of Sighet, studying Talmud and, against his father's wishes, often

Kabala. In Sighet, the boundaries of Wiesel's life were heaven above, holy words in holy books, and the worries of his Orthodox but pragmatic father that Kabala would make him unstable, crazy, mad. He wasn't alone: parents in Sighet warned their children that anyone who studied Kabala was "hurtling to their own destruction. Keep away from them."[1]

For ten years after liberation, Wiesel silenced himself. "All I know is what I have words for," Wittgenstein had said, and Wiesel also knew the limits of words. Indeed, no one had the words. There were no letters, no syllables, no sounds for what he'd seen, for where he'd been. Vocabularies and alphabets failed before this abyss. Silence was the only speech.

And then, while working as a journalist in Paris for an Israeli newspaper, he interviewed the French writer François Mauriac, who started talking about the suffering of Christ. Wiesel exploded: "Ten years ago, I knew hundreds of Jewish children who suffered more than Christ, and no one talks about it." With that, Wiesel wept, and the decade-old dam inside him started crumbling.

Wiesel began writing. Incessantly. First came an eight-hundred-page memoir. Wiesel winnowed that down to the one hundred twenty-seven pages of *Night,* which contains the most widely quoted passage in Holocaust literature:

> Never shall I forget that night, the first night in camp, which has
> turned my life into one long night, seven times cursed and seven times
> sealed. . . . Never shall I forget those flames which consumed my faith
> forever. Never shall I forget that nocturnal silence which deprived me,
> for all eternity, of the desire to live.

An avalanche of books followed *Night,* forty-four at last count. With that prolificacy and the sobering warnings he cast at the universality of pain (Rwanda, Cambodia, Kosovo, Soviet Jewry, and more), he became a walking conscience for the world, a role institutionalized, as it were, when he received the 1986 Nobel Peace Prize.

"I have tried to keep memory alive," Wiesel said in his Nobel address. "If we forget, we are guilty, we are accomplices. . . . We must always takes sides. Neutrality helps the oppressor, never the tormented."

As sobering and grim as all this is, when you meet Wiesel, there's a surprise: he's not all doom and gloom, not stooped by the burdens of Auschwitz and its various permutations that have visited the world since 1945. He does smile. His eyes do have a twinkle. He can take a joke, and he can tell a joke. He can even take some gentle teasing. He has a wife and a son and a life and is not stuck forever in the death camps, a grim visage, relentlessly scouring the world for the latest evil, the newest savageries. A-7713 is tattooed on his arm. It is not necessarily tattooed on his soul.

In a sense, though, he does live a double life: at seventy-seven years old he is a man—a statesman—of the world, yet he is also a child, still, of Sighet: "All roads lead home. Sighet remains the only fixed point in this seething world."

In Sighet, his father, Shlomo, was respected and admired. In Sighet, his mother, Sarah, was both a modern and a traditional woman: one of the few Jewish women in the region to complete high school, she admired Goethe and Schiller, and still she was a visionary, certain of the Better World, for she trusted the Word of God. In Sighet, there were many Jews and many rebbes and at least one madman, and "we all," said Wiesel, "awaited the Messiah." There, Elie Wiesel had his bar mitzvah, an event so brief, so fleeting, so barely notable by modern American standards that it could have been a hasty afterthought, an accident of timing and coincidence. But no. As Wiesel told me, the entire event was "inner," a refraction of honest and unbreakable faith. All the rest, as they say, is commentary.

In 1964, exactly twenty years after I left, I returned to Sighet for the first time. I wanted to see whether the house was still there, whether the people were there, whether I am there. Nothing had changed in the city. The houses were the same, the sky was the same, the gates were the same, my house was the same, the well was the same. Because it was all the same, I thought, "It's not my city." I was seized with terror being there, as though caught in a whirlwind of hallucinations. I waited for a window to open and for a boy who looked like the child I had been to call out to me: "Hey, mister, what are you doing in my dream?"

Inside my house, nothing had changed: the furniture was the same, and the tile stove my father had borrowed money to buy, the beds, tables, and chairs, all were ours, still in the same places. Strangers were living there. They had never heard my name. My feverish eyes wandered left and right, up and down. The only thing missing was a picture that I had hung over my bed of Rabbi Israel of Wizhnitz. I had loved him, and I hung the photograph the day he died in 1936. I can still see myself, heavy hammer in my hand, driving in the nail and hanging the frame, crying for the rabbi's death. Now, the nail was still there. It was holding a cross. And I realized that, sometimes, a very small detail contains much of the tragedy. The nail had become a witness.

All of a sudden, it dawned on me that the last night in that town, the last night in my home, everybody had hid something in the family garden. We were like makeshift gardeners. My little sister had hid her toys; my parents hid jewelry and money. It was very strange. We were all digging, digging, digging, hoping to come back one day and find it. I now went into the garden, alone, and dug with my bare fingers and found the one present I had received for my bar mitzvah—my grandfather's gold watch, a pocket watch. I loved that watch. Not because it was gold, but because it was my grandfather's.

That night in 1964, my grandfather's watch was the only object that linked me to my past. Somehow I felt, "I cannot take it away." Something of me, something from me, something of my family should remain there, in that city that once had twelve thousand, fifteen thousand Jews. This had really been a Jewish city. On Shabbat, the streets were empty; even some non-Jewish stores were deserted. Many, many non-Jews spoke Yiddish. They knew of the Jewish holidays. Our servant, Maria, knew as much as we did. Maybe one day, ten years from now, one hundred years from now, somebody will, by chance, find the watch. And it will remind that person that once upon a time, there were Jews here.

We were not rich, but we were well-to-do. We had a grocery store. My father was always busy with communal affairs. Before the holidays, we all helped in the store; even I stopped my studies and helped. But when I went back for the first time after the war, I couldn't believe how poor we were. There was no running water, and we had only a few rooms in the house. And everybody owed us money. I remember discussions my father had with my mother at night: "Should we buy a coat for our little girl or not? Should we buy a stove?" We didn't even have money for necessities like that.

I absolutely loved to study. This passion of mine was there all the time, even when I was very young. I would get up at six o'clock to go to heder; in the winter, I would get up with a lantern because there were no lights outside. I studied all the time, usually Talmud during the day and Kabala in the evening and late at night. One man in town, Kalman, was a master of Kabala. He had three disciples. I was one of them. One of my friends who studied Kabala along with me went mute, then the other. They lost the power of language. One night, I went to Kalman's and recited for hours passionate verses laden with mystery, then fell asleep and woke up hours later sweaty and delirious as Kalman sat on the floor, racked by sobs, hitting his head against the wall. I felt madness lurking. Even today, I remain convinced that if the Germans hadn't entered Sighet the following spring, I would have suffered the same fate as my two unfortunate comrades. There is no doubt in my mind. Thus, it was the killers who "saved" me.

I started heder when I was five or six, and of course, I knew that up ahead was something called a "bar mitzvah." But it was nothing. It simply meant that this was an important day because afterward you have to think and behave differently. "Bar mitzvah" does not mean that you are *doing* "mitzvah" [good deeds]. It means you are a man who is obligated to do them.

My bar mitzvah was celebrated in September 1943 in a shul across the street from our home. There were many shuls in Sighet, but this was the closest and we would go there all the time. The Rebbe of Borsher celebrated my bar mitzvah. I was called to the Torah and read the appropriate blessings. In Sighet, we did not read the haftarah aloud. I read it silently; to this day, I do not recall it. After the service, the faithful were invited to Kiddush, and Rebbe Haim-Meir'l helped me strap tefillin onto my left arm and forehead for the first time. He had a long black beard. Nobody gave any speeches. No one even said "mazel tov." Nothing. That was it. But they did think, "From now on, we can count you as a man."

It was totally, totally, totally the opposite of what we see in America. I wore a jacket and trousers. No tie. The same people were in shul who were there all the time. It was nothing special. We didn't send invitations to anybody. It was all very internal. The main thing was that you were now responsible and you would work harder and you would study harder. But did I feel like an adult? No. Of course not. I didn't have to work. I was protected and shielded and continued studying. For me, it meant that I was, internally, on my own. For now on, if I did a good deed, I was rewarded; if I did a bad deed, I was punished. I was very pious and believed that you were punished for sins. And what was a sin to me then? If I forgot to say a *bracha* [a blessing] when I got out of the toilet or when I washed my hands, or if I had a certain thought when I saw a beautiful woman. Those were sins.

But all this was very internal, just as knowing that from now on, I'd try to put on tefillin every single day. The fascinating and, to me, the perplexing thing was that I put on tefillin even in Auschwitz. A Pole had somehow smuggled tefillin into Auschwitz, and someone had traded a dozen rations of bread for them. In the morning, my father and I would get up before the general wake-up call, go to a nearby block, and strap the tefillin onto our left arm and forehead, quickly recite the ritual blessings, then pass them on to to the next person. There was no need to do this. It was dangerous. And it's not one of those [Jewish] laws that you must risk your life for. Every morning, a few dozen prisoners sacrificed their sleep, and sometimes their rations of bread or coffee, to perform the mitzvah, the commandment to wear the tefillin. We practiced religion even in a death camp. My father did it because *his* father had done it all his life. And I did it because my father did it. In Auschwitz, I didn't question why we did this. Only afterward, and then not immediately after the war. I wanted to know: Where was God? I had a very profound religious experience.

Even now, my faith is a wounded faith. The covenant was broken, but it's up to us to renew it. We *must* renew it. The first set of tablets of the Ten Commandments was broken. But it was kept in the Holy Ark with the true Ten Commandments. Yet that broken set is as important as the other, just as a broken covenant is as important as one that is intact.

In my life, the word "responsibility" is important. Why? Because often I'm asked what is a response, theologically or psychologically, to a tragedy? And I don't know the answer. I say that all I know is that "response" lies in "responsibility," that we are responsible to respond. So what does it mean to say, upon your bar mitzvah, "From now on, you are responsible"? It means that *you* give a response, that you receive a response, that you are a response. If you attribute those kinds of meanings to the words "bar mitz-vah," then those two words become richer.

I tell you, these days the American way of having a bar mitzvah is just ridiculous. Here, a bar mitzvah is a small wedding. I don't understand it. I know people who took out loans with the bank to be able to finance these. Some of these affairs were outrageous; some even had belly dancers. But this is America. Everything is the biggest and the best and the rich-est. And how can you not do it, with all the peer pressure on the children?

I don't go to many bar mitzvahs or bat mitzvahs, and I don't want to sound critical of them because they're Jewish customs and Jewish customs may be holy customs. Their value depends on the parents, the rabbi, and the child. If the child feels that he needs that expression along with the love that goes with the expression, then it's okay. But he might not even need that. I didn't need such luxurious affairs to know that my parents loved me. But the whole system was different. The whole civilization—the Jewish civilization—was different. I can imagine that what occurs here must be valuable, or it wouldn't be.

And yet, all this should *mean* something. It should not simply be a lux-urious dinner or a room full of belly dancers. It should not simply mean that you get a lot of presents, or a lot of money, or a trip to Jerusalem. We need meaning now more than in my time. Because today it's too easy to be Jewish. In my time, it wasn't easy. It was *normal* to be Jewish, but it was not easy. Also, at that time there were so many other forces that drew you to Judaism: there was study and there was celebrating every hol-iday. On Rosh Hashanah in Sighet, we used to say that the trees in the forest were trembling and the fish in the water were trembling and that *we* were trembling. These *were* the days of awe. When they have Rosh Hashanah here, it's not the same. Maybe in [certain Orthodox commu-nities in] Brooklyn, but not in Baltimore or Philadelphia or Manhattan. Not at all. Therefore, I think that an event such as a bar mitzvah has to have a special meaning.

We must tell our sons or daughters, "Look, an event is coming for which we have to prepare you. This is not only a matter for celebration and bring-ing friends and being happy and dancing with the orchestra. It's an inter-nal thing. You must feel something." How do you create such a feeling?

And yet we all have different experiences and different reasons for those experiences. I am not God's policeman. All my life, my adult life, I've fought against fanaticism. I still fight against fanaticism. Fanaticism is against culture. It's against civilization. It's against humanity. It's against religion. The enemy of religion is not atheism. It's fanaticism. And therefore, if a person says, "I want to be a Jew the way I see fit," I say to them, "Go ahead. Go ahead." If you feel enriched by it and justified by what you are doing, go ahead. It's your right and your prerogative and your privilege.

PART THREE

HINDUISM

Coming to Brahma, Knowing Nirvana

I am holding this staff which will suppress my impudence and will make me follow the righteous path. May it protect me from that which will induce fear.

INVOCATION SAID BY HINDU BOY AT HIS INITIATION

THE THREAD OF LIFE

"I bugged my father a long time for this," Ajay Kumar told me a few weeks after his sacred thread ceremony. "I thought it would be cool."[1]

Cool, indeed. So cool it was probably the most exotic rite of passage that anyone who attended Ajay's middle school in Gaithersburg, Maryland, had ever seen. And so exotic that the only way he could remotely get people to understand what he was doing was to say that it "was sort of like a bar mitzvah"—everyone knew what that was. The comparison wasn't exact: a bar mitzvah culminates years of training, while an *upanayana* (the Hindi word for the ceremony) *begins* a Hindu's religious education. According to Hindu belief, every reincarnation has a purpose, and maybe Ajay was living in the suburbs of Washington, D.C., so he could patiently explain to his friends that Hindus aren't pagans and they're not polytheists and they really worship the same God as everyone else (just more of them, although they each embody specific qualities of the One God, the Ultimate God, the All-in-One God). That's a big job for any thirteen year old, but now that Ajay has his sacred thread, he just might be up to it.

Ajay's an upfront kid. He doesn't beat around the bush. "I didn't really understand much of the ceremony," he confessed. "I just did what I was told to do and I said what I was told to say. I'd only been to one other sacred thread ceremony, and that was when I was two years old."[2]

Maybe so, but Ajay followed directions like a pro. For two hours, he and his father and their short, pudgy priest who was from South India and only spoke a handful of English words performed ablutions, squatted, stood, rang a hand bell, poured ghee (purified butter) into a small fire, and chanted mantras and prayers to a battery of gods, all while a small audience watched and smiled and wandered in and out of the ceremony: *upanayanas* are immensely informal events. (In the United States, they're also immensely shortened. In India, they last for days; in the United States, they're a mere few hours.)

Near the end of Ajay's *upanayana,* the priest handed him a wooden staff, a symbol of the long journey toward perfection on which he was embarking; the priest also gently touched Ajay's heart, a sign of the communion between the two of them—the learned man and the eager boy. At one point, Ajay went "begging" to his mother and aunts, imploring, "Bhavati bhiksham dehi." "Whichever honorable person is present, please give alms." And they did, offering up a few grains of rice, a small symbol of what boys used to be handed while begging door-to-door, bowl in hand, for years after their *upanayana.* But that was another era: initiates haven't gone begging like this for several hundred years.

Briefly, Ajay went outside to address the sun. Looking upward, he recited a mantra he'd learned barely half an hour before while huddled under a blanket with his father and the priest—a safeguard so anyone not initiated would not be privy to the holy syllables. Ajay also implored the sun's "divine light" to "illuminate our minds," intoning one of Hinduism's most venerated mantras, so potent it reportedly relieves disease, wards off misery, removes evil tendencies, instills virtue, sharpens the intellect, and improves the power of speech. With such benefits, how could Ajay balk at one of his new obligations: reciting the Gayatri mantra—a shibboleth of the Indian subcontinent, a hymn of hope and virtue—three times a day for the rest of his life, morning, noon, and night?

The mantra's actual words are

Om Bhur Bhuva Suvah
Tat Savitur Varenyam
Bhargo Devasya Dhimahi
Dhiyo Yo Nah Prachodayat.

which translates

Om is the source of everything
That Lord is the one who is most worshipful
We meditate on that all-knowing Lord
May He illumine our minds.

The Gayatri mantra is not a secret, not with its wide availability to the public, even through the Internet. A more private mantra is conveyed when a guru adopts someone as a student in a ceremony known as a *guru diksha*. That mantra is known only to the student. In either case, since a mantra has power only if revealed by a competent guru to a deserving disciple, mantras conveyed through the Internet or pamphlets really have limited spiritual value. That value comes solely through the blessing, grace, and love of a guru. The Gayatri mantra, along with many other mantras, carries the weight and sanctity of the Hindu tradition. If introduced to people who revere and love the tradition, a mantra mingles timeless tradition with a marvelous and mystifying magic.

And where was the thread in Ajay's sacred thread ceremony? He received it near the beginning of the ceremony. Actually, he received *three* threads, each about two feet long, all tied together with a knot. There's little concurrence about why there are three threads, which is not surprising, given that Hindus don't agree on much. With its thousands upon thousands of deities, Hinduism can sometimes resemble a religious free-for-all—a theological bazaar where you can find just about anything to suit your taste: there's something for ascetics and aesthetes, for introverts and show-offs. One sage says that the three threads represent the three major gods of Hinduism—Brahma, Vishnu, and Siva—who keep the universe in balance. Another says that the threads represent any Hindu's essential obligations: respect your ancestors, your teachers, and your gods. And a third (but far from the last) explanation is that the threads symbolize the three paths of energy that must be purified to reach God: two ethereal nerves that curl upward around the central column of the spine and the spine itself.[3]

No matter what it means, the sacred thread is worn across the chest, from above the left shoulder to under the right. During funerals, it's reversed, hanging across the chest from the right shoulder. During physical activity, it hangs straight down from the neck; while bathing, it's looped securely around an ear. However it's worn, it represents holiness and goodness, which is why Brahmans working at tea stalls in India sometimes strip to the waist: their sacred thread, now visible, guarantees the purity of the food they're selling, sort of like an Indian version of the *Good Housekeeping* Seal of Approval. (And speaking of good housekeeping, people don't wear the same thread their entire life: it's replaced at an annual ceremony, usually held in late summer.)[4]

Getting the thread is the first stage in Ajay's religious life. In another decade or two, he will marry and work and have children; now is the time for him to learn and study and spiritually fortify himself, to be ready for a future which has only one certainty: it will be more complicated and more taxing than anything he had known until now.

The really odd thing was that all this was going on in Lanham—a Maryland town a few miles north of Washington, D.C., better known for strip malls that give good architects bad headaches, for KMarts and Sears and Dunkin' Donuts, and for split-levels and ranchers with barbecue grills in the backyards and a plastic pink flamingo or two out front. The Sri Siva Vishnu Temple, where Ajay's ceremony was held, was just down the street from all this stuff, stuff that has turned into the guts of just about any American suburb. This didn't necessarily make Lanham an inhospitable location for a massive Hindu temple. Just an improbable one.

The all-white temple has six low, squared-off towers on its flat roof, each crammed with bas relief scenes from Hindu holy books—vignettes from the Ramayana and the Rig-Veda and the Bhagavad Gita, all with gods and goddesses cavorting and loving and wooing and playing flutes or games: not the kind of scenes you'd see outside a church or synagogue. Tall, wooden doors at the end of a long plaza open onto a vast hall with dozens of shrines scattered about, each large enough to walk into and each to a different deity: Rama, Durga, Siva, Lakshmi, Hanuman, Vishnu, Ganesha, Parvati, Krishna, and more. (The number of Hindu deities is a mystery: there's never been a census.) Everywhere in this immense room, people are praying or meditating or fingering their *malas* (prayer beads), and after a while, between the din of all the mantras and the press of the crowd and the smell of the incense, the only thing that assured me I hadn't fallen through a time/space warp into India itself was not seeing a sacred cow milling about.

Ajay's *upanayana* was one flight down from all this, in an auditorium that was absolutely plain: no decorations, no shrines, no statues. But an explosion of color on the low stage at the front of the hall relieved the drabness: oranges and bananas and coconuts were spilling out of bowls on the floor, vivid flowers were everywhere, the priest was wearing a gleaming white robe, and Ajay and his father were wearing *dhotis* (long strips of white cloth wrapped around their waist and between their legs). The three of them were bare-chested, with broad lines of white ash on their foreheads, signaling their devotion to Siva, the god of destruction. Every few minutes, as the priest ladled more ghee into the fire, there'd be a new burst of color; he later told me that each flame was a "postman," carrying prayers as far as the heavens. Given his broken English, the metaphor was surprisingly apt.

Upanayanas initiate boys into their faith. Before their sacred thread ceremonies, Hindu boys have no religious duties. They can't even mouth prayers and chants. But suddenly, after their sacred thread ceremony, their life—indeed, their next several lives, once you adjust for reincarnation—is in their hands. Now the karma they're producing can bless them or damn them, as they create their own fate, their own destiny, partly inherited from previous lifetimes, partly molded by what they do in *this* existence.

Upanayanas also initiate boys into their caste—at least, into the three higher castes. Sudras—the lowest caste—don't merit an *upanayana;* tradition claims that they are "contaminated" by their lowly occupations, indeed, by their very lot in life—a very miserable lot. This stain disqualifies them not just for a sacred thread ceremony but also from having more than a cursory involvement with Hinduism. Hinduism teaches that each caste has a prevailing trait—a trademark, if you will. Sudras' trait is survival. All they can do is drag themselves around, miserable and wretched, happy that they're just getting through the day, although even the very notion of "happiness" may be beyond them, for their task is simply to exist, to endure. Contemplating eternity, a prospect available to Hindus of the three higher castes, would just confuse them, maybe even raise their hopes for a life and a fate to which they are not entitled and from which they are thoroughly and irrevocably barred.

Meanwhile, members of other castes are thriving and doing well, progressing through life and through their latest incarnations: Brahmans, the priests, seek the meaning of life; Kshatriyas, the warriors, are often in government or law and maintain the social order; and Vaisyas, the farmers and merchants, help the community prosper by raising cattle and crops and by practicing various trades. Everything is preordained, everything is in order, and everyone knows their place.[5]

It's the sacred thread ceremony's link to the caste system that discourages many Hindus living in the West from having one. One man who moved from New Delhi to Virginia over a decade ago scoffed that the *upanayana* "has no meaning for us." Now in his twenties, he's "too modern," he declared, too "democratic" to tolerate a ritual that propagates the archaic, regimented caste system, a system which substitutes fate for freedom and destiny for choice. It's no honor, he said, to have an *upanayana*. They're throwbacks and artifacts that should be abolished so Hindus can join the twenty-first century.[6]

And yet, even as many Hindus in the West spurn their sacred thread ceremony, there's an incipient movement, especially outside of India, to extend *upanayanas* to females. At Ajay Kumar's sacred thread ceremony outside of Washington, D.C., his sister, Vani—ten years old and thin as a rail—was a busy girl: sometimes sitting on the stage or giggling or twirling around to the music or talking quietly with a close family friend, occasionally glancing over to see what her brother was up to. This was as close to an *upanayana* as she might ever get, unless the reformers have their way. Girls stopped having sacred thread ceremonies about eighteen hundred years ago, although why is somewhat speculative. One theory is that, in ancient Vedic times, girls and boys were *both* trained in the ways of Hinduism at home—their parents were their teachers, their gurus, in effect. But as Hinduism got more complex and as the caste system strengthened, the Brahmans, in particular, held sway, and young Hindus had to leave their homes and study with gurus elsewhere. Girls stayed home, perhaps to preserve sexual mores (for who knew what might happen once they were beyond their parents' watchful eyes), or perhaps because of worries about "female pollution" during menstruation, or perhaps because study and knowledge were becoming the sole province of entitled, privileged males. Barring females from sacred thread ceremonies also meant that they, like untouchables, could not participate fully in Hindu life: they were barred from reciting the potent Gayatri mantra, which illuminates and opens the mind; and from studying and reciting the Vedas, the most ancient body of sacred Hindu texts; and from becoming priests. In time, rather than acquiring religious merit from their own actions, women acquired it from their husbands. If a husband did well, the wife acquired good karma; if he behaved badly, she acquired bad karma. Her fate was inextricably linked to his. It was simple as that. Weddings became their *upanayanas;* husbands became their gurus. That doesn't mean that men are perceived as superior to women. Rather, just as boys surrender to their guru, women surrender to their spouse, with everyone—guru, husband, and wife—trying to boost their humility, curb their ego, and serve God. In the greater scheme of things, all are different, but all are equal. Everyone has their place and their duty, and everything is ordained by karma and by fate.

Yet a Hindu lawyer living in Annapolis, Maryland, offered a more modern, neo-feminist reason for girls not having an *upanayana.* "Boys need the sacred thread ceremony for protection," she said. "They're entering a phase of study, and some of what they learn can be dangerous, especially if they don't use it right. The sacred thread insulates them from danger. But girls are born with the right amount of protection. Boys have to get it from a guru."[7]

This modernism—girls are strong, boys are weak—may not fly in New Delhi or Benares or Calcutta or in the hundreds of thousands of villages where three-quarters of Indians live on the Asian subcontinent. Hidebound traditionalists, most of these people are quite content with how things are and don't seek further explanations for who's eligible for a sacred thread ceremony other than this is how things always have been and how they always will be. Many better educated, more modern Hindus, especially those who reside in the West, also don't gravitate toward a rationale that posits that girls are protected and boys aren't. For these more cosmopolitan Hindus, such a hypothesis is pure hogwash. They favor full, uncompromised equality, with neither males nor females elevated above the other, but both given comparable access to Hindu truths and teachings. Ironically, extending the sacred thread ceremony to females could satisfy ultraconservatives as well as reformers, since it would be as much a return to the ancient Vedic era (when females received the thread) as a nod to contemporary egalitarianism, which rankles at the strictures of rigid castes and fossilized piety.

Since the late nineteenth century, a reform-minded group called Arya Shastra (the Noble Society) has led the charge for expanding sacred thread ceremonies; founded in India, it now has branches around the world, including the United States, Canada, the United Kingdom, and the Caribbean. Recently another group, Navya Shastra (New Scripture), has also been lobbying for girls to receive the thread; this organization has about a thousand members, mostly in North America and the Caribbean. In fact, when Ramya Gopal, a sixteen year old whose mother cochairs Navya Shastra in the United States, first heard about sacred thread ceremonies, she thought, "What the heck?" A lifelong resident of Detroit, Ramya calls herself an "ABCD girl"—an "American-Born Confused *Desi*," a designation that pleased her little. She was quite content with being American born and had no quarrel with being a *desi*. She just didn't like being confused. (*Desi*—Hindi for "from my country" and pronounced "THEY-see"—is a colloquial term for people who trace their ancestry to South Asia, especially to India, Bangladesh, and Pakistan. In 1996 an article in the *New York Times* about the South Asian party scene in Manhattan described a *desi* as a "Hindi version of homeboy or homegirl." This was as irreverent as it was accurate.)[8]

And why was Ramya confused? As an American Hindu—a star-spangled, red-white-and-blue, "Yankee Doodle Dandy" Hindu—Ramya "was lost on the topic of *upanayana*" when first hearing about it. "We've seen some of our friends' dads or our own dads wear the thread," she said, "but that's the extent of our exposure to this holy sacrament."[9]

To many American Hindus, the thread was an artifact from another world, another culture, another time, something they had a hard time relating to, since here in the West, no one was sent off to live with their gurus, as still happened in some fairly isolated areas of India; few parents knew enough about Hinduism to properly teach it to their children; and America's ostensibly fluid social egalitarianism, the only milieu most of these Hindus knew, had little use for a ceremony which, in part, ushered young Hindus into a rigid and impermeable caste.

To many female American Hindus, the thread was more than an artifact. Part of the straitjacket of almost two thousand years of Hindu tradition, it mocked them, teased them, derided them—a constant reminder that in the up-to-date secular West, they were the equal of kings and plutocrats (at least, under the law), while their own religion cast them among the lowest of the low—as unworthy of Hinduism's highest knowledge and teachings as any untouchable, heretic, or apostate. Simply by virtue of their gender, they were expelled from their faith's greatest wisdom. They were worse than second-class citizens: they were hardly citizens at all.

Thoroughly steeped in American ways, Ramya Gopal compares the inequities of the sacred thread ceremony to "the old voting rights that were limited in America. But instead of being reserved for white American men, *upanayam* is confined to upper caste, young Hindu boys. This leaves out the lower castes and women." Rejecting as "irrational" Hinduism's arguments for keeping its restrictions on sacred thread ceremonies, Ramya noted that, in other religions, initiations once barred to females—say, communion for Christians and bar mitzvahs for Jews—are now available to both genders, "leaving Hinduism the only religion yet to modify our religious practices. . . . Unlike other societies, we haven't moved on to change with the times, and those who want to learn the Vedas . . . are forced to break the traditional rules. Aren't we 'hypocrites,' saying that 'we are one,' yet insist[ing] that there is enough of a difference that some cannot go through with this ritual?"[10]

Ramya's mother, Dr. Jaishree Gopal, who emigrated from southeastern India to the United States in 1988, ventured that Hinduism is the last holdout for a rite of passage reserved only for males because "people in India got their freedom [from colonialism] just a few decades ago. We need a critical mass" to tip the scales toward reform, a venture that could take years, she implied, since Hinduism has no Vatican, no chief rabbi, no synods, not even an annual meeting of all the priests and gurus in the same town. With such a decentralized religion, such an almost institutionally inchoate religion, and with tens of thousands of temples around the globe, each essentially autonomous, the only way to make any progress is by proceeding temple by temple. Realizing that this is an agonizingly slow strategy, the reformers have wisely decided to first focus on the more influential gurus, hoping for a trickle-down effect that will gradually revolutionize this most disorganized and disparate of religions.[11]

But Ramya Gopal, at sixteen and with her whole life ahead of her, has little patience. She wants Hinduism to change—now. "I want to feel that I am more of a part of my own religion," Ramya said emphatically. Since learning at the age of fourteen that females (even females like her who come from the highest caste, the Brahmans) are ineligible for sacred thread ceremonies, she has been working to reverse the situation, partly to partake of all of Hinduism's knowledge and rituals, but also so she can have an opportunity to educate her non-Hindu friends about her faith, a faith about which they know little. With its galaxy of deities with strange names and strange myths and stories, Hinduism was alien to Ramya's friends in

Detroit. Interfaith knowledge may be the order of our day, especially after the horrors of September 11, but Hinduism is rarely part of the ecumenical conversation.

"If I had the thread," Ramya said, "my friends would want to know what it is. That would give me a chance to tell them about Hinduism," an opportunity often lost in the United States, where Siva and Vishhu and Kali may now be worshipped by Hindus living here, but where these gods have also been appropriated by marketers looking for cool images for lunch boxes and T-shirts—all to create "style," from which holiness and meaning have been bleached, all in the cause of profits and the look du jour.

Ramya's yearning to explain her faith is admirable in a culture that often ignores context and meaning and purpose, all of which might make people reconsider the common sense of wearing a Krishna T-shirt at the same time as a crucifix is dangling from their neck. America prides itself on pluralism, on faiths nestling up to each other with a rough semblance of peace and tolerance. But tolerance without understanding is an empty civics lesson, and Ramya Gopal's passion to tell her friends about what's really going on with those godly images from the other side of the world has the potential to be a splendid antidote to empty-headed designer éclat. But first, of course, Ramya needs her thread.[12]

In that sense, she differs with a certain Hindu reformer who preferred that the thread ceremony be suspended until the entire faith became more democratic. For all his demands that Hinduism discard its caste system and all his proclamations that men and women were equal ("Woman is gifted with equal mental capacities [as man]. She has the right to participate in the minutest detail of the activities of man. . . . The soul in both is the same"), Mahatma Gandhi never lobbied for giving the thread to women. He had other priorities. His personal evolution regarding relations between men and women was gradual and nuanced and, certainly, highly advanced for his time and culture and traditions. No doubt, it took courage to state that "woman has the same right of freedom and liberty" as man. This set him against thousands of years of cant—and not just in India. And yet so many of his pronouncements about equality within Hinduism focused on advancing Sudras—untouchables. Far, far less did he attempt to bring women entirely into the Hindu fold, maybe because if, as Hinduism claims, all humans are (theoretically) equal since they have a soul, then giving the thread to women would have been superfluous and unnecessary. Or maybe he believed that it was wiser to bestow the thread first to untouchables and, in time, to women: society could handle one major reform at a time, and bringing the thread to male untouchables, however jolting that might be, was still less jarring than bringing it to women.[13]

And yet, Gandhi had an early fascination with the *upanayana*. "When I was an urchin of ten," he wrote in his autobiography, *The Story of My Experiments with Truth*, "I envied the Brahman lads sporting bunches of keys tied to their sacred threads and I wished I could do likewise." He did—almost. A few years later, he was invested with the thread, and while he "had no occasion to possess a bunch of keys, I got [a thread] and began to sport it."[14]

Eventually, Gandhi's fascination with keys—and with the thread—dissipated. When his thread gave way, he didn't replace it; years later, he didn't even remember if he missed it. "But I do know," he wrote, "that I did not go [to a temple] for a fresh one."[15]

Over the course of Gandhi's career, several "well-meaning" efforts were made to give him another thread. He resisted all of them. "If the *shudras* may not wear it," he argued, "what right have the other *varnas* [castes] to do so?"[16]

In his midforties, while deeply engrossed in conversation with a swami, the holy man pressed Gandhi on the matter of another investiture. Gandhi was touched that the swami was pained that he was not wearing the thread, but he did not yield. He saw no need for the thread, he said, "when countless Hindus go without it, and yet remain Hindus. Moreover, the sacred thread should be a symbol of spiritual regeneration, presupposing a deliberate attempt on the part of the wearer at a higher and purer life. I doubt," Gandhi insisted, "whether in the present state of Hinduism and of India, Hindus can vindicate the right to wear a symbol charged with such a meaning. That . . . can only come after Hinduism has . . . removed all distinctions of superiority and inferiority, and shed a host of other evils and shams that have become rampant in it. My mind, therefore, rebels against the idea of wearing the sacred thread."[17]

Gandhi's aversion never left him. The untouchables never received the thread, and Gandhi never received another thread. To this day, untouchables and women are still excluded from wearing the thread. It's interesting and disturbing that Gandhi sought equality for all castes while not for both genders. In that sense, his instincts were half-right: he semi-understood what was keeping Hinduism from an even more glorious future. And now, more than fifty years after Gandhi's death, Ramya Gopal and her mother and the thousand members of Navya Shastra and other reform groups are seeking to go one step beyond Gandhi. If successful, they will affirm one of Gandhi's last statements, one he made just nine months before his assassination: "I make no distinction between man and woman. Women should feel just as independent as men. Bravery is not man's monopoly."[18]

Ajay Kumar, of course, didn't have this problem. Since his sacred thread ceremony at the Sri Siva Vishnu Temple, his father has been teaching him how to be a good Hindu: the days when boys move in with their gurus after an *upanayana* are long over. Brahmans, especially, needed to be close to their gurus for their twelve-year apprenticeship. For them, this was really vocational training: they made their living from teaching and performing religious ceremonies. Boys from other castes stayed just long enough to learn personal and domestic rituals and no more.

But no matter who Ajay learns from, the ultimate goal for any Hindu is right there in the Bhagavad Gita (5:24):

Only that yogi
Whose joy is inward,
Inward his peace,
And his vision inward
Shall come to Brahma
And know Nirvana.[19]

No one expects such peace for Ajay. Not today. That takes many years and much wisdom, and Ajay is only thirteen—years away, maybe reincarnations away from nirvana. For now, he's still a kid in the suburbs, a kid who plays a mean game of basketball, has a knack for languages and a passion for music, and plans to be a doctor. But he's seen the "postman"— the ritual fire at his sacred thread ceremony—carry his "letters" to all those gods and goddesses who bicker and love and peer down at our funny, weird, tragic, strange, very human predicament. If a strand of thread can sort out the mess we're born into, maybe we should all wear them. They might help us find our own "postman." Lord knows, we need him. Too much of our spiritual correspondence ends up in the dead letter office.

RELIGION IS FREQUENTLY IDIOTIC

What do you do when *Time* magazine includes you in the top one hundred icons of the twentieth century, when Mikhail Gorbachev calls you "one of the most lucid and inspired philosophers of our time," when someone far less famous than Gorbachev compares trying to absorb your "ceaseless wisdom" to "attempting to take a sip of water from a fire hydrant"?

What do you do? You enjoy it, and why not? But you also continue to write books—thirty-five at last count, with translations into over thirty languages and more than twenty million sold worldwide. And you offer your mind-body programs at the five-star La Costa Resort and Spa, just north of San Diego: the high-end mecca on the holistic healing/meditation/yoga circuit. And you produce TV specials about holism and spirituality and lecture at Harvard's Divinity and Business Schools.

That's what we'd be doing if we were Deepak Chopra. But we're not, so we watch at a remove how this former chief of staff at the New England Memorial Hospital morphed into a New Age guru extraordinaire in barely two decades. Trained at New Delhi's All India Institute of Medical Sciences in the 1960s, Chopra interned at hospitals in New Jersey and Virginia, specializing in internal medicine and endocrinology. In the early 1980s, he left traditional medicine when warned that he would suffer from heart disease unless he changed his lifestyle. Taking up Transcendental Meditation, he learned about the five-thousand-year-old Indian system of healing called Ayurveda. Attributing most disease to the accumulation of toxins, Ayurveda seeks to balance the *doshas,* the three basic metabolic principles connecting the mind, body, and soul. These principles are deemed to be responsible for regulating the body's functions by cleansing physical, mental, and spiritual impurities from it. In India, being an Ayurvedic practitioner is a licensed profession, requiring almost as much training as a Western medical degree. One of Ayurveda's many virtues, says Chopra, is looking at patients in their entirety: an Ayurvedic doctor doesn't ask, "What disease does my patient have?" but "Who is my patient?"[1]

Now a one-man international conglomerate—Chopra virtually embodies spiritual globalization—Deepak tirelessly pursues his mission: "bridging the technological miracles of the West with the wisdom of the East." He melds heart with mind and mind with body and both with meditation and herbal medicine and what he calls "quantum healing"—"healing one mode of consciousness, mind, to bring about changes in another mode of consciousness, body." All this, he says, opens us up to "the infinite possibilities contained within human potential. . . . I want a day to come when perhaps we will see a world of peace, harmony, laughter and love."[2]

You can't argue with that. But many scoffers say Chopra is selling snake oil to the meek, the susceptible, the ignorant. Christian critics, especially, wonder if Chopra's patients would practice Ayurveda if they knew that its "real purpose . . . is to contact the essence of the Hindu God, Brahman, and to . . . recreate oneself as God through occult practices."[3]

The carping doesn't bother Chopra. He's busy saving lives, expanding consciousnesses, making this a safer, saner planet. Even Gandhi didn't set his sights so high: he was only concerned with saving one country—India. Chopra has his sights set on the world.

Since Chopra is the most famous Indian in the West, I figured he was also the most famous Hindu in the West. Not so. His father was a Sikh, his mother was a Hindu, and Chopra identifies with neither faith: "I am not at all religious. As soon as you label yourself, you confine yourself. I say that I was born a Hindu, but that I draw inspiration from Vedanta, which is the eternal source of wisdom that Hinduism comes from."[4]

Conceivably, living with a man whom millions believe has The Answer can be daunting. But to Chopra's two children, both in their thirties, he's just their father, not a sage. Mallika says she and her brother had "a wonderful childhood—not only because of the fascinating people we met, but because we were taught to look at the world with magical eyes, curiosity, and passion." And Gotham, Chopra's son, says he is "very close" to his dad: "We speak probably about three times a day. I consider him a friend. . . . The key to our relationship is that we don't get stuck in traditional roles—'He's the father and I'm the son,' or 'He is the teacher and I am the student.' We just know how to have a lot of fun together."

Asked if his spirituality influences his career, Gotham said, "Very much. I make a lot of my decisions via intuition—how I feel about what it is I want to do and the people I want to work with. I consider that the ultimate expression of spirituality. I guess you could call that 'spirituality in action.'"[5]

Spirituality, apparently, runs in the Chopra bloodline. But not *upanayana,* since both Deepak and Gotham, with their Sikh ancestry, are not eligible for a sacred thread ceremony. (They would certainly qualify if they were 100 percent Hindu: they are in the second-highest caste, the Kshatriya caste.) But each Chopra has essentially the same view of rites of passage: by drawing lines between religions, they separate us into competing, often misunderstood niches. The Chopras long for the day when we stop clinging to our religious ideologies and see each other for what we are: humans caught in that most peculiar of circumstances—our own humanity.

I discussed this lack of *upanayana* by phone with father and son. Not adjusting for the three-hour time difference between Baltimore and Los Angeles, Gotham asked me to call him at 9 A.M. When I woke him shortly after dawn Los Angeles time, he asked that I call back in a few hours: even the son of the high priest of cosmic harmony needs his sleep. Deepak was a slightly different story: focused, friendly, but a tad didactic, he inquired as the interview started whether I minded if he ate a salad as we spoke. It was 1 P.M. Pacific time. Of course I didn't mind. Harmony is one thing; a full tummy is another.

I have always felt that religion is quarrelsome and frequently idiotic and kind of a cover-up for insecurity, full of sexism and ethnocentrism and racism and what people would perceive as idolatry. If you look at the world right now, it's a total mess. We have war, terrorism, racism, bigotry, hatred, prejudice. Most of it is in the name of God. Why is that? If we are so religious, why is this the outcome of religion? And if one is very honest about it, very forthright about seeking global harmony and peace, Hindus have to stop thinking "I'm a Hindu" and Christians have to stop thinking "I'm a Christian" and so on. They have to believe in what Christ said rather than believing in Christ. If I'm pointing my finger at the moon, you don't worship my finger. You look at the moon. Unfortunately, what has happened is that religious identity has not kept pace with our understanding of who we really are. And if you want a global identity, then we have to shed these limited identities.

All rituals are just different forms of conditioning. They trap energy and information into a particular pattern that influences your consciousness and your behavior and your ethics and morality and allows you to have allegiance to a particular belief system. Why do we salute the American flag? Why do we stand up when the national anthem is played? Because we give significance to a certain process that gives us meaning in our life. At a certain stage, I think, one would like to go beyond that.

These rites condition someone to a particular belief system. And whenever you make something exclusive, it influences you into thinking that other beliefs and religions are not that great because you hold yours to be truer.

But I'm not even totally attached to what I just said. Many people who are part of a religion do absolutely astonishingly wonderful things. I know Christian missionaries who are doing amazing work in Africa and helping starving children and helping people with AIDS and helping those that are not privileged. I know Hindus who are doing extremely wonderful work as well. But I also know Hindus who would torch Muslims to death yet say they are kind vegetarians. So it's a paradox, a total contradiction.

We have to understand that human beings have been on this planet only for 200,000 years and the planet has been around for 3.8 billion years and the universe has existed for around 14 billion years. We've had written language for less than 5,000 years. In many ways, we are in our infancy in our evolution.

In the end, I think that the essence of true spirituality is to be tolerant and understanding and compassionate about the fact that we are full of paradox and ambiguity and contradiction. A rite of passage might be totally appropriate for someone and not appropriate for someone else. True spirituality allows us to say that *this* is the state of our evolution. This is where the universe is at this moment, and its pattern of behavior is fine. The best we can do is to try to understand it and be forgiving and compassionate and share in the confusion and the suffering of our fellow human beings. If we do that, maybe there is the birth of love; maybe there is a possibility for healing. That is a spirituality which is beyond religious dogma, although I would not deny religious dogma to people who find it nurturing and consoling and that it sustains some meaning or focus in their life.

I was born in New Delhi in 1946. My father, Krishnan, was a cardiologist. My mother, Pushpa, was a housewife. My father came from a Sikh background and my mother came from a Hindu background, but religion was never really a focus in our family. My mother used to read from the scriptures, mostly stories. We occasionally went to a temple, but I attended an Irish Christian missionary school where I frequented catechism classes, among other things. I was in a very eclectic environment with people of all religions.

The idea of a sacred thread ceremony never even came up. My father had been educated in England. He was a physician to the royal infirmary and a fellow of the Royal College of Physicians and was very Westernized. Even though we came from this background, we never really were part of it.

None of my friends had the ceremony either. Certainly not the friends I played cricket with. Some were Hindus or had a Hindu background; some were Jewish or Christian or Muslim. But they all went to a missionary school, so they couldn't have been very orthodox in their beliefs.

Buddha probably had a sacred thread ceremony, but he was so disillusioned by the ritualistic aspect of Hinduism that he created a whole new religion based on what he saw as the essential truths that were in Hinduism and Vedic philosophy. He was a reformer, and even twenty-five hundred years ago saw that some aspects of ritualism were not that relevant. And in the ninth century another reformer, Adi Shankara—the most important figure in Hinduism in the last twelve hundred years—was initiated in the sacred thread ceremony at the age of seven or eight, then left home at a young age and wandered as an ascetic for years. He died at the age of thirty-three, and his writing was more prolific than Shakespeare's. Yet in his entire body of literature about Hinduism, there was nothing about rituals.

I have written, "If you have happy thoughts, then you make happy molecules." Given this formulation, would Hindus who have happy thoughts need a sacred thread ceremony? If the ceremony makes them happy, then that's okay. That's what they need. Some people need a sacred thread ceremony because that's the conditioning of their culture, the conditioning of their parents, the conditioning of their environment. If somebody takes away that conditioning, they might become unhappy or insecure or lose their identity. I had a different kind of conditioning, even though I lived in a milieu where there was a lot of that other kind of conditioning.

Around the world, too much weight is placed on all these rites of passage. In our modern civilization, we have a very interesting situation. We have very ancient habits and we have very modern capabilities. So in a way, we are still very tribal, even as we have the Internet and nuclear weapons and biological warfare and the same violence that our ancestors had. Combining a tribal identity with these ancient habits and modern capacities can be very devastating. Even the violence today is the same as what we had, say, five thousand years ago, and our capacity to self-destruct and to destroy others is greater. Ultimately, the only hope for humanity is to go beyond tribal identity. I don't see it happening, unfortunately, and I've thought about it and agonized over it and struggled with it. And in the end, I've said to myself that maybe nature is saying that the human being is an interesting experiment that didn't work. So, let's try something else. Or maybe I'm wrong and in a couple of generations we'll transcend our tribal identities. But who knows?

Hindus take pride in what I do because much of what I use in my writings is borrowed from the Vedic tradition and the Vedic philosophy, which gave rise to Hinduism, although in a form that became ritualistic and ideological and dogmatic. [The Vedic tradition flourished in much of India in the first millennium B.C.E.] That is why I'm frequently seen as someone who propagates or talks about Hinduism. In my mind I don't do that. I'm taking the kernels of wisdom and expressing them. The Vedic system satisfies the intellectual curiosity of anyone who wants to understand consciousness and spirituality and the essential nature of reality. It never mentions "God." The Vedic system would be intellectually and emotionally fulfilling to anyone, even an atheist or an agnostic or a theist, because it talks about consciousness as our reality, with consciousness being the phenomenon that gives rise to physical reality. It further says that as long as you think of yourself as a person, then you have a person's stake in everything, and that is the basis of suffering, which comes from clinging to things that are transient and ephemeral and being afraid of things that are transient and ephemeral. It means identifying with a socially induced hallucination which you call a "person" or an "ego" or a "personality." It also means that you have a fear of death.

Henry James called it a complex fate to be an American. It is also a complex fate to be a Hindu. The word "Hindu" originally comes from the word "Indu," which refers to the people who lived around the Indus River [in northwest India]. The original Hindus belonged to the Indus Valley civilization. They were very sophisticated. They had one of the first universities that ever existed and delved into astronomy and philosophy and mathematics. They were not tied to a religion. But then as Mongols and Muslims began to invade India, these very civilized people started to say, almost as a resistance movement, "Oh, we also have a religion, and that religion is Hinduism."

Having said all that, if Gotham told me tomorrow, "Hey, Dad, I really would like to have the sacred thread," what would I say? I'd say, "Go for it. Go for it. If that's what makes you happy, go for it."

GOTHAM CHOPRA

Religious rituals can be very divisive, and that's unfortunate. The world is changing very fast. Change is good and change is inevitable, and it's our responsibility to adjust around that change. But for five years, one of the areas I covered as a journalist mostly related to conflicts and wars. I spent five years on the road—Chechnya, India, Pakistan, Kashmir, Sri Lanka,

Israel, Palestine. I witnessed wars and carnage and refugee camps. More often than not this was related to some sort of religious strife. That had a profound influence on me and solidified my perspective, a perspective that I didn't qualify as "religious." I certainly had a very spiritual upbringing, and spirituality continues to be a strong part of my life. But am I "religious"? Not necessarily.

The backlash toward fanaticism, which we see often in the world today, is not good, although it may be inevitable and eventually things will end up finding their right place. And while rituals have an important place in contemporary culture and society, everywhere, they can make people rigid and intolerant. To this day, I still have friends I grew up with who are so religiously rigid that it's bothersome. They were brought up with rigid views about the way things are. This is very stifling, but I've been taught that you can't control other people's views and you can't control the way parents raise their children. You can only focus on your own traditions and on how you are raising your children.

Strangely, people in the West expect the East to be more tolerant. It's not true. To this day, when I go to India, I see some of the same divisions that occur elsewhere. And in the United States especially, the people who are the least tolerant are those who are the least exposed to others. Those with the worst opinions of, say, Muslims or people in the Middle East have had no experiences with anyone from that faith nor have they been in that region. I've traveled a lot in the Islamic world and in the Middle East, and it's so complex that it's not easy to categorize as we do in this country.

To avoid this, people have to be exposed at a much younger age to a variety of different cultural and religious traditions. People get fixated on their interpretation of the divine and their way of celebrating it. Believers grow attached to their way as the right way and determine that others are blasphemous and sacrilegious. And since most people interpret religion within a very dualistic paradigm—sinners and saints, sacred and profane, good and evil—they are unwilling and unable to accept the contradictions of life and various spiritual traditions. Can this be overcome? Of course—as soon as believers let go of their need to be right all the time.

I was born in Boston in 1975, the first in my family to be born outside of India. I spent almost all my youth in the Boston area, until I went to college. My parents got married when they were twenty-one or twenty-two, and they immigrated to this country in the early 1970s. My dad had finished his medical school in India. This was during the Vietnam War, and there was a shortage of doctors in this country. He always had the intention of coming to the West, and this was a great opportunity for him. The recruitment of physicians was heavily underway.

At first, we lived in Jamaica Plains, which is in central downtown Boston. Not a great neighborhood at the time. We were there only about a year. Then we moved to Lincoln, a small, charming town about twenty minutes outside of Cambridge. It was a great place to grow up. We had a really nice house, with several acres of woods in the back. Many in my father's generation from India, and especially many in his medical school class, had immigrated, so we had a pretty solid community of people with a very similar experience. Several Hindu temples were nearby, but we went to them on very rare occasions. In our house, though, we had statues of Ganesha [the elephant-headed Hindu god of success], and during certain holidays we observed certain rituals, but we didn't really go to temples or anything.

Ironically, my family has really never qualified as religious. Spiritual? Definitely, although that may be parsing words to a certain extent. And, of course, I grew up with such a unique experience, although my father was not Mr. Spiritual his whole life. He was very much a traditional physician with a traditional lifestyle. When I was in junior high school, he started to transition. That was obviously a very formative time for me, and like many of my generation, religion wasn't a huge part of my upbringing. I don't want to make it sound like we were infidels. My parents were very observant of our cultural traditions and our religious traditions, but I was not told that the gods would punish me if I did not do certain things. That was not part of our vocabulary.

My parents didn't even have a problem with my going to church or chapel every morning at the predominantly Catholic school I attended. We went to chapel every morning and said grace before every meal. That may have been my most formal religious education. My parents' intention, I think, was always to expose my sister and me to a lot of different traditions. At the same time, I don't think we ever really questioned that we were Indian, although we were definitely more Indian than Hindu.

In fact, I've never really identified as Sikh or Hindu. I'm definitely more familiar with Hindu mythology and Hindu traditions. That's India to me.

I grew up with stories about Krishna and Ganesha. But frankly, there is a part of Sikhism with which I feel more comfortable. It's more of a practical religion, and it was born, historically speaking, out of a real need from people who had kind of lost their way.

I never had a sacred thread ceremony, and truthfully, it doesn't interest me that much. I've never been that interested in traditional religious rituals. The closest we came to going through religious rituals was when we traveled to India, which was usually once or twice a year while growing up. My grandparents, and especially my grandmothers, were far more religious than my parents. My father's parents, who were Hindu, took us to temple, and we'd go through certain ceremonies there. These were sort of rites of passage, but my sister, Mallika (who's three years older than me), and I mostly interpreted these as part of the cultural experience of being in India. Quite honestly, we didn't come back feeling that we were "more" Indian. And every time we left India, we would do a puja with my grandmother, who would thank the gods for letting us come there safely and then tie a string around our wrist. We sort of smiled and endured it because it was important to my grandmother. We didn't take it very seriously.

And with my mother, who's fascinated with sacred sites and spiritual destinations, we'd go to temples and to different pilgrimage sites. In the north, we visited Amarnath [site of a massive shrine to the god Shiva]. This didn't involve serious mountain climbing, but we still had to trek up a mountain and cross a glacier to get to the temple. In southern India, we visited Tirupati [site of an elaborate temple to Lord Venkateswara, an incarnation of Vishnu, protector and sustainer of the world]. And with my paternal grandfather, we visited the Golden Temple, the holiest Sikh site, in the town of Amritsar and, in the old part of Delhi, went to one of the largest Sikh temples in the world—the Bangla Sahib Gurudwara. (I still go there with my grandfather every time I visit India, but it's now more of a tradition than a religious excursion.) And my grandmother, who recently passed away and was probably more religious than any of us, took us to a temple for a blessing that was supposed to make sure that we got good grades. It worked for my sister; for me, I'm not sure.

These visits essentially grounded me in being Indian and in being Hindu/Sikh. They gave me an identity for the balance of a year, plus my father's brother and his family lived about ten minutes away from us. We were a very close family and always came together for certain holidays, such as Diwali, the celebration of lights.

The closest that I've come to going through a rite of passage is Rakhi, which stems from one of Hinduism's seminal myths, the Ramayana, which is basically the story of Ram, a hero-god who, with his brother, goes in pursuit of his wife when she is kidnapped by the demon king. When they save Sita, she recognizes that Ram could not have saved her without his brother's help. She ties a string to Lashman's wrist, acknowledging that now he is her brother too, and like Ram, he will also be her protector.

Every fall, my sister and my cousins and I celebrate Rakhi. They tie a string to my wrist, saying, "You're my brother and you're going to take care of me." That's the closest to a sacred thread ceremony I've come. We've done this from birth, and we still do it, and now my two young nieces do it with their older cousins. In my family, the string is usually red or gold, and you wear it until it eventually falls off, which can be months.

When I was younger, there was more ritual around Rakhi, and we either did it in the temple or had a party for it. Now, I live close to my sister and we may do it at her house. But my cousins who live in Boston or India may send me rakhis—that's what we call the strings—in the mail, and my sister will tie them on me on their behalf.

Does it work? My sister is now married and has her own protector. But Rakhi reminds me that I still have a certain responsibility, which is nice. I would certainly pass this ritual on to my kids.

With no formal rite of passage, do I feel that anything is lacking in my life? No. Even when I went to friends' confirmations or bar mitzvahs when I was a kid, I never had a lack of fulfillment at a spiritual level. Our trips to India fulfilled that. We had our own culture and we were very proud of it. I think the experience of going through these rites is more valuable than actually understanding them at the time. I'm not sure that anybody really understands them because, if you logically attempt to explain a lot of these things, they don't make sense to begin with. They're fairly arbitrary. Even going to the Sikh temples with my grandfather was really a sort of male-bonding experience between generations. That was as much a part of it as actually going through a ceremony once we got there.

There are now certain rites of passage that I look forward to, such as having a child. Even when I got married, it was not that important to my wife and me that we go through any of the traditional ceremonies. She comes from a Chinese American background, and we chose the Sikh ceremony because we felt that it wasn't overly religious. And all the ceremonies *around* the wedding were more cultural and secular. We had a Chinese banquet and also an Indian celebration called a *sangeet* [consisting of music, dance, food, and sometimes hired entertainment]. So no, right now, I don't feel that I've missed out on anything. That may change. Who knows?

PART FOUR

BUDDHISM

Original Perfection versus Original Sin

> Buddhism has the characteristics of what would be expected in a cosmic religion for the future: it transcends a personal God, avoids dogmas, amends theology; it covers both the natural and the spiritual; and it is based on a religious sense aspiring from the experience of all things, natural and spiritual, as a meaningful unity.
>
> ALBERT EINSTEIN

WAKING UP

A few years ago, a student at a Zen monastery went crying to her roshi. She was scheduled for *jukai* the next day—a Buddhist initiation ceremony— and the whole thing, she sobbed, was a big mistake. She wasn't worthy, she wailed. She wasn't a good Buddhist. She wasn't even a good person. "You don't know me," she said through her tears. "I can be so awful."

"We can all be so 'awful,'" the roshi, or Zen teacher, told her. "That's why the precepts you're about to take are so important."[1]

Everyone gets the jitters before a coming-of-age ceremony. But it's different when, like the woman who wanted to back out of *jukai*, you're thirty-five years old—not ten or eleven or twelve. For one thing, you have a keener sense of the enormousness of your undertaking. Too often, kids comprehend little about these ceremonies, often doing them to placate parents and clergy and not be the oddball in their circle of friends. But also, since Zen cultivates an awareness of *everything*, then someone really ready for *jukai* is very aware—or should be aware—of personal anxieties and fears and reservations. That doesn't mean Zen Buddhists suffer from anxiety disorders—only that, having tuned in to their own demons, they may be better aware of them than many of the rest of us.

The precepts that the roshi mentioned to his jittery student encapsulate Buddhism's core teachings; and *jukai*, which his student so desperately wanted to avoid, is a serious and sobering commitment to them. Simple and austere, *jukai* can be as subtle as Zen itself and as one-pointed as a mind sharpened by years of deep meditation. It's entirely voluntary. You're not penalized if you don't take it, and you don't get any new privileges if you do. It doesn't even make you a better Buddhist. But it does say that you are serious about Buddhism, that now you're not an amateur and you're not a dilettante. You are a Buddhist. It's that simple, and that complicated. *Jukai* has been widely misunderstood. Some people say it's Zen's equivalent of converting or of being confirmed or inducted into an order of monks. It's none of these. Strip away all the rituals, and at its heart *jukai* is a public expression of your long-term commitment to Zen. Of course, in Buddhism, "long term" could be several thousand reincarnations.

Several hundred years ago, another rite of passage was common among serious Zen Buddhists: pilgrimages. Today, we think of a pilgrimage as a visit to a sacred place or teacher—having a specific purpose and destination. But a Zen pilgrimage was essentially random and almost, to our Western eyes, pointless. A monk who had completed training might go off into the wilderness and wander around—randomly and, you could say, capriciously—for several years, with no intention of going anywhere in particular or visiting certain teachers. The monk simply wandered, existed, *was*. It was a matter of losing oneself to the moment, the world, the forest, the path: to whatever came one's way.

Many koans record the travels of monks who were on pilgrimage. One of the best known is an encounter between Master Dizang and Fayan:

"Where are you going?" Dizang asked.

"I am wandering aimlessly," Fayan answered.

"What is the purpose of your wandering?"

"I don't know."

"Ah! Not knowing," Dizang said. "Very intimate, very intimate indeed."[2]

Intimacy didn't emanate from a plan or a map or a route, from a full-fledged "knowing" in advance where Fayan would spend the night, what he would have for lunch, whom he would study with and where. He was enriched by the moment, not by the next moment, for that was a distraction, a decoy. The further he could sink into the moment, into his wandering, into his presumably pointless, random, capricious wandering, the more focused, the more one-pointed, the more Buddha-like he became.

Jukai literarily means "to receive the precepts," although its real meaning is much broader. Gary Shishin Wick, roshi at the Green Mountain Zen

Center in Lafayette, Colorado, defines *jukai* as "revealing *yourself* as the *kai*"—as the fundamental truths of Buddhism which are within us but which we have yet to fully realize. And from the other side the continent, John Daido Loori, the roshi of the Zen Mountain Monastery in Mount Tremper, New York, says, "At the heart of *jukai*, at the heart of any ceremony . . . is 'the beholding mind.' This is the mind that has insight . . . , the aware, conscious mind which . . . give[s] life to the precepts."[3]

Both definitions come down to mind and to self, to examining what Loori calls "the catastrophe" of our existence—catastrophic because it insulates us from who we really are.

In that sense, Buddhism is the reverse of Christianity. Buddhists believe that years of conditioning make us forget the perfection with which we're born; Christians believe that we're born tainted and stained, contaminated by Adam's horrible sin back in the Garden.

Original perfection: we're born pure, clean, whole.

Original sin: we're born corrupt, debased, defiled.

The first glows with cheery possibility; the second dims with a dreary gloom. Which could be why *jukai* is voluntary and why baptism is more or less mandatory: Buddhists are sure we'll all be enlightened—eventually; Christians worry that, without a baptism, we'll die exactly as we were born: weighed down by sin and helpless against the temptations of the devil himself.

Zen students and teachers wait for the right moment for *jukai*, a moment when readiness, awareness, and more than a little wisdom come together, when everything is as right as Buddha's Eightfold Path—right view, right thought, right speech, right action, right livelihood, right effort, right mindfulness, and right concentration.

For the whole week before *jukai*, candidates gather, usually in a monastery or meditation center, sewing a *rakusu* for themselves—a black, quilt-like square, roughly twelve by twelve inches, that they wear across their chest after *jukai*, almost like an oversized fanny pouch hitched up in the wrong place. With each stitch, the students softly chant, "Being one with the Buddha. Being one with the dharma [the teachings of the Buddha]. Being one with the sangha [the Buddhist community]." This is sewing as meditation, as a device to quiet minds, to still egos. By the end of the week, if all goes well, the chant and the stitch and the Buddha and the dharma and the sangha all come together in the *rakusu,* which symbolizes not only Buddha's life but also our own enlightenment.

The *rakusu* is entrusted to the roshi who will officiate at *jukai;* the roshi will then present it to the candidate at the ceremony—a public statement of the value of having a group and a teacher to meditate and learn with: anyone can sew a *rakusu,* but only a Buddhist community can endow it with the right spirit and the right intent.

At the end of the week, the sangha and parents and the close friends of the candidates gather, and the ceremony begins with nine bows: three to a statue of the Buddha, who signifies enlightenment; three to the roshi, who represents the many teachers who have transmitted the Buddha's teachings; and three to the parents, who represent the candidate's personal lineage. If someone's parents are not present, candidates bow in the direction of their home; if they're dead, they bow in the direction of their graves.

Next, the candidates promise to abide by the essential Buddhist teachings: the Three Treasures—the Buddha, the dharma, and the sangha; the Three Pure Precepts—practicing good, actualizing good in others, and not creating evil; and the Ten Grave Precepts, which prohibit killing, stealing, lying, and denigrating others or elevating yourself above them. Twice, the roshi asks the students if they will maintain the precepts. Then, more firmly, he asks, "Will you *really* maintain them well?" Finally, the students receive a Buddhist name and the *rakusu* they had sewn in the past week.

Deliberateness and consciousness underlie *jukai.* That's its strength, and yet *jukai* can easily be misused. Sometimes, said John Daido Loori, people disappear not long after taking their vows, never to be seen again. Apparently, they took *jukai* lightly, maybe treating it as a spiritual lark or thinking it is "like getting a badge of some kind or a diploma that assures them they'll have a better moral life. They think they're 'graduating' after getting *jukai.* Really, all they're doing is committing themselves to a lot of hard work."[4]

No one is *entitled* to *jukai.* Buddhists don't get it automatically because they've reached a certain age or have studied a requisite number of years or have memorized whole texts and volumes. If a wise roshi senses that someone wants *jukai* for the wrong reasons—say, pursuing *jukai* more to get status in the community than as a matter of heart—he asks them to wait and let their patience mature. Many people don't come back. Apparently, they have little patience.

These admonitions—"Be patient." "Don't rush."—stem from Buddhism's acute appreciation of the human predicament: we suffer until we are liberated, and we're not liberated until one final reincarnation reminds us of the perfection with which we were born. With so many rebirths, we have lots of time—millions and millions of years—best used by waking up, being aware, becoming conscious. That's the heart of Buddhism and the heart of Buddha's teachings. Shortly after Buddha was enlightened, people gathered around, stunned by his aura, perplexed by his peacefulness.

"Are you a god?" they asked.

"No," Buddha responded.

"An angel?"

"No."

"A saint?"

"No."

"Then what are you?"

Buddha answered, "I am awake."[5]

BORN A BUDDHA. DIE A BUDDHA

Zen is an austere practice, and the Zen Mountain Monastery is one
of the more austere Zen centers in the United States—two hundred
twenty-five acres located within Catskills State Park, ten miles from
the town of Woodstock, which will always be known as the place where
three days of peace and love—the Woodstock Music Festival—did *not*
occur. (The festival actually took place in Bethel, seventy miles southwest of Woodstock.) But real Buddhists don't need seventy-two hours
of manufactured harmony: the universe provides its own harmony.
You just have to find it, which is never easy, not in Zen and not even
at this monastery, despite being enveloped by a silence so deep it
can be nearly impenetrable. But you can try.

Originally, the monastery had nothing to do with Zen but a lot to do
with other religions. Built as a Catholic retreat center in the 1930s, it
later served as a Lutheran summer camp. In 1980 it finally entered
Buddhist hands and in 1994 was placed on the National Register of
Historic Places, a well-deserved designation, since the building is a
unique blend of traditional Norwegian architecture and the Arts and
Crafts motif common in upstate New York in the early twentieth
century. This gives it cachet to the mavens of preservation. But it
stands out from the crowd for another reason: from the right angle,
and there are many of them, it looks less Norwegian or Arts and
Crafts-y than ancient and Japanese, the sort of heavy-lidded building

that Akira Kurosawa would have cast in one of his sweeping epics about good-hearted samurai and black-hearted bandits. It doesn't so much sit on the ground as squat on it. Possessing the earth, it is as immovable and stoical as Zen itself, even if it does need new windows and stone steps and an overhaul of its entire electrical system. But just as the Buddha's body fell into disrepair, parts of the monastery are the same way. What's important is that Buddha knew what lives, what is the changeless essence of all sentient beings. If any building (well, any building in Mount Tremper, New York) could be said to be Buddha-like, to evoke changelessness, it is this one: there for the long haul—hermit-like and as rock solid as the mountains that loom above.

Raised a Catholic in Jersey City, John Daido Loori later trained as a physical chemist. Not especially comfortable with Catholicism as a kid, as an adult he explored various religions, finally finding his way to Zen, which he studied for fourteen years before becoming a Zen priest and returning to the East Coast from California to teach. Even after studying Zen's lay and monastic traditions, Loori is thoroughly American—a childhood in Jersey City is hard to put behind you. But he's also thoroughly Buddhist and sees Zen as adapting, over and over, to specific cultures while never losing its integrity and power, using its ancient wisdom to take Master Buddha's Traveling Enlightenment Show from one country to another, from one millennium to another.

"For forty-seven years," Loori told me, "Buddha taught 'no soul and no self' in a country where everyone else was doing the 'soul/self thing.' Nobody tried to kill him. He lived a full life. Buddhism would go on to China and India and Japan and other countries that practiced Hinduism and Confucianism and other religions, where it was embraced, because it did not oppose them. It embodies them. It's the equivalent of a Black Muslim minister going down to Mississippi back in the sixties, and not only preaching but converting the governor."

Loori and I talked in a small room just off of the monastery's main meditation room—a massive space with a thirty-foot-high ceiling and a floor of oak and white pine. Just over six feet, Loori spilled out of his chair that was in front of a clear, leaded glass window—a reminder, along with the tall Christ figure on the building's facade, of the monastery's Catholic origins. If anything was now catholic—deliberately spelled with a small "c"—about Loori, it was his appreciation of every faith. Maybe not how some of them are practiced or interpreted, but the healthy teachings at their core. No Zen supremacist—a flagrant oxymoron—he was more of a Zen universalist, a card-carrying religio-civil libertarian.

A pattern soon emerged. Whenever Loori would tell a story, he got fairly animated and spoke more rapidly, carried away by the scene and the events. But whenever he returned to his more general comments about religion and, especially, about Buddhism, he slowed down, speaking more deliberately, more thoughtfully, choosing his words more carefully. The stories buoyed him; the religious talk braced him. Both engaged him. Both delighted him.

About half an hour into our discussion, a student attending the ninety-day retreat that was then in session brought us herbal tea and sugar cookies. They were welcome. Seventy-year-old buildings with three-foot-thick walls of granite may look stable and evoke enormous confidence, but they get chilly on rainy days. We sipped the tea and nibbled on the cookies, all the while discussing gentle priests, wise monks, the two hundred *jukai* ceremonies Loori has led, and why he hit a nun with an eraser.

My first *jukai*, when I "officially" became a Buddhist, wasn't even a ceremony. My teacher, Eido Roshi, just announced to the sangha [a Buddhist community] at dinner, "John has a new name. His name is Daido, [which means 'The Great Way']." That was my initiation. It took place in 1971 at Dai Bosatsu, a Zen center in upstate New York. He told me to make myself a *rakusu*, which I never did. In 1975 my second teacher—a Japanese master in Los Angeles—actually *did* the ceremony. And he gave me a *rakusu*.

That first *jukai* affected me, to a certain extent. The name I was given is also the beginning of the Faith Mind Sutra by the third Zen ancestor, Sengcan. It was, and continues to be, an important teaching for me, so much that I purchased one hundred booklets on the sutra and distributed them to all the people I thought would find it valuable.

That *jukai* was not as significant as the second one. Then Maezumi Roshi gave me the name "Muge," which literally means "No hindrance" and completes the opening of the Faith Mind Sutra: "The Great Way is not difficult."

Also, this *jukai* was entirely in Japanese. When it was over, I got a copy of the ceremony and started asking questions: "What does *this* mean? What does *that* mean?" Basically, I educated myself about what was really happening, and that became the foundation for what I later did as a teacher. Now I do some of the chanting in Japanese, because I can chant faster in Japanese. And everything is repeated three times—once in Japanese, once in English, and again in Japanese. That way, the students understand what is being said. Probably, the next generation will do it all in English. In fact, I used to complain to my teacher, "Why are we doing all this Japanese stuff, Roshi?" And he'd say, "Daido, I'm Japanese. When your turn comes, you do it in English." But I do it in two languages, Japanese and English, because I'm just a transition figure: a first-generation American Zen master. So I still have one foot in each place.

I take *jukai* very seriously, and I take my commitment to the students very seriously. Even if they burn their *rakusu* and say, "Screw you!" and leave, I'll still be here for them, as much as I can possibly be, as long as I live.

What does it mean to really receive these precepts at a *jukai* ceremony? It means to embody them. And essentially, what you're embodying is the life of the Buddha, someone who doesn't elevate the self and put down others, someone who is compassionate, someone who lives life out of the realization of the unity of all things, someone who recognizes that this very body is the body of the universe, and who *acts* that way.

I try to awaken them through a series of lectures that they need to attend, and particularly through my work with them that last week before *jukai*. I poke at them. I probe at them. I try to bring all their "stuff" to the surface.

I tell the students that they can't get "divorced" from *jukai,* although some of these people disappear and I never hear from them again. Or some may pop up after a number of years and say, "I got married and this is my kid." Or some of them may come back to the training after being away for ten or twelve years.

Often, the first thing I see months after someone has *jukai* is a self-consciousness. After a few months that disappears, and I get a sense that they're taking it to heart. I know that because of the questions they bring to our face-to-face teaching. During periods of meditation every day, students come individually into this room and we sit face-to-face for an encounter. They can ask questions or I can test them. It's here that I get a sense that they're working with all of this. If some of this is backfiring, if they're using *jukai* to expand their ego, then I nail them. And that's an opportunity to teach. You know, all of this—the liturgy, the face-to-face teaching, the lectures, the zazen [meditation]—all of it is a skillful means to get people to realize that they already have what they're looking for. It's a way to get them to recognize that they were born a Buddha and they will die a Buddha. It's a process of discovery. I don't have anything to give anybody. They already have it. But you have to discover this before you can use it.

Rites of passage for youngsters must do *something*. You can call this "transformation," but, you know, it's very easy to "transform" the mind of a seven year old or an eleven year old. Another word for this might be "brainwashing" or "indoctrination." You don't have the ability to discriminate when you're eleven, twelve, thirteen. Unless you're very precocious. When I do *jukai,* I'm dealing with adults, and often some very sophisticated adults: doctors, lawyers, professors, teachers. So the whole thing is on a totally different plane than when I had my confirmation.

This is one of the reasons that this monastery does not have religious studies for kids. I've resisted this, though the parents do badger me. What we do have are classes in which Buddhist principles come into play without naming them "Buddhist principles." We take kids into the woods and teach them about the wilderness. We have them express themselves through art projects. We discuss practical aspects of human relationships— "There's an argument between two people. How can we resolve it?"— rather than have kids sit around and memorize chants. This is a way to teach kids to use their mind, their consciousness, that incredible gift of human birth, without filling it with a bunch of predetermined stuff.

But in principle, I think, these various rites of passage are fundamentally the same: they mark a transition. They are a way to relate to a spiritual practice, to go from one level to another one, to a deeper one. They make you a part of something. They are designed to ground teenagers in the religion, to bond them with the religion, to identify with the religion. The language and the way they express it may be different. But once you get past all that stuff and get down to the nitty-gritty beneath it, they all have the same origins and intentions. When I had my first communion, for example, I was seven and living in an Italian neighborhood in Jersey

City. *Everybody* was Italian, and everybody spoke Italian, and all my little friends were Italian. All the adults made a fuss over my communion: it was a cultural event and a community event. In a sense, it was similar to *jukai,* which is also a public event. It's one thing to make a vow, and another to make it publicly. Leading up to *jukai* are a number of workshops in which students deal with moral and ethical teachings on an intellectual level. But when they take the vows publicly, and I say, "Will you maintain this?" and they say, "I will," and then I ask, "Will you *really* maintain this?" and they say, "I will," I want eye contact from them and I want to *feel* their answer. I do a lot of chanting, and the students do a lot of chanting, and the community that's gathered does a lot of chanting. Because in Zen, it's not just between the officiant and the recipient. It always includes the sangha, one of the Three Treasures. We have the dharma, the teachings; the Buddha, who is the historical Buddha, but also all beings; and the sangha, the community of practitioners. The community, the public ceremony, takes *jukai* away from the intellectual. It makes it *real.*

Growing up, I went to Holy Rosary School—until I hit a nun with a blackboard eraser. I'd been cutting up in class a lot, and at one point, this nun came up from behind and slapped me. I had an eraser in my hands and threw it at her. It made a white, chalky mark on her. She grabbed me by the ear and dragged me to Mother Superior. They called my mother and expelled me for a few weeks. After that, my mother put me in public school.

My parents were both born here, but *their* parents were immigrants. My father died when I was eight, so most of what I know about him is really stories—hearsay. He was held in very high regard. People loved him. My mother went to church occasionally, but her mother went all the time. Every day, she'd walk to church for the morning service, and she'd pray at home. My grandmother was the "fanatic" in the family.

As a kid, I was always questioning things. I was very interested in science, and when a nun would say to the class, "Who made the world?" and all the kids would answer in unison, "God made the world," I would put up my hand. And she would say [Loori's voice hardens in a mock imitation of the nun], "What is it, Mr. Loori?" And I'd say, "Well, how do you *know* that?" And she'd say, "Go see Father Santori." He'd be outside playing softball with the older kids. "Loori," he'd say when he saw me coming, "are you here again? Why don't you just go in there and shut your mouth? Stop annoying Sister Sunta." And I'd say to myself, "They don't know. They don't know." And I secretly declared myself an atheist.

And yet I did have my first communion, when I was seven, and my confirmation, when I was eleven. I had no idea what was going on, especially for the confirmation. I was in a state of trauma and just mouthed what I was told to. We had to learn a lot of stories, like one about a guy who wanted to identify with the pain that Christ had felt carrying the cross. I forget what he did, but I know what I did: on my way to catechism class one day, pebbles got in my shoe and I let them stay there. It was my way to identify with Christ.

The mystical aspects of communion were a bit curtailed because I knew how they made the host. I helped. The nuns made it, the same nuns who taught at the school. Inevitably, I would be punished for something and be sent to the nunnery. While I was there, they'd say, "Okay, you can help with this." And I would be working with the host: they had this bread that they rolled out flat, then used these little circular cutters to go boom, boom, boom on the bread, and pulled out the circles. That was the host, and what was left we could eat. So for me, there was little mystery in the whole thing.

To do your first communion, first you had to go to your first confession. For me, this was like a blackboard, with a list of all the bad things I'd done. The priest forgiving me at confession was like erasing the blackboard with a wet sponge. I felt fresh and clean . . . for about ten minutes.

The girls wore white dresses, and the boys wore black suits, and everyone wore a white bow on the arm. That signified purity. For confirmation, the bows were red. That signified the blood of Christ. Later, when I explored other religions and especially Buddhism, I decided that even though the *experience* of the confirmation was kind of special to me, I felt that nobody really understood what was behind it.

Here at the monastery, we have a rite of passage for teenagers, but this is not a traditional Buddhist event. Keep in mind that Buddhism is essentially monastic, and very little was offered for laypeople. But in America, 25 percent of Buddhists are laypeople, so we began to look at the fact that we'd been in existence for twenty-five years, and some people who had been coming here from the beginning now had kids who were teenagers. Partly to place American Buddhism on a par with other religious traditions in the West (Christianity, Judaism, Islam), we devised what we call a coming-of-age ceremony. Preceding that are classes in sex and sexuality and mutual respect. It's all about human relationships. It's not otherworldly, but this world. So we've adapted, and in a very practical way. This is for fourteen year olds, which is when kids are first starting to feel their oats and are getting mature. Eleven year olds are too young for this or for the sort of esoteric stuff they get in other faiths.

At the ceremony, the recipient has two dharma guardians who vow to see to the spiritual education of the child if both parents die. The sangha chants the Gatha of Atonement, the preceptor recites an invocation, then the recipients take refuge in the Three Treasures. Finally, they receive the Five Lay Buddhist Precepts as well as a rakusu, a mala, and a certificate. The ceremony ends with chanting the Four Bodhisattva Vows. [A gatha is a terse, pithy summation of Buddhist teachings; the Gatha of Atonement apologizes for actions born of greed, anger, and ignorance. The Three Treasures are the cornerstone of Buddhism—the sangha, or community; the dharma, or knowledge; the Buddha, which refers to the historical Buddha and to all beings. The Five Precepts are a Buddhist's basic, minimal observance of moral conduct. A mala is made up of beads used during prayer or meditation. And the Four Bodhisattva Vows pledge to eliminate suffering in the world and guide others toward enlightenment.]

Having a Jewish bar mitzvah at thirteen makes a hell of a lot more sense than having a Catholic confirmation at eleven, and I think there's a value to some of the religious education that the church is doing at these ages, although these classes should be less myopic and more ecumenical and broader. They should examine other religions. In Japan, when a teacher walks into a classroom, he faces students who all have the same history and the same religion and the same background. In America, there's such diversity that we need to understand all religions to *survive.* We need to respect our differences and not be frightened by them. What you don't understand is always frightening.

Only a charlatan would try to get people to believe that they have something that the other guy doesn't. Yet the fact remains that when someone takes *jukai,* when they take these precepts that are the manifestation of the life of a Buddha, it is an act of faith. These precepts are how a Buddha lives his life, but the students have to take my word for it. And they take the word of the literature for it. But the process doesn't end with them taking their vows. It continues for the rest of their training. Some people here have been in training for seventeen years. By then, these precepts are no longer something that's come from the outside. They've been transmitted mind-to-mind and become a manifestation of their life.

No doubt we've Westernized some of our teachings. But we haven't watered them down. We've just as tough-ass as we've always been. And we have barrier gates of entry. You can't just come in here and plop down your $35. Anybody's welcome, but it's a different story if you want to become a student. They have to go through five barrier gates of entry. They take the place of the barrier gates of ancient times. Then, somebody would come and sit outside the gate of a monastery. A monk would come out and say, "What do you want?" and he would say, "I've come to study with the teacher." The monk would say, "He doesn't want any more students. Go away." If he wouldn't leave, some monks would pick him up and throw him onto the road. And he would come back, and come back again. He *had* to show perseverance. If we did that here, nobody would be here.

We've replaced that with other barrier gates. The first is a weekend workshop so they know what they're getting themselves into. The second is going before a council of seniors and explaining why they want to practice here. Some people are looking for physical well-being. We send them to a health spa. Or they're seeking psychological well-being. We send them to a therapist. But if they're asking, "Who am I?" "What is truth?" "What is life?" then they stay. Those are religious questions, and that is what we do.

The third barrier gate is sitting for a solitary day of meditation. The fourth is asking me for the teaching. The fifth is entering the sangha. And after about two or three years, they can petition for *jukai*.

You know, goals suck. They separate you. You get preoccupied with the goal and forget the process. The process and the goal are one reality. They're not separate. So many people say, "Is practice something you do to get to enlightenment?" In fact, practice and enlightenment are one. And just as practice *is* enlightenment, *jukai is* wisdom, *jukai is* joyfulness, *jukai is* humility.

In Japan, it's not common for people to do *jukai*. Only the more devout do it. It's definitely not as common as bar mitzvah among Jews or confirmation among Catholics. It's not an imperative the way it is here.

Certain people want *jukai* because they confuse it with the practice. But my feeling is that they could practice these precepts without taking the religious vows. A few years ago, some nuns were here who insisted on wearing our student robes. "Why don't you wear your own habits?" I asked. "We don't want to stand out," they said. "We want to identify." I relented. I could understand that.

I LOOKED LIKE HENRY MILLER IN DRAG

Tibetan Buddhism is to Manhattan's Upper East Side what the Himalayas are to Cole Porter: an oxymoron that screws up everything—every assumption, every premise that rationally links A to B.

The problem is that Robert Thurman, America's premier interpreter of Tibetan Buddhism, detonates all this neat logic. Raised on the Upper East Side, his life has been one part upper drawer, two parts doing the unexpected, and three parts rebellion/curiosity/dedication/scholarship. He encapsulates the roving, restless mind that finally settles down, but in an almost raffish James Dean way. How else to explain Thurman's raft of nicknames? The Red Skelton of Tibetan Buddhism. The Buddhist Billy Graham. A dharma-thumping evangelist.

Thurman shrugs off the appellations, insisting, "I am not an evangelist in the sense that I am trying to get people to be Buddhist. But I believe that every liberal academic—'liberal' in the sense of liberal arts—is an evangelist for wisdom. . . . Buddhism means 'awakening,' so I am an evangelist for awakening. . . . 'Awakened' means understanding what's going on, being kind to others. I don't mind being accused of being an evangelist for wanting to help people awaken to that."

Thurman's life has been a constant succession of awakenings. While growing up, Isadora Duncan's brother conducted weekly dramatic readings in the Thurmans' living room, with Robert reading parts alongside Laurence Olivier. Later, Thurman ran off to fight with Fidel in Cuba, married a wealthy heiress his first year at Harvard, then split for India, wandering around with long hair and a scraggly beard until called back to the United States for his father's funeral. While here, he met his first guru at a Tibetan monastery in New Jersey (of all places!)—a sixty-one-year-old Mongolian monk. Thurman learned Tibetan in ten weeks, helped build a temple, meditated, studied, and "fanatically" wanted to be a monk. Finally, his guru agreed to take Thurman to India to meet the Dalai Lama. The two hit it off—Thurman was twenty-three; the Dalai Lama was twenty-nine. They taught each other—sort of. "Basically," Thurman says, "he got my Exeter and Harvard education in a year and a half. We met once a week. I'd say, 'What about this problem in *madhyamika* thought?' And he'd say, 'Oh, talk to blah blah blah [another teacher] about that. Now what about Freud? What about physics? What about the history of World War II?'"

In 1965 Thurman became the first Tibetan Buddhist monk from the West. His head was shaved. He wore maroon robes. After he returned to the United States, his guru in New Jersey eventually convinced him that the world did not need a "white *geshe*"—a monk trained in important Buddhist scriptures. There was a better alternative: he could become, in Thurman's words, "a 'Protestant monk.' That is, a professor."

Thurman has done that with a vengeance, teaching at Oxford, Cambridge, Harvard, Wesleyan, Smith, and Amherst. Now at Columbia, he occupies the only endowed chair in Buddhist studies in the United States. He's written more than seventeen books, translated ten others, and as the Dalai Lama's informal cultural liaison, he uses his megawatt connections—Richard Gere, Natalie Merchant, Michael Stipe, and Harrison Ford, not to mention his daughter Uma—to advance Buddhism in this country.

For the interview, we met in Thurman's cramped study, with its pink walls offset by white trim, located along Riverside Drive in Manhattan. Sitting behind his marble-topped desk, the sleeves on his red flannel shirt rolled up, Thurman seemed less a classically serene Buddhist than a guy completely engaged with the world. George

Bush had been reelected three days before, and Thurman kept riffing on what went wrong, on Republicans' dirty tricks, on the stupidities of American voters. But when prodded, he steered back toward rites of which he knows much: Tibetan Buddhism is full of them. And so is Thurman's life—pre-Buddhist and after.

When I became a Buddhist monk, my mother said she should've known something like this would happen because I had kicked over the baptismal font as a baby, drenched the priest, and barely got baptized. The priest was very annoyed and wrung out his cassock on my feet. Being a Buddhist now, can I say that this was symbolic of anything? Who knows? Looking back from my current sense of life (or of lives), I think I felt this was a kind of barbarian, faraway Western country, that I was born in an outpost faraway from the bastions of civilization in India and Tibet.

It's very funny: my wife has pointed out that my memories of my youth deal a lot with having to put up with a bunch of frenzied people all the time. And yet she points out that in pictures, baby pictures and the like, I have the broadest smile on my face and I look much more cheerful than anybody else around me. I'm always grinning. Still, I have a memory of being bothered all the time.

Maybe because I'm too much of an intellectual, I don't claim any memories of past lifetimes, although I have had some flashes. I was definitely in Mongolia and places like that for quite a few lifetimes. And when I visited certain spots in Tibet, it was like, "Ooh, now I'm back." But somehow I never took the time to look into this. It's important to me to know that there was something, but exactly what it is will not really help me. It'll probably make me more depressed about living in this loony country.

While I was growing up, we lived on Eighty-first Street between Park and Lexington [in Manhattan] and went to a brick church around Eighty-ninth and Park. But we didn't go often. Usually only on holidays and family events. In the 1940s in New York, most people weren't that religious. I went to a school—St. Bernard—that so much wanted to be in England that teachers actually used the cane on us. But there was no chapel there and no services.

Then I went to Exeter, which I loved. I was quite gung ho about it and quite popular: it was like family to me. After that, I never really went home:

in the summer, I visited friends or worked in foreign countries. But there were aspects of this that I resisted. I could have just followed the track of the American WASP establishment and gone on to Harvard with my National Merit Scholarship and headed for the State Department. That was the expected "rite of passage." Instead, I was kicked out of school and almost not allowed to enter Harvard.

It was April 1958. Graduation was in May. A lot of my friends came from wealthy Latin American families, yet at Exeter they were rather idealistic. I was really into the Spanish personality, and we all read a lot of poetry. Knowing that I'd been admitted to Harvard, it was like my whole future was programmed. Theirs, too. They would go back to their homeland and be the bosses, the *patrones*. Then someone read one of Castro's poems and said, "Well, we'll never really have this kind of idealism. We'll never fight for our principles the way Fidel is." A Mexican friend and I went, "Oh, yes, we will," and soon we were on a train heading for Miami to sign up for the revolution. Someone had given us a pistol that he'd been hiding under the bed in his dorm room; I didn't even know how to shoot a gun. We registered under assumed names in Miami and went to a bar that we'd heard was doing recruiting for Castro. They laughed and laughed and rejected us. But they were interested in my friend because his family owned huge territories in the state of Vera Cruz. They asked us to go to Mexico to spread support for Castro. When we got there, we were practically arrested by his family. I was sent to a farm somewhere, and he was sent to work on a road gang and was whipped like a peon.

When we finally got back to Exeter, we were told we could graduate if we pleaded temporary insanity. We were willing to apologize and say we'd been foolish, but we wouldn't admit to a moment of insanity. They threw us out. I found out years later that the lacrosse coach wouldn't let the faculty off the hook. We were both on the lacrosse team—I was cocaptain—and somehow we'd both forgotten the game with Andover [another exclusive private school and a major rival of Exeter's].

Harvard told me to get a job or a high school diploma and I'd be readmitted the following year. Eventually, they let me in even though I never did those things.

In some ways, losing my eye could have been a rite of passage. It was just an accident. I was working in a garage on a car I used to race when the tire iron popped in my eye. I was unconscious for three days. It was a death/rebirth experience. When I woke up, the world was flat. I have depth perception now. The mind creates it; the brain recomputes it. But at first, when you don't have parallax vision, it's like, "Whoa!" That involuntary rite of passage gave me insight into impermanence; it helped me realize that everything changes, that *we* will change, and that time cannot be relied on.

But my first *real* rite of passage was becoming a monk. I did that against the advice of my original teacher, who said I should just live *like* a monk and study. He was sure that I wouldn't stick with it. But I felt like I belonged, and that my life should be like this.

In Buddhist society, it's wonderful to be a monk. It's like a lifelong Mac-Arthur Grant. You can do what you want. You can study. People respect you. They feed you. You don't have to worry about a pension. You're developing your spiritual potential so, at some stage, you will serve people. In these cultures, it's such a privilege to be a monk that people are overjoyed to support you. They don't want you to thank them when they give you lunch. You might say this to be polite, but they want the merit of giving without the reward of the thanks. That sort of uses up some of the merit they're getting.

I was twenty-four years old. There were two stages to becoming a *bhikku,* a monk or mendicant. The first stage is the renunciative part; the second stage is more comprehensive. The real transition is the first one and was given to me by the Dalai Lama's senior teacher. The Dalai Lama gave me the full-fledged thing. He never did the first thing. Those were always done separately and to a group of fifty or a hundred people. Of course, I was the only white person there.

[Thurman's book *Essential Tibetan Buddhism* has the full vows that a monk takes. During the first stage, an abbot asks the student a battery of questions, including whether he is a "fanatic," a "slave," an "invalid," a "famous bandit," a "hermaphrodite," a "serpent," or "a mannish woman." The abbot also asks if the student has killed his mother, father, or a saint and if he has albino hair. The most perplexing query—"You have not changed your sex three times?"—suggests that it's acceptable to change your sex "only" twice.

Next, the student bows to his teacher, takes refuge in the Buddha, Buddha's teachings, and the Buddhist community, and promises to refrain from drugs, liquor, violence, and "lustful sexuality." Finally, the teacher says, "It is the method. It is good!" and the student responds, "It is good!"

Monks taking the second set of vows—the one for celibacy—receive a begging bowl, robes, and a water filter (the filter screens any living creatures from the monk's drinking and washing water). Prayers are chanted, flowers are scattered, the community chants, "May his banner of liberation be firm! . . . May he enjoy the pure ethics of the transcendent in all his lives!" The monk pledges to stop adhering to the duties of a "householder"; his master chants, "This is the method of achieving transcendent renunciation! You are excellent!" and the monk replies, "This achievement has been excellent!" With that, he sets his life on a new, and leaner, course.]

The first ceremony when becoming a monk is called "from leaving the home to homelessness." Personally, my home was a loony bin. I had a theatrical mother. I'd divorced my wife, and now I was mentally leaving the marriage. I had a daughter from that marriage. I was not happy about leaving her, but I had to.

Being a Buddhist monk is not like being a Western monk. Even "monk" is the wrong word. "Monk" comes from the Greek *molos*, which means "alone." It carries an aspect of solitude. But when a Buddhist monk says, "All beings are my family rather than any particular family," you're chanting "families" and taking on a communal role. You become a monk to avoid distraction and develop your mind and your meditative ability and your ability to understand yourself and the world. It's like embarking on a super-intense advanced psychology program; it's very scholastic, academic, experiential, and meditative.

In Buddhism, the goal of liberation is not being saved by a god, but understanding the world and developing your own wisdom. In the process of doing that, you give up property and the idea of earning your living. You almost give up your life. And you rely on people to support you. It's a radically different way of orienting to the universe. You risk being homeless, and you put all your energy into understanding everything. The drive is not so much to pray and be holy as to learn and be wise.

When I came back to America, my mother thought all this was nuts. My daughter, who's seen a picture of me in my robes, says I looked like Henry Miller in drag. My teacher, the guy who'd told me not to be a monk, kept teasing: "You think people want a white Tibetan?"

I left after about two years. I had a *fantastic* time. My learning, and my clarity, and my meditation were just tremendous. It was a great time in my life. But remember the Vietnam monk who burned himself to death? [In June 1963 a monk, Thich Quang Duc, immolated himself at a busy intersection in Saigon to protest the repressions of the Vietnamese government.] Stuff like this was going on in our society too, in different ways. Schoolmates were engaged in civil rights protests and beaten up in Birmingham. Other friends were going crazy on drugs. I realized that what my old teacher had said was correct. I was quite happy but had no leverage to help anyone with their disasters.

I had a problem resigning my robes. There was a rite of passage for that, too. It's better that you resign rather than just take off your robes and get married or have a girlfriend. My old monk guru said that he would not accept my robes and I'd have to give them directly to the Dalai Lama. In fact, when I took off my robes at his monastery, I realized I had no clothes. I was ready to ask someone to buy me some jeans or something at a nearby five-and-dime when the monk said, "Never mind." He went into his closet and pulled out all my clothes—everything I'd thrown into a garbage can when I came back from India wearing my robes. He had retrieved them without telling me because he knew I would not last. I was mad because he hadn't believed that I was sincere. I was also happy because he had had the foresight to see that I would change my mind. He was a great old teacher.

I wrote to the Dalai Lama and never got an answer, I think because he was upset and annoyed with me. The Tibetans were in exile, and he had thought that I—their first Western monk—was a great hope for them. About seven years later, I met an old lama, who said, "Oh, they didn't accept your resignation? That's terrible. I'll retroactively accept it." And he did a little ceremony. To my surprise, I felt good about it. I'd always been under a shadow because they wouldn't accept my resignation.

At that time, the Dalai Lama hadn't been out of India and had fled Tibet a few years before. To him, in a "normal" society, *anybody* wants to be a monk. It's a great thing to be and it's a lifelong fellowship. Today, he knows Western society and he has traveled all over. He is much more knowledgeable. And much more careful.

I developed a theory that monasticism would never work in the modern world. It was too obsolete. Then, from studying Buddhist history and getting into the issue of militarism and demilitarism and having insights about the role of monasticism in history, I became very pro-monastic. For the last fifteen years, the Dalai Lama has been telling me that I'm the most enthusiastic *ex*-monk about monasticism that he knows. He chuckles kind of sardonically but appreciatively. I may even be more determined about monasticism than he is. He has kept it at the heart of the Tibetan exile. It's key to his culture. But maybe he's not so sure it's usable worldwide.

Since resigning as a monk, I've attended many Tantric initiation ceremonies, such as introductions into the mandala and visualization sequences where you are reborn in a different deity embodiment. You can definitely tell when the teachers who are giving the initiations are just performing a ritual and when they really have an experience that they are transmitting. In a way, you could say that what is being transmitted is the seed, or the potential realization, of insight. Basically, Buddhists say you can't transmit understanding into the mind of another person. Otherwise, Buddha would have transmitted his enlightenment to everyone. Although in a sense, he *did* transmit it to everyone in the form of his teachings.

Tibetan Buddhists don't use the term "initiation." They don't even use "ordination." They use "graduation," because you are graduating out of a certain lifestyle into another. Some people call these ceremonies "empowerments." Why? Because they really *do* open doorways. In fact, *any* rite of passage in any religion has value; it's the interpretation of these religions that's critical. We need a new type of theological education that takes the results of about a hundred years of critical religious studies about all world religions so that when people are trained to be clergy, they don't become fundamentalist fanatics and they don't appeal to the baser levels of people and they don't insist on literalist interpretations of ancient mythical documents that prevent people from living a more humane and scientific life. Religious education is very valuable and the rituals are very meaningful. But they shouldn't be used to imprison the faithful. They should guide us to a glorious and harmonious liberation, to a liberation of humanity. Faith is stronger when it's reasonable, when there's no exploitation of the simpleminded. Otherwise, it's just going to mess them up.

PART FIVE

ISLAM

Seven Essential Words

To Allah do belong
The unseen (secrets)
Of the heaven and the earth.
And to Him goeth back
Every affair (for decision);
So worship Him
And put thy trust in Him.

QUR'AN 11:123

Many ways of life passed away before your time. . . . Go about the earth
and behold what happened.

QUR'AN 3:137

ALLAH IS ONE

You'd think that every world religion would have a major event to initiate people into the faith—a baptism, a reading from a holy text, or a public pledging that you'll follow a certain path. All these events, in one way or another, tell youngsters that they are ready to move on to a new phase in their lives or that they are old enough to seriously begin their religious schooling. These events signal that kids are ready for new responsibilities: whether a girl reads from the Torah at her bat mitzvah or the Holy Spirit descends upon a Catholic boy at a confirmation, both youngsters are elevated to a higher plateau, and both are empowered to confront the world (and themselves) in new and maybe less silly ways. Ahead lies adulthood. Behind lies childhood. And now comes the awkward phase when children learn to negotiate what they are becoming.

And yet these events—as powerful and as common as they are—are not universal. In Islam, *nothing* chronicles the transition from young to not-so-young. The second-largest religion in the world has none of this. No now-you're-cleansed-of-sin baptizing. No now-you-are-a-man bar mitzvah. No promising before an audience that you'll observe certain wisdoms and precepts and teachings. Islam is the only major religion with no ceremony marking the onset of puberty, although Muslims entering puberty *are* considered legally responsible for their actions. They just don't make a big deal about it. In fact, they don't make any deal at all.

Of the major religions, Islam has the fewest life cycle events and the most minimally decorated houses of worship. This minimalism is spiritually functional: it throws you back on your own resources. With no intermediary between Muslims and God and no images of God in which to take refuge or that might trigger speculations about personality quirks of Allah or why the artist chose a certain shade of blue for an obscure corner of heaven, there really is less of an opportunity to hide—from yourself or from God. Everything else is a distraction; everything else keeps you from Allah.

Having said this, Islam is *not* void of rites of passage. During the *aqiqah* ceremony, the head of a two-week-old baby is shaved, and the equivalent weight in silver or gold is given to charity. Muslims in southern India practice the *bismillah* ceremony, which marks the beginning of a child's formal education: not long after the child turns four, he or she publicly recites the first chapter of the Qur'an and part of the ninety-sixth chapter, which was the initial revelation to Muhammad. And the *ameen,* a party for a boy or girl, is usually held around the age of eight. It marks the first time the child has read the entire Qur'an. But none of these have the universality or the rigor or the formal bestowing of early adulthood that are common to initiation rites in other faiths.

For some Muslims, another event could plausibly be called a rite of passage: leading services at their mosque, often at a young age. Yahya Hendi was eleven when he led a service for the first time in the mosque in his village on the West Bank of Palestine. "I stood in the pulpit. I led a sermon. I gave the prayers just like the eighty-three-year-old imam. My village has a history that goes back thousands of years, and I was the youngest to ever give a sermon. The sermon was about love, specifically about Muhammad ordering his followers to cater to the needs of a cat that needed help. And how Muhammad told the man who cared for the cat that he would enjoy Paradise because of his actions."

There was more to the sermon than a youngster's fondness for felines. Hendi, now an imam and the Muslim chaplain at Georgetown University in Washington, D.C., had "seen that people were not kind to cats. They didn't feed them. They kicked them. They transmitted their anger and aggression to the cats." So the sermon was really about compassion, not cats. Some people were offended by his message; others, by the fact that a boy his age had given a sermon. A few were surprised that he was so erudite and spoke classical Arabic and could quote the Qur'an with such skill and ease.

But was this an initiation? Hendi wasn't willing to take it that far. "Of course," he said, "it had great meaning for me. But not every Muslim does that. So I would not undermine those who have not gone through that experience. On the contrary, I know people who memorized the entire Qur'an at age five. Word for word. So everyone goes through a rite of passage differently in Islam. And at different times in their lives. It's all very fluid, but it almost always involves going to the mosque and feeling that you are part of the *umma,* the world community; and learning the Qur'an; and speaking the language."[1]

To keep the essentials of Islam with them around the clock, to burnish them into their consciousness and make them palpable and unforgettable, Muslims have the *shahada,* the tightly compressed testimony of faith: "La ilaha illah'Liah. Muhammadun rasulu'Liah" ("There is no god but Allah. Muhammad is the messenger of Allah"). (As the essential creed in a faith, only Judaism's "Sh'ma Yisrael Adonai Elohaynu Adonai Echad" ["Hear, O Israel: the Lord our God is one Lord"] rivals the *shahada* for such terse profundity.) The *shahada*'s seven words lay down the essentials of Islam: without this statement about God's oneness and Muhammad's finality, there *is* no Islam. You are a Muslim *only* if you accept Allah and *only* if you acknowledge Muhammad as the last of the prophets. Not as a god. Not as the son of God. "Only" as a prophet. (Muhammad took to heart the cautionary tale of Jesus, whose true paternity will forever divide Christianity from the other faiths that derived from Abraham—Islam and Judaism.) If Islam literally means surrendering to the will of God, then the *shahada,* when said with right intention, is *the* act of surrender—an inner prostration to Islam's laws, ethics, origins, and destiny. Everything else in Islam, even its four other "pillars," as its elemental concepts are called, flow from the *shahada.* Minus Allah and minus Muhammad being the final prophet, there's no reason to fast during Ramadan or go on hajj. Even charity, another pillar, takes on a different complexion, a lesser complexion: it becomes less a function of ego.

Muslims say the *shahada* so often and in so many ways that it is integrated into their very fiber, their very being: they breathe it; they hear it; and they say it when they need strength and when they need assurance and when they want to remember Allah and His Prophet. Fathers whisper it into the ears of their newborn babies. "Life does not start at eleven or twelve or thirteen," said Imam Hendi, referring to the usual age for confirmations or bar or bat mitzvahs. "Life starts the second a child is born. That's when you put him or her on the path of righteousness. They may not seem aware, but they are *spiritually* aware." A woman in the middle of childbirth may suddenly fall silent and remember the *shahada;* a nervous student taking a test might, barely audibly, recite the *shahada,* then return to the exam, relieved and comforted; a businessman, jittery during a high-stakes negotiation, might duck into the corridor, say the *shahada,* know that Allah is with him, and return to his deal making. Every day, in just about every way and at almost any age, Muslims say the *shahada.* Hendi's two-and-a-half-year-old son "knows the *shahada* by heart and says it all the time. He doesn't pray and he doesn't eat without saying the *shahada.*" In Muslim countries, five times a day, at dawn, noon, midafternoon, sunset, and evening, muezzins climb the minarets in mosques and sing the Call to Prayer, which includes the *shahada;* and five times a day, Muslims turn away from what they've been doing and bow and prostrate and pray their lengthy prayers that, of course, include the *shahada.*[2]

In Islamic countries, the *shahada* is everywhere: an unwavering constant of the spirit. A few years ago when I was in Mauritania, a country high on Africa's western coast that's 99 percent Muslim, I was surrounded by the *shahada.* It was recited on the radio, shouted from the minarets of mosques, and heard in the prayers of the three million people who were barely getting by in this terribly poor country that gets less than an inch of rain a year and where finding firewood can take an entire day. Here, the *shahada* was an anchor against the drifting of the sand and the howling of the desert wind; it was one of the few comforts for these people, who wanted to know that there was more to life than brushing sand out of your bed first thing in the morning or watching it coat all the merchandise in your tiny stall in the bazaar by midafternoon.

Driving east from the capital city of Nouakchott into the Sahara itself, the *shahada* was the only thing that could be counted on. Sand obscured so much of the one road that connected eastern and western Mauritania—the two-hundred-mile-long Route de L'Espoir—that drivers had to navigate parallel to the road, zipping through stubbly fields and dry riverbeds and quiet villages, dodging goats and children and sheep while searching for the elusive macadam. We were always losing the road, but Allah and the *shahada* were always there. Five times a day, no matter where we were, my driver faced Mecca and said his prayers. He'd pray in a corner of a roadside café or go outside, placing a prayer mat on the ground as gently as if he was setting down a tablecloth. If we were driving in the middle of nowhere, surrounded by sand dunes and scraggly brush, he'd pull over to the side of the road and walk about thirty feet away from our pickup truck, face east, place his prayer rug on the ground, and pray as stiff winds whipped sand all around him. Five times a day, the same prayer—"In the name of Allah, the Merciful, the Compassionate . . ."—then back to the truck he'd come, and again we'd go hurtling down this road that needed the intervention of Allah to make it worthy of the name to which it never seemed to live up: the Road of Hope. Here in Mauritania, on this road that just about any other country would have condemned, hope came from the *shahada:* seven words that are the fundamental, rock-bottom essence of Islam.

Strictly, the *shahada* is *not* a rite of passage. It doesn't transform a single moment, a particular phase, or a certain juncture of someone's life. It isn't scheduled by the sun and the moon and the stars or occur when someone turns a certain age—maybe because, as Imam Hendi said, "I look at my daughter, Nourjannah, who knows many *surahs* [chapters of the Qur'an], and I know that she is mature. Not as mature as you or I, but she is a mature seven year old. And she will grow in maturity. At age fifty, she will still need to grow in maturity. We are all maturing. Islam tells people that they are no different from or inferior to someone else because of their age. On the contrary, they are equal to everyone else." If everyone has a certain dignity and maturity, regardless of their age, then a rite of passage for attaining a certain age is superfluous. Life can't be divided into discrete "stations," not if it's a single journey of turning toward Allah, turning toward our origins. The real passage in Islam begins when we come into this world. This is the moment when we forget about our "preconceptual life," the existence that our soul had before its birth into a human body. With that incarnation, we forget about the higher realm our souls had enjoyed. (Which explains why *insan,* the Arabic word for "man," is related to the word *nisyan*—"forgetfulness.") Our task is to remember where we came from and who made us and who guided us. Hence the *shahada:* an almost-constant humming in the ears of a Muslim that Allah is the Creator and Muhammad was the Prophet and all Muslims owe each of them their lives.[3]

For anyone born into Islam, the *shahada* is as natural as breathing in and breathing out; for converts, saying the *shahada* for the first time is their initiation to the faith. And since faith is a pact between you and Allah, totally inward and personal, saying the *shahada* for the first time is also, usually, inward and solitary. You can say it to an imam, or to someone of another faith, or to no one at all. You can say it in the middle of a crowd, in the middle of a forest, in your car, while walking down the street, while shopping, while emailing, even while you're dying. The location and the timing pale beside the intent. "Uttering *shahada* is between you and God," said one imam. "What matters is acknowledging God's glory and that Muhammad is but a messenger. *Shahada* is the passage into Islam. Your full soul has to be given to God. The beauty of the *shahada* is in its simplicity, but practicing what it leads to, especially observing Islamic law, takes a lifetime. When you first utter *shahada*, you accept it with your tongue and your heart. But you have not lived it. It increases with the way you translate the *shahada* into practice and decreases when the *shahada* is no longer effective in your life."[4]

There's no hoopla, no hubbub when the *shahada* is said for the first time. It may be the most minimal religious ceremony ever devised. Find someone and say it to them; find no one and say it to yourself. But sometimes, in certain American mosques, the word goes out that a convert will take *shahada* in a few minutes, and whoever is available gathers around: we Americans like audiences and public affirmation. While the scale of these off-the-cuff events is almost hermetic compared to the throngs that attend bar mitzvahs or confirmations, this public display of conviction still disturbs many Muslims. For them, it detracts from the inner-ness that *shahada* traditionally reflects; from the authenticity of an open heart meeting a powerful and compassionate God; from what Thomas Merton (who was not a Muslim but whose wording applies here) called "the deepest psychological ground of one's personality, our inner sanctuary." Recalling such a public taking of *shahada* at her mosque in Baltimore a few years ago, a Muslim woman in her midtwenties turned her nose up. "I didn't like it," she said. "Why should someone be congratulated for professing their belief? The *shahada* is supposed to be a turning of the heart, something that's only between you and God. Doing this in front of an audience turns it into a bit of a show."[5]

In fact, the most elaborate *shahada* in the United States was in Philadelphia in the early 1990s: about thirty people took *shahada* together. "To me," said Imam Hendi, "this was not so much about the converts as about the audience. It made the audience feel good about their own faith."[6]

Even with this increase of public display, there is still much for which to be grateful. Compared to other public rites of passage, the "show" is subdued and introspective. It lacks the glitz of a bar mitzvah, the mass scale of a confirmation, the sensuality of a sacred thread ceremony. In two sentences and fifteen syllables in Arabic, it's over. (In the United States, converts usually say the *shahada* in Arabic, then recite its English translation. This yields a total of four sentences and thirty-three syllables—still pretty skimpy for a pivotal moment in someone's spiritual life.) With *shahada*, someone who did not know Allah before can plunge deeper into God, deeper into the Qur'an, deeper into themselves. What matters most, whether taking *shahada* or having a bar mitzvah or confirmation or *jukai* or *upanayana*, isn't necessarily whether the "magic" works on the day of the rite of passage. It rarely does. We're dealing here with subtle "magic." Not Penn and Teller magic. This magic creeps up on you—gradually, imperceptibly. If it were more obvious, it might be suspect. Sometimes the best transformations are the "sneaky" ones: those with less drama but more permanence. And anyway, whether you take *shahada* silently, publicly, alone, or in a mosque full of Muslims, no one can really gauge its effect. As the Qur'an says, a believer "avoids vain talk" and "guards . . . [his] modesty." The *umma* and the convert and the imam who may have taught the convert can't judge it. Only Allah, who gives life and death and is the wisest of all judges, can measure the effect of someone taking *shahada*. And that verdict is not revealed until this life is no more and the afterlife has begun.

JUST BEING SENTIENT
IS CAUSE FOR RAPTURE

Until I heard of Coleman Barks, I knew of only one guy who was born in Tennessee, the greenest state in the land of the free—Davy Crockett. If we're to believe the Disney version of the Crockett story, Davy was an all-around guy: trapper, explorer, politician, and patriot, a nineteenth-century Renaissance man who killed a bear when he was only three, fought Indians with one hand tied behind his back, and died a hero at the Alamo, swinging his musket at onrushing Mexican soldiers.

And then Coleman Barks, poet and visionary, walked into my life. Bearded, slightly disheveled, and fond of flannel shirts, hiking boots, and jeans, Barks's idea of a good time is getting his hands dirty in his backyard, riding around in his 1972 Dodge convertible, and for his daily shot of caffeine, walking up to Jittery Joe's—a coffee shop that used to be a Shell station.

"Everything is church," says Barks, so why not tune into the divine when your ragtop is down, or when you're playing with your grand-daughter, or when an ice storm that tears the phone lines off your house gives you time for a "spontaneous family celebration."

Barks's vim and vigor belies his age (sixty-eight) and echoes another

poet's. Just as Walt Whitman proclaimed, "I am large; I contain mul-
titudes," Barks has announced, "I am everything! Why not a Hindu? I
love the dancing Siva. Surely St. Francis and Boddhidharma would get
along fine. They wouldn't have an argument. They would laugh
a lot, and laughter's pretty holy to me. It's right at the core where you
lose your boundaries."

This disregard for boundaries made Barks the right guy to translate
poems by Rumi, the most beloved of mystical poets. The project began
in 1976 when Barks took up the challenge of resuscitating the poems
from dreary, stifling translations that had drained them of their ecstasy
and joy. By now, he has published over fifteen collections of Rumi's
work, turning the Persian into the best-selling poet in the United
States and the Rumi-Barks collaboration into one of the most successful of all time—for poets, that is. He's been charmed by the poems'
"unpredictable spontaneity, the push-pull of great tenderness and
great loneliness, . . . of drifting at ease inside the unsayable."[1]

Of Rumi's many lines that speak to him, Barks particularly gravi-
tates toward

> Out beyond ideas of wrongdoing and rightdoing,
> there is a field. I'll meet you there.

"I love the idea of human companionship in a region beyond judgment,"
Barks says, "beyond the mind, and language."

And he's been thrilled by the unexpected correspondence between
himself and Rumi. "The universe," he says, "is just so incredible that
we're all spoiled. . . . [As] Rumi said, 'The eye is meant to see things;
the soul is here for its own joy.'"

Indeed, joy *is* Rumi. The founder of a branch of Sufism that celebrates ecstasy, Rumi studied for several years with a somewhat mysterious man—Shams-i-Tabriz. Rumi's intense devotion to Shams so
alarmed his own followers that they pressured Shams to leave their
teacher's presence. When Shams disappeared in 1248—most likely he
was murdered—Rumi became increasingly distraught, turning away
from the affairs of the mind and focusing his energies on music and

dance, eventually finding great relief by holding onto a pole that supported his tent and walking in circles around it, achieving states of ecstasy which would become the foundation of the *tariqa Mawlawiya,* or whirling dervishes.

Eager to invite people to the realm of the heart, Rumi spent the next twelve years dictating over twenty-seven thousand verses. These honor the self and the soul, warn about the limits of the intellect, and advise about spiritual life. Each poem is infused with Rumi's joy; each is illuminated with eternal Spirit.

From his home in Five Points, an older neighborhood in Athens, Georgia, with many oaks and almost as many people walking the shady streets, Barks has breathed new life into Rumi's poems—an American energy that would do their author proud. And like Rumi, Barks came to the poems through a mystical experience of his own. A few months after he began the translations, Barks had a vision— "a ball of light" in which a Sufi master he had never met (and never even heard of) "told me the Rumi work had to be done. You, of course, can believe that or not. I don't have the luxury."

What does any of this have to do with Davy Crockett, who, as far as we know, was not prone to visions and was neither a mystic nor a poet? Not much, except that both Davy and Coleman Barks started out in Tennessee. Each had a certain wanderlust—Davy's was more external, Barks's more introspective. Both broke molds and defied expectations, and in the early 1950s, when Barks was around fifteen, the two of them actually crossed paths when a few scenes for a Disney TV film about Crockett were shot at Baylor School, the boarding school in Chattanooga where Barks's father was headmaster. Baylor was historic (its red brick buildings date back to the turn of the century), pastoral (its 670 acres overlook the Tennessee River), and tough (it's one of the top prep schools in the country). It's also where Barks began to understand the power of imagination. That primarily stemmed from the creative freedoms in his own family, but also, on a slightly lesser scale, by seeing—in the flesh!—Fess Parker, the actor who played Davy. This was place and history as a transformative experience, as magic and alchemy and conjuring. Rumi would have approved of all this, even without knowing anything about TV or Davy Crockett. After all, Rumi wrote,

anywhere you put your foot, feel me
in the firmness under you.
How is it with this love,
I see your world and not you?[2]

Barks never took *shahada:* mystics usually don't take vows. It's the
experience that sways them, not the words. In fact, he professes that
he is not a Sufi ("All I know about Sufis is that I met one") and that
everyone is a mystic ("Just being in a form and sentient qualifies you
for that"). Yet thanks to Rumi, he entered a luscious, fertile Islam
thirty years ago—an Islam devoted to the soul's return to God. From
that, everything else followed, and Barks became that most unique of
creatures: a poet devoted to words, seeking to get beyond words.

I'm one of those unaffiliated mystics. I honor the traditions of all the in-
wardnesses that I have shared and those I have not. This seems to be what
religion is trying to do—get us to a place where we share our inwardness
in an almost wordless way. I do love that. Sufis call it *sema*—the deep listening to text and music and movement. Maybe the Dalai Lama would
call it simplicity or kindness. A Zen master like Rinzai might call it des-
olation or silence. [The Rinzai school of Zen emphasizes sudden enlightenment and uses tools such as koans, riddles that defy the rational
mind, to achieve this end.] John Keats might call it "the vale of soul making." And the Knights Templar might call it the communion of the Grail.
Heraclitus called it fire.

They're all talking about the same thing. Nasruddin [the Sufi mystic/
jester] might call it laughter. Rumi, in fact, has a wonderful theological
metaphor: Maybe, he says, God is the impulse to laugh and all of us are
the different ways of laughing. Isn't that a beautiful way to express this?

When I have to use the word "Sufi," I define it as just people of the
heart, of the open heart. St. Francis is one. As are those wonderful Jewish Hasidic mystics. And probably Shakespeare and Chaucer. But I don't
like setting up categories. I'm interested most in dissolving boundaries
rather than designing "-isms" to divide us. Rumi said that God is in between you and what you love; in that space, you will find the mystery. He
also said when you look for God, God is in the look of your eyes.

In the end, I don't really have a sense that there is a category of sacred literature. It's more that everything I love is sacred: the poetry, the lyrical prose, all the great stories and all the great places, like the amazing Taktsang monastery I visited in Bhutan, built while Milton was writing *Paradise Lost.* It honors the place where Padmasambhava arrived on the back of a legendary tigress and meditated for three months in a cave. It's an amazing cliffside monastery, perched eight thousand feet up. You could fall at any moment. I love finding places where I can be alone in my solitude and with the feeling that Jesus calls "the kingdom of heaven," which is within you and all around you. The Gospel of Thomas says, "Lift up a stone and I am there. Break a stick and I am there." [The Gospel of Thomas is an ancient collection of sayings attributed to Jesus that was discovered in the Sinai in 1945. Some scholars suggest that it was collected from New Testament sayings; others believe it springs from a completely independent author.]

I may be too dismissive of the organized religions, but as Rumi said, if you think there's an important difference between a Muslim and a Christian and a Jew, then you are making a division between your heart, what you love with, and how you act in the world. That's a radical thing to say, but he said it in the thirteenth century with such authority and gentleness that they didn't kill him.

To cultivate this sort of wonder and ecstasy, you have to use whatever it is that you love, and that might not be constant. Not at all. It might change daily. But you have to be able to recognize what it is you're drawn to. Whatever that is. And you have to follow that. Love, in any form, is from the divine, no matter how unexpected or mundane or scandalous it may seem. Whatever draws people together is part of one motion.

Baylor School, where I grew up and where my father was headmaster, is located in one of the most beautiful places in the world—right off the Tennessee River, five miles north of Chattanooga, on a site that has been inhabited for fifteen thousand years. It had been sacred to the Cherokees and is on a hill overlooking the river. The beauty of that place made me a nature mystic at a very young age.

We lived in an apartment at one end of a dormitory. I had every meal with four hundred people in the school's dining hall, so I had a lot of "brothers" and a lot of "mothers" and "fathers." It was tribal, an amazing, grandiose environment for me because I had the run of three hills and four football fields. I especially loved it when school was out, say during the Christmas holidays, and I and the football coach's son roamed all these acres and we had all these buildings to ourselves, including two gymnasiums. Every time I had a birthday, I'd stand up on my chair in the dining room and four hundred people would sing "Happy Birthday." I had this huge sense of self—I was kind of a prince—and I've never lost it. I told my mother at seven years old that this was the age I wanted to stay, and I have successfully done that, pretty much.

I was brought from the hospital when I was born to that place and I stayed until I was seventeen and went off to college. To this day, I feel very proprietary about the place. I recently gave a talk there and spoke about the trees that were missing, that they had cut down. I adored the trees—beautiful old oaks and black locusts and persimmons. Beautiful trees. They're gone.

There was a lively literary atmosphere. Something called the Round Table got together every month to discuss a book we'd read—Chesterfield's *Letters to His Son* or Conrad's *Heart of Darkness*. And all the time, almost no matter where you were, there was kind of an ongoing literary discussion on that hill, and there was a goofball, ecstatic Latin teacher, James Augustus Pennington, who would yell across the quadrangle, "Young man! Young man! I love words! I love words!" or some Latin phrase, "Quo usque tandem abutere, Catilina, patientia nostra?" ["How long, O Catiline, will you abuse our patience?"—the beginning of Cicero's first Catiline Oration, his denunciations before the Roman Senate in 63 B.C.E. of his friend who had plotted to overthrow the government.]

My mother, too, was kind of a hoot. We're not sure what she did, because she didn't have to cook any meals. She got them at the dining hall. And every week, the laundry would go out, then come back perfectly folded. She didn't have to clean the house; she had a live-in maid. She did page through *McCall's* and *Better Homes and Gardens,* but other than that she just laughed a lot and told jokes and had a lively interest in language. She sort of presided over the campus. But she was also my ecstatic teacher; she danced and sang around the house.

I had a christening as a baby. In town, we attended the First Presbyterian Church. I didn't much like it. The preacher did that ministerial intoning thing that people have accused me of doing. But anyway, it felt kind of fake. There's an ease about it that was repulsive to me. It was sort of "country club Presbyterian." But at Baylor on Wednesday nights, there was prayer service in the chapel. It was voluntary; you went over there and put your head down on the bench in front of you and listened to the music. It was wonderful. *All* of this was magical. Looking down the river toward Lookout Mountain. Looking down the other way toward Walden's Ridge. The curve of the river and boats coming along it at night. The sacredness of the literature at Baylor. All so magical.

Translating Rumi is an amazement to me. I don't know why I should get so lucky. It seems like Shams was playing a joke on Rumi: "Yeah, I'll give you a translator. Here's one! A horny poet from Chattanooga! Go ahead! Use him!" And yet I do feel so close to Rumi, his sensual ecstasy and his humor. He was a hilarious mystic. And he loved the wonderful indignity of being a human. Just consider the contortions we go through to have sex. Rumi is always putting that into a metaphor for spiritual desire.

This all started when Robert Bly handed me a book of Rumi translations by A. J. Arberry, a Cambridge Islamicist. Published by the University of Chicago, they were stilted and scholarly and unpoetic. Bly said, "These poems need to be released from their cages." I began working on that in the fall of '76; I'd go downtown after three classes of explaining what poetry meant and sit at the Bluebird Café, have some hot tea, and start rephrasing these poems. It felt like such a relief, like deep rest, to get into this world which could not be explicated. Rumi's poetry can not be explained. It can only be inhabited.

My only credential for working on the Rumi poems is the dream-vision I had on May 2, 1977. I was sleeping right here in my bedroom in Athens. In the dream, I was sleeping on this bluff above the Tennessee River in a sleeping bag. I woke up inside the dream in the way that you can sometimes when you're not entirely awake but you're lucid. Essentially, I was awake inside the dream realizing that I was inside a dream and that I wasn't awake in the normal sense. A ball of light came up over Williams Island, across the river from Baylor. I was sleeping out in the backyard where I grew up. The ball of light came and hovered over me. Inside was a man sitting with a white shawl over his head. He was all in white. He raised his head and said, "I love you." I said, "I love you, too." I don't know what my life would have been like if I hadn't said that. I can't imagine *not* saying it. The whole landscape, the whole world, felt drenched in dew, and the dew was love. The process that formed the dew was love.

In the fall of 1978, I went to Philadelphia to visit a friend who was teaching law at Rutgers Camden Law School; for some reason, he had read some of my Rumi rephrasings to his law class. A student named Jonathan Granoff wanted to know who wrote them. Jonathan started writing to me, saying, "There's a teacher up here that you should meet." So I called Jonathan, and he said, "Let's go over and meet Bawa." So we visited this man—Bawa Muhaiyaddeen, a Sufi from Sri Lanka—about 9:30 that night. I was so stunned that I wasn't able to say, "Oh, my God! You're the man." He just sat on his bed and looked at me and said, "Will you meet me on the inside or on the outside?" And I said with a kind of English teacherly ambiguity, "Isn't it always both?" I wish I'd said, "Inside. Inside. Meet me on the inside."

Until his death in 1986, I would visit him in Philadelphia four or five times a year, or he would visit me in dreams and teach me. Once I started telling him about a dream, and he said, "You don't need to tell me. I was there."

In one of these dreams, he taught me how to take tiny little sips from a glass. I asked, "What does that mean?" "You want to be wise too quickly," he said. "You want to take gulps. Just take a little sip of wisdom and then assimilate that." And often, face-to-face, he would point at himself and say, "Don't love this. Don't love this. Go to something beyond this." But I couldn't do that.

His eyes were so beautiful that I said, "If you had a blindfold over your eyes, I might not come up here. I come up here to look in your eyes. What I see in your eyes, can it ever come up behind my eyes and look out?" "Well, if you want it bad enough," he said, adding a pun, "Not until the 'I' becomes a 'we.'" I learned that, somehow, you've got to become plural to get out of your ego and personality.

Bawa was a totally surrendered human being. He sang songs spontaneously and loved to cook, and the food was always free. The wisdom was always free, too. He would never let anybody charge for his talks. Being with him was about the only initiation I ever had. I think he initiated me into the opening heart. And that is still occurring even though he's dead.

I think he would say that there are no limits once the heart opens. Your compassion doesn't have any rules about it. You don't have it for some and not for others. It was amazing to meet somebody on the level of Jesus and Buddha. Someone enlightened.

That was my initiation, but everyday, somewhere, young teenagers are having more formal, more traditional rites of passage. Obviously, some kind of passage happens in that period to help an adolescent become a useful member of society. It seems to be more important for young men than for young women: girls become women by a change in their body, mostly, and by some instruction from older women. But young men, in many cultures, have to forcefully be removed from the presence of their mother by the older men of the community, taken apart and instructed, given new food to eat, new stories, and a new sense of self in a certain way. In our culture, we have a lot of uninitiated males because they just didn't have that. A black police chief in Chicago says he sees young men every day that never see a grown-up man until they meet him. My theory is that's why all the graffiti and the tattooing and gangs are happening. It's a howl, a savage lament and rage for not being initiated. They're trying to initiate themselves, and it can't be done.

What's missing for these kids is that, at a certain point, they didn't see a human being that was fully ecstatic, fully alive and competent in the world. They didn't see someone who was comfortable with morality and with ways of being and living that come out of an authentic and personally experienced faithfulness. They didn't learn that just being in a form and sentient is cause for rapture.

Look. Here's a Zen story. A man is drunk. He goes to sleep on top of the covers with his clothes on. During the night, inexplicably, someone comes and sews a jewel of incomparable beauty and brilliance into the hem of his robe. That jewel is identical to the universe and all that is. It seems true to me that such is the situation we find ourselves in. We have fallen asleep in our drunken enthusiasm. We wake inside this bright jewel of consciousness and galaxies and conversation with no way, really, to express the beauty of it.

FLOATING ON A CLOUD OF MERCY

> Morning has broken, like the first morning
> Blackbird has spoken, like the first bird.
> Praise for the singing, praise for the morning
> Praise for the springing fresh from the word.

You could say that morning broke for Cat Stevens when he stopped being Cat Stevens. But that steers us into a nomenclatural house of mirrors, since before he was Cat Stevens, he was Stephen Demetre Georgiou—the third child of a couple living above the restaurant they operated in London's West End. Over the years, names and institutions always seemed to shift for Stevens, along with varying levels of comfort with himself and the world. And now, finally, he is Cat no more and Mr. Georgiou no more. In their place has come Yusuf Islam, a man at peace with himself and with Allah, and who can sing with a new and deeper conviction one of the first songs he made famous:

> Sweet the rain's new fall, sunlit from heaven
> Like the first dewfall, on the first grass.
> Praise for the sweetness of the wet garden
> Sprung in completeness where his feet pass.

Islam's father was Greek Cypriot; his mother was Swedish. They divorced when Islam was around eight years old; eventually his mother moved back to Sweden and took him with her. In his mid-teens, he returned to London, briefly attended art school, took up folk music and cut some hits ("Peace Train," "Wild World," "Moonshadow") that sold forty million albums by the time he was thirty.

Then to the dismay of his fans, this guy with the bedroom eyes and the black shoulder-length hair, who once looked out knowingly from the cover of *Rolling Stone* and filled up astrodomes and had a few too many affairs, bid farewell to glitter and fame and press conferences and a fawning entourage. In 1977 he took a new name, a new faith, a new identity; as he explained to Larry King on CNN twenty-six years later, "[I] needed a break, wanted a break. I hadn't known any other life, just hotel rooms and concerts and recording studios. Here was a chance to jump off that wagon and see life for real."

The stability found in the religion of Islam offset certain vagaries from Islam's youth: with a Greek Orthodox father and a Swedish Baptist mother, attending a Roman Catholic school produced a spiritual dissonance, a confusion of the soul. His yearning for some kind of certainty was accelerated in 1976 by his near-drowning off the coast of Malibu. Pleading for deliverance, he said to God, "Please, I'll do anything for you." After he took *shahada* the next year, "Cat Stevens" essentially disappeared from the music world, a detour he later attributed to his early misunderstanding about Islam's attitude toward music. His rare public performances or recordings were invariably propelled by charitable motives, such as the 1985 Live Aid concert for famine relief in Ethiopia. (He never actually performed the song he'd written for the occasion—Elton John's set ran too long.) By the mid-1990s he had learned enough about Islam to understand that lyrics in English were allowable, made several recordings with Paul McCartney, David Bowie, and even Dolly Parton, and appeared at the 2003 concert that Nelson Mandela organized in Cape Town to fight the worldwide scourge of AIDS.

But being a Muslim is not all promises of paradise and salvation. In 1989 Islam's comments about the fatwa against Salman Rushdie were so misconstrued that headlines in England blared "Cat Says Kill Rushdie." In reality, while he had told university students in London that Rushdie's controversial novel, *Satanic Verses,* was "blasphemous," he had also stressed that Islamic law compelled Muslims to obey all civil laws that didn't restrict their basic religious duties.

And in 2004, while flying from London to Washington, D.C., Islam's plane was diverted to Maine, where the FBI detained him, then flew him to England the next day. Federal authorities believed he had links to potential terrorist activities. All this may have been no more than a matter of mistaken identity: the name of the man on the FBI's watch list was actually spelled "Yousaf Islam." The next year, Islam won an apology from two British papers which had reported that the U.S. had been correct to turn him away. The articles had not only defamed Yusuf Islam; they'd also implicitly refuted the citations he'd received for his charitable work: in November 2004, the Man of Peace award from Mikhail Gorbachev's foundation and, a year later, an honorary doctorate from the University of Gloucestershire for his services to education and humanitarian relief.

Throughout all this, Islam says he "remains an optimist. Common sense and justice will prevail. I was brought up to believe that if you wait until the end of the story, you get to see the good people live happily ever after." Which may be another way of saying,

> Mine is the sunlight, mine is the morning
> Born of the one light, Eden saw play.
> Praise with elation, praise every morning
> God's recreation of the new day.

When my brother came back to the United Kingdom following a visit to Jerusalem in 1976, a festival of Islam was taking place in London, and suddenly there were books and exhibitions about Islamic culture in bookshops and museums. He saw the Qur'an in a bookshop window and thought to himself, "That's the Bible of the Muslims." He decided to buy it and give it to me as a gift.

It was astounding to me that I hadn't discovered Islam before. But in those days, there was little news about it. It was almost a secret. There were only some Oriental books about it—this was before the Iranian Revolution [when the media exploded with stories about Islam].

When I started to read the Qur'an, the first thing that I did was try to keep an open mind because so many preconceived images were already built up within me. Many times, I'd visited my favorite spiritual bookshop in Los Angeles, The Bodhi Tree, but never had I even bothered to look at the "Islam" bookshelf. Perhaps that was because my father belonged to a Greek Cypriot culture and, therefore, anything connected to Muslims seemed inimical to me and my upbringing. There is long-term animosity between the Greeks, who are primarily Christian, and the Turks, who of course are Muslim.

But the more I read the Qur'an, the more it struck me, deep down. This wasn't sudden. I'd been looking at several religions—Buddhism, Taoism—while also reconsidering my Christian upbringing. I was interested in different ways of looking at this universe. I'd gone through many developments in my identity, in my art, and I still wasn't satisfied. I hadn't found what I was looking for. I didn't have peace. And if you listened to my songs and if you actually followed my path, you would know I was always searching. Ever since I can remember, I was searching for the meaning to life.

I found that Islam was not quite that "foreign" religion which I had come to expect. First and foremost, it was talking about belief in one God, the master of the universe. And it talked about the unity and the indivisibility of the universe. That message is also contained in the Bible, but the greater clarity, for me, of this message in the Qur'an left a much deeper impression.

The Qur'an also talked about humanity as one family, and it mentioned many prophets, including Abraham, Moses, Jesus, and Muhammad, all as brothers, equally teaching the same message of unity to mankind, and all of us being the offspring of Adam and Eve.

After a few months of carrying the Qur'an around with me while on a world tour, I read the chapter called "Joseph" [Yusuf]. My God! My life seemed to melt into a mirror of this story. Up to then, I instinctively felt that, like Joseph, I too had passed through many stages. Joseph had been sold in the market by his brother, much as I was being sold in the market of the music world. The section of the story that really shook me was when his brothers, who had thrown him down the well, were face-to-face with him. Unaware that Joseph was in front of them, they were talking badly about him, slandering him. But he kept it within himself. Something resonated inside me, perhaps it was those words I wrote in my song "Father and Son": "All the times that I've cried, keeping all the things I knew inside." At that point, I wept. That chapter opened my heart.

About a year later—on a winter Friday in 1977—I took the dramatic step and walked to the mosque in London's Regent's Park to declare my faith. Out of the greenery of the trees shone the golden dome of the mosque. I had never really seen this before. In a way, that was the epitome of everything that I was now discovering: suddenly it was where it hadn't been before. Now I realized that I must get rid of my pride, get rid of my ego, and face God.

After *jum'a* [congregational prayer], I went up to the imam and declared my wish to become a Muslim. I was sat down and asked if I believed there was only one God and that He is absolutely unique, without partners. I affirmed that. Then I was asked if I believed that Muhammad was the last of the messengers. At that point, it became absolutely clear to me that no prophet could come without God's permission, and no prophet could create a true religion unless it was inspired by God. I knew that Muhammad was exactly what he said he was: the slave of God and His messenger. To the imam, I affirmed my belief, saying, "I declare that there is no God except the one God [Allah]; and I declare that Muhammad is His servant and messenger."

From that moment on, I felt I was floating on a warm, invisible cloud of mercy, carrying me upward from my past entanglements and worldly confusion. I was still making records, but—like Moses and the magicians—the truth had to win, the truth about Islam's position on music. Interestingly, there wasn't anything in the Qur'an directly mentioning music. It didn't say music was forbidden. The chief imam in the London Central Mosque encouraged me to continue composing and recording; at no time was there ever an ultimatum for me to choose between music or Islam. But many things about the music industry contravened the Islamic way of life—fornication, intoxicants, idolatry, competition, greed, selfishness. The music business was full of that stuff. How could I really accumulate wisdom and get closer to the angels if I stayed in that world? I found it very difficult and I was new to my faith, so I simply decided to give up the music business. This helped me concentrate fully on learning and practicing the five pillars of Islam and striving to get close to Allah through my knowledge and worship. [The five pillars are the foundations of Islam: *shahada,* praying five times daily, giving to charity, fasting during Ramadan, and going on pilgrimage to Mecca.] At the time I said, "I have suspended my activities in music for fear that they may divert me from the true path, but I will not be dogmatic in saying that I will never make music again." You can't say that without adding, "insha Allah" [if Allah wills].

At last, when I got a chance to escape from the hell of the burning limelight, I grabbed it. My last record was *Back to Earth* in 1978. The only real regret I have is that the link that existed between those who listened to my songs and me ceased to exist. For a long time, I lost that privileged link of communication by cutting myself off from musical creativity, although this was not necessarily a severe break: by doing it, I joined the wider human race. But at that time, it was very difficult to stay on the straight path with both feet amidst all the destabilizing drama of rock star existence. Today I'm trying to redress that balance and find a way to allow my creative side to flow within the generous rivers of Islam's cultural landscape. The great thing is, I'm still floating.

Would I have liked to have been born a Muslim? Oh no, although, of course, whatever the Lord wants. I am so grateful for this journey. I am also a surprise gift for the Muslim community, a proof that Islam is not a heritage based on tribal homogeneity.

Now I have a better balanced perception of myself and my music. I had rejected everything for a while. I was so happy with what I had discovered, I did not care about anything else. Now I understand that the past is part of my self; without it, I would not be where I am today. I have realized that music is part of our lives, and I have fit it into the way I look on life today. Now I understand that Islam does not prohibit music, but it does not encourage it either. It took me twenty years to reach that conclusion. The problem with Muslim music is that it is dominated by a conservative musical element originating in Saudi Arabia. It is not the genuine music you'll find in Malaysia, Indonesia, or Turkey. There are also people who preach that Islam is against music. I have studied the sources. There was a feast when music was being played in Muhammad's presence, and someone said, "Music in front of the Prophet? Stop it!" But the Prophet intervened. "Let them!" he said. "They are having a feast." Which means that, under proper circumstances, people are allowed to play or listen to music.

If I had not stopped performing when I did, I would have kept on doing the same things. I wanted to be honest with my fans. Although I had found what I was looking for in music, music was not taking me where I wanted to go. It paved the way, but it did not give me directions. I was seeking answers. Great truths. I could not lead my fans anywhere when I did not know where I was going. Hypocrisy is not my style. I still feel loyal to them. Is it not said that the secret of a truly successful person is knowing when to stop?

23 · *Michael Wolfe*

I FEEL LIKE A MONOTHEIST
WITH EXTRA CREDENTIALS

When a Jew converts to Christianity, Jews are stunned: why leave Judaism for a religion that persecuted Jews for centuries, and anyway, how can anyone believe all that malarkey about Jesus?

When a Christian converts to Judaism, Christians say he's forsaken the Messiah and will probably end up in Hell.

And when a Jew or a Christian converts to Islam, everyone is confused: the convert is now keeping company with his "enemies." The shadow of Middle Eastern politics falls every which way, even the way of personal salvation; worse, few Westerners really understand Islam. They haven't since before the Crusades, and now, with Islam's image hijacked by homicidal con men hiding behind the skirts of the Qur'an, they understand even less.

Michael Wolfe went against the grain. Jewish, smart, well educated, talented, and curious, he was pulled to Islam intuitively, almost as if it was a current he couldn't resist. For him, Islam wasn't the great bugaboo that terrified Westerners. It was monotheistic, inherently democratic, egalitarian, tolerant. And it offered a mystical tradition he deemed "attractive." Islam deeply resonated with Wolfe. Its emphasis on liberty and individual responsibility and correct action gave it such a rightful place in America that he half-jokingly proposed that America is a Muslim nation.

More of an alienated Jew than a discontented one—he never felt especially at home in the faith—Wolfe's path to Islam was circuitous, almost random, fed by a long spiritual yearning and a sense that, somewhere, there was a canon and a code and a discipline that would speak to him and strengthen him.

Born in 1945, Wolfe grew up in Wyoming, a mostly gentile suburb of Cincinnati. In this leafy, almost pastoral village, Jews and Christians got along, although with churches all around him—Catholic, Protestant, Episcopal, and Baptist—it was a twenty-minute drive to the nearest synagogue. He was adept at straddling: his father was Jewish; his mother was raised in the Church of Christ. "Both faiths," he later wrote, "were undoubtedly profound. Yet the one that emphasizes a Chosen people, I found insupportable; while the other, based in a mystery, repelled me."[1]

In synagogue, Wolfe learned to read passable Hebrew; in high school, he sang Christmas carols with the choir; when he was fifteen, while dating an Episcopal minister's daughter, he had a confirmation, which for many years the Reform movement substituted for a bar mitzvah. He was an all-American kid, whose friendly town Norman Rockwell could have visited for inspiration, and where the lines between faiths—at least beyond their individual houses of worship—were porous and permeable.

Wolfe's father had about as non-Jewish a job as you can get. He was a private detective, a guy with a fedora and a Lugar—"a cocky product of the Roaring Twenties," says his son. For years, David Wolfe worked for one of the largest investigative agencies in the Midwest. He quit upon overhearing an anti-Semitic remark, vowing to start a firm that would be even larger. He kept his word: eventually, the Associated Bureau of Investigation had offices in Chicago, Indianapolis, Cleveland, and Cincinnati. It also did some work overseas and took occasional assignments from the Anti-defamation League.

By the time he hit twenty, Wolfe had drifted away from all religions, dismissing them as empty and divisive—useless accessories for a decent, thinking person, especially someone like him, a religious "mongrel," in his words, who could see both sides of an argument or creed. Finally, when he was in his midforties, he wanted something to soften his cynicism, something that would provide "new terms by which to see." While living in Africa for three years, he'd been impressed with the tolerance of the blacks who lived there, people for whom the color of skin was irrelevant, immaterial. Wolfe found their outlook "transcendent and refreshing." Perhaps, he considered, it was no accident that all these people were Muslims. When it came time to contemplate embracing a religion—"an escape route from the isolating terms of a materialistic culture, an access to a spiritual dimension"—he was pulled partly by accident and partly by memory to Islam, a religion that, most likely, few of his ancestors, Christian or Jewish, would have understood or approved of.

Now living in Northern California, Wolfe writes books and produces documentaries, often for PBS and often about Islam. His book *Taking Islam Back: American Muslims Reclaim Their Faith* won the 2003 Wilbur Award for "Best Book of the Year on a Religious Theme." Like any good Muslim, Wolfe prays five times a day and has gone on hajj. And unlike just about any Jew in the world, he has taken *shahada,* a brief ceremony which changed his life.

In 1982 I was in an auto accident in California. I escaped the worst, but my back was badly injured. About a year later, when I could move around easily again, I walked into a bookstore one day and found a $3 paperback of the Muslim prayers. It was printed in Meerut, which is north of Delhi in India, and had little photos depicting the various postures, and the accompanying prayers were written out in Arabic and English. There was also a transliteration in English of the Arabic sounds. Using a rubber band to hold it open, I set the book on a music stand, so I could read it while standing and attempting the postures. I just stood there and looked at it for a while. Gradually, I found that when I performed the postures three or four times, my back felt better. I was doing other exercises at the time; I had a whole regimen. I added this to the regime, and it was a big improvement.

Then I thought, "Well, words go with this. Maybe I'll learn them, too." I had memorized a lot of Greek and Latin poetry in my day, so it wasn't really hard for me to memorize sounds without knowing the language. Within a few weeks, I was fairly proficient. I was only thinking that this was making me feel better. I wasn't thinking about going to a mosque or going to Mecca. I was lucky I could walk!

I was living in Bolinas, a tiny town in Marin County in Northern California. There were about fifteen hundred people in town and certainly no Muslims. Once I could perform salat, the daily Muslim prayers and prostrations, efficiently, I began to do a little reading. One of the works I ran across was a two-volume travelogue about the Muslim pilgrimage, the hajj, to Mecca by the early-nineteenth-century Swiss Muslim explorer and ethnographer J. L. Burckhardt. I learned that the hajj was not merely a journey. As one of the five pillars of Islam, it was a major spiritual requirement for Muslims. Travel had always been a major path to knowledge for me. Being somewhat restless, my ability to absorb working knowledge in schools and universities was limited. I learned best, it seemed to me, when I was on the road. And now I began to think, "Well, what about this hajj?" But living in California and nowhere near a mosque, I set the whole subject in parentheses for the time being.

I first encountered Islam in Africa, where I lived and traveled for three years in the late 1960s and early 1970s while on a poetry fellowship—first in Morocco and later in West Africa. That was my substitute graduate school, you might say. I was in a Muslim milieu almost all the time. Like many of my contemporaries, I had managed to graduate from a good university without learning a thing about Islam. Now, in Africa, I realized that Islam was a major world religion, not a cult, and that it bore a close relationship to Judaism and Christianity—with a monotheistic view of the divine, and reverence for the prophets of the Bible, and a sacred book of its own. Entertaining a positive attitude toward new faiths was not unusual to me. I grew up in a time (the 1960s) when many people I knew routinely stepped clean out of the tradition of monotheism in their attempts to reach new spiritual plateaus, adopting practices from Zen Buddhism or Hinduism, for example. Islam, by contrast, is a thoroughly Western religion, with much the same cultural and theological background as Christianity and Judaism. The more I learned about Islam, the more I saw that these three faiths are cousins.

But I was not a religious person then, nor were any of my Muslim friends telling me what a great religion they had and that I should convert. Muslims were not wearing Islam on their sleeves. I found that attractive.

I returned to Morocco in 1981 and again in 1985, for pleasure and also to pick up some manuscripts. I had started a publishing company, Tombouctou Books, and among the titles I was publishing were translations by the American novelist Paul Bowles. Bowles, who lived in Tangier, was putting into English oral stories invented by Moroccans who were terrific storytellers but not literate writers. In Tangier, I met one of these storytellers, Mohammed Mrabet. Through him, I had further inklings of the hajj and a new notion: now that I could perform salat and had read Burckhardt and other reports by hajj travelers, I thought that I might go to Mecca some day. But when Mrabet finally said, "Michael, I have nothing left to do in this life. Let's go on hajj," I was taken aback. I knew that what he proposed wasn't a vacation. The hajj had been going on annually for fourteen hundred years; millions of people had gone to Mecca from around the world to perform it, and a whole way of undertaking this complex rite, almost from the moment you left your door, had evolved around it.

I returned to America, but Mrabet's words stuck in my mind. I read more about the hajj and more about Islam. The more I read, the more I wanted to go—although, of course, in order to go, I actually had to be a Muslim.

The hajj was really essential to my converting. Learning more about it pressed me to comprehend religion in terms of desire and passion. Performing a hajj, I now understood, would not be about accompanying somebody somewhere or having a travel experience. And so, I tried to figure out how to go, thinking it might be best to first be in Morocco for a month or two, spending Ramadan there and really immersing myself in a fairly traditional culture that I already knew something about.

I don't want to sound naive: after two years of performing the salat, I knew what I was doing. I was learning to pray. And the effects of that were powerful. I had never really done this in the Judaism of my youth, where the spiritual side—the concept of a relationship or a conversation with God—was not emphasized. I had never put on a pair of phylacteries, for instance. So this was a whole new experience, and I was simply appreciating it for what it was, as something quite new yet somehow oddly familiar.

Perhaps the most powerful effect of my new experience with prayer was a sense of proximity, of nearness to life's Creator. I did not hear voices. I did not get instructions. But I do have a sense of being in partnership with something much larger than us.

There was a point where I wanted to go on hajj more than I wanted to be a Muslim. Then I crossed that, and I wanted to be a Muslim, too. When I tell people this, they think, "Oh, you confused one with the other." But Muslims understand it. For them, the hajj has a magnetic quality. They are tuned to the notion that, when you get into your thirties and forties, the hajj takes hold of you. Mecca, the geographical lodestone of the faith, starts dragging at you, and you go! You get the money together, you tell your family, you say goodbye to relatives and friends or (even better) you make the journey with them. People have been doing this for many centuries. Among Muslims, the compulsion to go on hajj, while not perhaps universal, is familiar, rational behavior.

Around this time, some people who knew about traveling to Mecca told me that I should sign up with one of the many "pilgrim tour" companies that would take me on the hajj for a modest sum, including airfare, hotels, and guides. I would be in a group of fifty or sixty other Muslims from around the country. This seemed efficient, if a little too organized for me. There was, however, a catch-22: I needed a visa to get the airline ticket, and to get the visa, the Saudi Arabian embassy required a document from a mosque that essentially said, "Michael Wolfe is a Muslim and two witnesses have signed this paper to say so."

By now, I had moved from Bolinas to a larger town about half an hour from a mosque in San Jose. I began to drop by the mosque on Fridays, the day for community prayer. At first, I only watched from the sidelines. After a few months, I thought, "I'm here. I know what these people are doing. Why am I not doing it, too?" I had no answer, so I stood up and joined the prayer. It was a dramatic moment for me; one could imagine music swelling in the background. For the other people in the hall, I suppose, it was just a normal Friday prayer with an additional congregant who hadn't participated with them the week before.

Several months later, in January 1989, I took the *shahada* after the Friday prayer. Sometimes a convert declares himself before a whole congregation. When I did it, only a handful of people were still in the building. That was fine with me. It felt more intimate, less a matter of display. Two people signed as my witnesses: a gentle retiree from Lebanon and a businessman who lived in Mountain View, a nearby town. They signed a photocopied sheet of paper that looked a little fuzzy from being photocopied too much. Nothing fancy about it: it had no gilt edging or elaborate calligraphy or ribbons. I mailed the paper to the embassy along with my visa application; the visa office returned it with my visa. I still have it. When I went on hajj, no one ever asked to see it.

The *shahada* is a door, an entry point. You know you're crossing it when you say, "There is no god but God, and Muhammed is His prophet." The sentence has an interesting construction. It doesn't say that Muhammad is the *only* prophet. In the context that I took it, and that I still take it today, Muhammad is the culmination of a long line of prophets, including Abraham, Moses, Jesus, and many others.

There is no requirement that the *shahada* take place inside a mosque. Saying the one-sentence declaration is the only requirement of the ritual, which, for me, was brief and not at all dramatic. It had absolutely no fanfare. It is the opposite of, say, the average modern bar mitzvah in the United States or the regime of catechism classes that are required of most converts to Christianity. In this regard, I sometimes think of Islam as the stripped-down model of monotheism. Other religions seem more elaborate. There is the ritual grandness of the Orthodox Catholic mass and the Roman Catholic mass. Judaism's High Holidays services can be quite dramatic, too. But my experience is that ritual in Islam is more succinct. There may be a very specific reason for the *shahada*'s briefness and lack of melodrama. In its early days, Islam underwent an enormous amount of conversion: millions of people in Iraq, Syria, Iran, India, China, and North Africa took it up in a century or two. That's a lot of *shahada!* No wonder the ritual of entering Islam is easy to execute.

When I took the *shahada,* I knew I was invoking a ritual with public and social consequences. I just didn't know what they were. The place where I first felt the full effect of becoming a Muslim, socially, was on the roof of the Grand Mosque in Mecca during the hajj. In this building, large enough for a million people to pray in at once, I really experienced joining a community and participating in a communal religious experience. In San Jose, I had engaged in a modest form of group prayer—fifty or sixty people came together. By comparison, Mecca was enormous and transformative. You might compare it to making a cake—you bring together all the ingredients, mix them up, and put them in an oven. Only there do they fuse and turn into a cake. Or, it was like taking a bunch of flowers that aren't much more than buds and placing them in a forcing house where, overnight, they bloom. Mecca was like that for me.

I stayed in Mecca for a month. I was among the first people to arrive that year. I was among the last to leave. I wanted to see it all, be a part of it all. And though I could not have foreseen it, that is when I became a Muslim.

It would be churlish to tell a story like mine and not take into account other people's reactions. I am sometimes asked how I could possibly have become a Muslim when I was raised as a Jew and had a Christian mother. What did my friends and family think of what I did?

Generally, friends were somewhat shocked—not necessarily that I should become a Muslim, but more that I should take religion seriously enough to actually want to join one. I was mostly surrounded by skeptics, I suppose, by friends who might entertain some spiritual interest or another but who didn't have much interest or trust in established religion. I may have been more like them than they supposed. Islam appealed to me partly because it has no hierarchy, no priesthood, no intercession between a believer and God. The whole practice, the whole conversation, as it were, is up to the individual and God. That is how I conceived of it, and that, in part, is what attracted me.

Those friends who had confused headlines linking Islam to terrorism with the actual religion were especially concerned. A handful cautioned that I should be very careful about going on hajj. One suggested I wear brown-tinted contact lenses to blend in with the crowd. These fears were not well founded. Socially speaking, the hajj was a peaceful affair from first to last. No one with a geopolitical ax to grind mistook me for my national flag. No one thought it puzzling that a person who looked like me, with white skin and hazel eyes, was a Muslim. They figured I was Turkish or Bosnian or Russian or South American. When they learned I was American, they either passed on to other matters or they got very excited and asked me to sit down with them, have some tea, and tell them about being a Muslim in America. Some believed that it must be almost torturous to be a Muslim in the United States, since American foreign policy seemed so unfriendly toward Islamic nations. Just as many Americans were mistaken about Islam, Muslims from abroad were mistaken about life in America.

My mother was still alive when I became a Muslim, but she was ill and it was difficult to communicate with her. She died the following year, while I was in Mecca. My father had died fifteen years before this. My mother would have been amused by my choice, in the way that many things amused her. I suppose she would have backed up my decision, strange though it might have seemed to her. My father would have questioned me—at length. But he probably would have gotten it in the end because he was an interesting combination—hardheaded yet gentle, and blessed with a sense of humor. He really loved my brother and me. He could be strong willed, but he could also be very accepting.

My mother was from a rather poor family; my father's family was somewhat better off. He was raised an Orthodox Jew and moved away from Judaism for quite some time. He came back to it later in life. My mother went along with raising us as Reform Jews. She held a dim view of Christianity—for a while, her mother had been raised by nuns who beat her. So perhaps she wasn't giving up much, although to my knowledge she never officially converted to Judaism.

Probably eight Jewish families lived in our town. There was no temple, but my father made sure that we were involved with Rockdale Temple, a very progressive temple about thirty miles away. He also made sure that we attended the High Holiday services and had a Passover Seder at home. But we had Christmas and Easter, too.

Rockdale was one of the most gorgeous buildings in Cincinnati. In front were very imposing Greek columns and a long flight of steps leading to the entrance. The sanctuary had a beautiful red carpet and very high ceilings and lots of chandeliers. The Torahs were kept behind high gold doors, and behind that was the large choir loft, and behind that were thirty-foot organ pipes rising up to the ceiling. It was a very impressive place for a little boy; it looked like a pretty good religion to me.

The rabbi, Victor Emanuel Reichert, took a real liking to me, and I to him. He was very literary and a beautiful speaker and was a close friend of Robert Frost, whom he brought to the temple to speak to the congregation numerous times. I got my love of books from Dr. Reichert. My relationship to Judaism was really literary rather than social, because most of my friends where I lived and went to school were Christian, whereas I spent only a few hours a week in Sunday school at Rockdale, with a separate set of friends who were Jewish but more like distant cousins.

And yet I was very satisfied with this. From the age of five until I was sixteen, I attended classes at Rockdale, first Sunday school and then, at the end, almost a full year of classes on Saturdays leading up to my confirmation. [Confirmations are held in many Reform and Conservative temples; in early Reform Judaism, it entirely replaced the bar mitzvah. Confirmation may reflect a greater knowledge and personal commitment to Judaism than a bar mitzvah. A side effect is that it ensures that a Jewish education will not end when children are thirteen but rather continue until their confirmation, which occurs when they are fifteen or sixteen.]

About twenty of us met with Rabbi Reichert in the library at the temple, sitting around a table in leather chairs for what was essentially a two-hour seminar discussing religion and Judaism and life in America. We also read, in Reichert's English translation, portions of the *Tahkemoni* of Judah al-Harizi, a thirteenth-century Spanish Hebrew poet. It was ideal for me: I was a little egghead.

As the president of my confirmation class, I had to give a speech at the event. I ended it with a poem by W. H. Auden. The last lines were

Follow poet, follow right
To the bottom of the night,
With your unconstraining voice
Still persuade us to rejoice . . .
In the prison of his days
Teach the free man how to praise.

Don't ask me why, but I thought this was important at the time.

Confirmation meant two things to me: that I had completed a great year in the presence of a special man—Rabbi Reichert—and that I had finished my time with the institutional side of Judaism. I still attended Rosh Hashanah and Yom Kippur services, but I knew that I was free in a certain way. So it had the opposite effect of what was probably intended: to make me part of the community. But that was really never in the cards, because I didn't live in a community into which Judaism was fully integrated. I traveled across town once a week to a temple. The rest of my life I lived in Christian American society, and that became the culture in which I grew up. Judaism was important to me, but in the end it didn't "take" as a religion.

For the next few decades, I was totally secular. By the time I could drive a car—1961—I was on to other things. Jack Kennedy was then president, Vietnam was just beginning to heat up, and I was a junior in high school. I had a Christian girlfriend, the daughter of a minister. I was playing basketball and smoking cigarettes behind the barn. I was always the poet, always the literary guy. I was also kind of wild. Judaism ended then for me. There was no great moment of rejection. I remained what some people might call a "cultural Jew"—those were my roots and I didn't appreciate wisecracks and slights on the subject. But in no way did I practice a religion. Part of the reason that I found it rather easy to become a Muslim was that I didn't have to give up as an adult what I had never had in my youth.

Since Islam incorporates Jewish and Christian teachings, I feel like a monotheist with extra credentials. I don't think that being Muslim detaches me from my youth or my American roots. I was born here. I was raised here. I don't plan to move. I don't want to wear different clothes. I don't want to speak another language. Since Islam's core values are essentially those of Judaism and Christianity, I would like to see these three religions join hands and help reinvigorate people's faiths. Islam's simplicity and directness might help on this score.

Some people believe that Islam is inimical to America. I disagree. Islam is suffering a lot of turbulence today because many Muslim societies today are premodern and only reluctantly on their way to modernity. This transition is causing great political upheaval in traditional Muslim nations. Americans and Europeans feel that they are the victims of the fallout from this process, but what's occurring is more like collateral damage. The war is not with the West, though al-Qaeda would have you think otherwise. The war is within Islam. Entrenched rulers are resisting change. Religious leaders are uncomfortable with the pluralism that's all around them. Opportunists and fanatics wrapped in a religious flag see an opportunity to create chaos through terror and drag whole societies back to the seventh century. The wacky arrogance of this vision is astonishing, and the stakes are real and high. The danger to much of the world's oil supply is only part of it. The greater threat is to an open, global society. This will be resolved more quickly and with better results if the majority of Muslims, who are clearly appalled by the current epidemic of violence, develop the vocal muscles to speak up and lead their communities away from it. This is already happening. Islam *is* finding its modern voice. That's what bringing Islam into the present is all about. Certainly, one of the great responsibilities for encouraging this process lies with us—we Muslims who are living in the West.

WOULD ANYONE RIDING BY
ON A HORSE EVEN NOTICE?

This book began on a personal note. It will end on a personal note: I have three daughters. Not one of them had a bat mitzvah. That has more to do with me than with them. Early in my career as a father, I reasoned that, since my own bar mitzvah was such a dud, my children should not be subjected to such a dull, unsatisfying, enervating experience. What benefits could possibly accrue? If the only wisdom that would be imparted from such an event was that religion was boring, insufferable, and irrelevant, then certainly there were better ways for them to spend their time, and for me to spend my money, since the cost of a bat mitzvah—the training, the schooling, the planning, the hosting, the partying—can equal the GNP of a small Third World country. (And that doesn't even consider the hand holding, the hand wringing, and the general, all-around anxiety, which may persist for months, even, I hear, for years. This is no fleeting enterprise; for some families, it is no fleeting misery.)

My daughters have never complained about missing their bat mitzvah. That silence may come from their good manners or from relief at avoiding years in Hebrew school, then "performing" before a full congregation including out-of-town relatives, many of whom would have been strangers to them anyway. And yet, I worry: one persistent theme of this book is that coming-of-age ceremonies bind us to certain wisdoms and rituals, to a timeless past and an endless future. But if you don't have a rite of passage, what are you bound to? Does tradition mean less? Do you and successive generations drift away from religion until your spiritual patrimony is a vague memory, a distant and meaningless abstraction?

Working on this book has convinced me otherwise. There is no surety that coming-of-age ceremonies will bind anyone to God or religion with permanence or ferocity. These are neither implacable guarantors of faith nor surefire remedies for lost, wandering, or inquiring souls. Invariably, they are stabs in the dark—seasoned stabs, if you will, because various permutations of these rituals have been performed again and again, in many places and over many centuries. Nor, in the long run, do these ceremonies necessarily impart profound and illuminating insights. They can, and ideally they should. But that's so rare, so unusual, so peculiar that almost everyone I interviewed scoffed when I inquired if their coming-of-age ceremony had generated revelations and insights. Apparently, my question was too naively apocryphal to be taken seriously.

In fact, there's really no way to tell how any of these rites will affect us. I say that after talking with Julia Sweeney: despite a commendable Catholic upbringing, she's now a devout atheist. And with Chinua Achebe: raised a Christian, he still misses knowing the secrets of his native tribe in Nigeria. And with John Daido Loori: an iffy student in Jersey City parochial schools, he is now a Zen master in upstate New York. And with Ram Dass: a nice Jewish boy from Boston who's been on the cutting edge of psychedelics and Eastern religions for decades, he now laments the lost potency of rites of passage, especially the bar mitzvah, which he had and which he still regrets for the emptiness smack at its center.

And let's not forget about Huston Smith: raised a Methodist, confirmed a Methodist, still a Methodist, he is armed with a curiosity about other religions that shames most interfaith mavens. And Elie Wiesel, who somehow managed to worship God from that hell known as Auschwitz. Their coming-of-age ceremonies were true journeys into maturity, a reflection of the spirit and an enrichment of the soul, even, in Wiesel's case, amid horrors that must never revisit this planet.

There's also no telling how the *lack* of a rite will affect us. Roz Chast never had a bat mitzvah and doesn't miss it. Abigail Pogrebin didn't have one until she was forty, when she came face-to-face with a void and a gnawing. And then there's Rabbi Jeffrey Salkin, who never had a bar mitzvah and still feels as Jewish as any of the four hundred kids at whose bar and bat mitzvahs he's officiated.

Also among the uninitiated are the Chopras—Deepak and Gotham—two transcendentalists who mirror, in their own way, William James's description of mystical states: "Our normal, waking consciousness, rational consciousness, as we call it, is but one special type of consciousness, whilst all about it, parted from it by the filmiest of screens, there lie potential forms of consciousness entirely different. We may go through life without suspecting their existence; but apply the requisite stimulus, and at a touch they are there in all their completeness."[1]

The Chopras are seeking that completeness, and to attain it, they are eager to jettison the very rites of passage that religious adherents say make us complete. From the perspective of the Chopras, these ceremonies shatter us into separate camps and labels and "–ologies." They are right. These rites *are* potentially divisive. They risk making us religiously provincial, insular, myopic, all of which would prevent us from appreciating truths beyond those into which we have been initiated, wedding us so tightly to our religious truths that we may belittle or scorn others' creeds and verities. Ultimately, that may be a comment on us, not on a rite of passage. Ideally, the wisdom imparted at such an event enables us to be porous and accepting, allowing us to see value and meaning even in a belief to which we do not subscribe and which may appear as a downright curiosity. The Chopras are apostles of a spiritual Esperanto, a revolutionary sphere which is enticing in the abstract but has little chance of progress when set against what seems to be a universal need for the very camps and labels and "–ologies" the Chopras assail. On the other hand, idealists in the field of religion and spirituality are precisely what religion—the ultimate arena for idealism—demands. But in this field of ultimates, of supreme good and supreme evil, voices for creative routes to amity are rarely heard and even more rarely heeded.

Just as each of us is unpredictable, the effect of these ceremonies is also unpredictable, which is why Ralph Waldo Emerson, who was right about so many things, erred so grievously when saying, in his later years when he was somewhat disillusioned, "We live amid surfaces, and the true art of life is to skate well on them." No, the true art of life is to live amid substance, to relish and welcome substance, to let it cradle and nourish us.

Otherwise, we are bereft, adrift, desiccated. And that is where these rites of passage come in: They might be alluring, annoying, majestic, inspiring, and in the end, their actual and specific fruits may be unknowable and absolutely unpredictable. (Anyone claiming otherwise is a snake and a charlatan.) But they are among the first occasions in our lives when we knowingly have the opportunity to find substance and direction, to reach a potential that we didn't know we had. Admittedly, that rarely comes, although with such a lapse in mind, maybe these events can offer a gift other than eternal salvation or an elevated standing in the community. Maybe their most incisive gift is ambiguity. Since life is uncertain, start to finish, maybe these ceremonies should just plunge people—headfirst—into the confusions that lie ahead. That would be a *real* lesson, although I must admit, it would detract from the vast, cosmic promises of so many religions, from their aura of suspense and improvisation, from the sweet, dramatic belief that, with these ceremonies, our life has just soared to a certain resolution, although of course, a lifetime of resolutions still lies ahead.

Perhaps in the end, being an adult really means taking nothing for granted, not happiness nor success, not revelation nor illumination. Everything has its price, and everything has its lessons. If rites of passage help anyone learn a fraction of this, then they're doing their job.

Sometimes the true rites of passage—the ones that really affect us—are those that don't occur "on schedule." A boy orphaned years before his confirmation matures in ways that his bishop can never anticipate. A girl bored during her bat mitzvah belatedly absorbs Jewish teachings about *tikkun olam*—changing the world—when, a decade or so later, she serves in the Peace Corps. A Quaker who doesn't know—*really* know—the inner light until he's in his thirties is no less a Quaker. He's just developed at his own pace, a pace no better and no worse than someone who's been communing with the light since he was ten. Maybe, when thinking about these rites, we should think less about someone saying a prayer or taking a vow or leading a service. Not much happens in a vacuum. These rites don't either. When trying to figure out how these events affect whoever's going through them, we should see how they connect the kids with "real" life, which, after all, is terribly long and complicated, full of detours and surprises and great pleasures and the deep, searing pain that is only noted by someone who thoroughly loves and cherishes life.

If these rites are really about connecting kids to their ancestors or a certain wisdom or tradition, then we have to look at how all that plays out over time. Subtracting part of life from the rest is just plain dumb. Saints don't walk out of baptismal pools; Jewish boys and girls aren't instant scholars after reading from the Torah; Hindus, Buddhists, and Muslims aren't necessarily wiser or more devout after receiving the Gayatri mantra or taking *jukai* or saying *shahada*. But they may be more open to the vastness of the world, to the richness of what is in them and around them—if not now, then maybe later.

Still, I fear that my daughters were shortchanged. When done right, a bat mitzvah (and any rite of passage) imparts a certain familiarity and comfort with faith, God, history, and self, with the textures, sounds, and patterns that will be with us our entire lives. They provide a frame, a window, a door—a context and also a meaning that can root us and ground us and comfort us as we wander through life, eager for purpose and ready for direction. These rites are a compass, and I hate to think I didn't offer one to my children. In fact, even if they had a bat mitzvah and didn't like it or if they had one and later moved on to another faith or to no faith or to a variation of Judaism that had never crossed my mind, I still think a bat mitzvah would have served a purpose: rites of passage (indeed, any rite) are either something that we're pulled toward or we push against, and the pushing can be as valuable as the pulling. Without something to push against in life, you stumble, losing your balance along with your perspective. The pushing is as indispensable a polarity as the pulling. These two are the vectors of our lives: always debating with each other, then, these two are the classic dialectics that we carry with us wherever we go—one is thesis, the other is antithesis. Eventually, we can hope, they come to terms and achieve some measure of peace, with each other and with the world.

The opportunity for my daughters to have a bat mitzvah has not passed: adult bat mitzvahs are more common every year. But that does not assuage my guilt that I stole a day from them, and that life should be rich with days—days of consequence and days of import. At best, they should have been told: "You *will* have a bat mitzvah"; at minimum, they should have been given a choice: "You can have a bat mitzvah. Think about it." Instead, only "You will not be having a bat mitzvah" prevailed, and that came about, really, as a cowardly default position, since neither my wife (who was raised Catholic) nor I were willing to firmly declare our beliefs and the beliefs that we'd like our kids to carry on. Rather I, in particular, clung to some nebulous aspirations that good hearts and kind souls would carry the day. This was really quite naive: even the best, most beneficent of hearts and souls need something—call it theology or community or the familiar, melodic power of hymns or the charged imagery of symbols and scrolls and texts—to plant them solidly on this good earth.

If, indeed, in dreams begin responsibilities, then those dreams—our own dreams or the dreams we have for others, for we have the right to dream for them too—must be sweetened and toughened and clothed, appealingly and attractively, with more truth to their substance than polish and sheen to their veneers. But what happened—the bat mitzvah–less raising of my daughters—was actually myopic and unfair, to them and to me. To them, because removing a choice from people can narrow their scope, even if they decide against it. To me, because if they had opted for a bat mitzvah, I may have been delightfully surprised: They might have enjoyed it; even *I* might have enjoyed it. There might have been the electric hum of knowing that we have touched something beyond ourselves, something larger and more potent, something with a greater sense of the eternal and the infinite than we can ever muster through our own solitariness. Maybe even better is that my daughters may have exceeded my rather dispirited performance at *my* bar mitzvah so many years ago, and it's always good for children to upstage their parents: humility is a fine tonic for a too-comfortable soul.

Finally, almost in desperation, I summon one last justification for withholding a bat mitzvah from my daughters: they have gone into the world with fine hearts, splendid souls, and keen insights about what is good and what is bad. They are kind. They care about others. They get angry at the injustices of this world. These are religious virtues: they are what patriarchs taught, what prophets preached, what gurus and the Buddha embody, and what various gods and goddesses ask of us: indeed, it is what they *demand* of us. Somehow, my daughters absorbed the truths of faith without necessarily being entrenched in faith. For that, I am grateful. Good people are hard to find, and I have no doubt that my trio of daughters— Sarah, Amy, and Molly—is as good as it gets.

And anyway, they may yet have a coming-of-age ceremony. It may be a bat mitzvah; it may be something bat mitzvah–ish and yet to be devised. And if they do, its meaning to them and to everyone else will be unavoidably different than it would have been if they had had it when they were thirteen: the onrush of years and experience and thought and knowledge will only enrich and, maybe, ennoble whatever rite they pass through. And since my daughters are all creative and thoughtful, whatever rite they choose, I'm sure, will most likely have different elements than the usual, run-of-the-mill initiation. All I ask is that it incorporate the consciousness of a *jukai,* the intense study of a bat mitzvah, the sensory satisfactions of an *upanayana,* the magical/mystical potential of a baptism or a confirmation, and the deliberateness of a *shahada.* For me, these are the most pungent, most exciting facets of a rite of passage. Together, they speak to our imagination, our senses, our emotions, our intellect, our awareness, our determination. Addressing us in our entirety, they make us whole.

In fact, the prime advantage my daughters may have over someone who had a rite of passage "on schedule" *is* consciousness and deliberation. If you approach a rite entirely of your own volition, *you* set the pace; to a large extent, you also set the content. I've forfeited doing that for my children, and quite frankly, at this point in our lives, it's fine with me if they never have a rite of passage. What's more important is that each day be treated as sacred, from rising in the morning to going to sleep in the evening. And that every encounter, even with themselves, be sacred too: that they live along what Martin Buber called a "narrow ridge," that thin boundary between absolute uncertainty and the even more alluring, more enticing confidence that every encounter in life will be rich, surprising, and quite wonderful.[2]

Having said all that, maybe more as a wishy-washy consolation to myself than as a definitive statement on the efficacy of rites of passage, maybe it's instructive to consider why certain people have little, if any, memory of their rite of passage and what this says about how these events meld into our lives. Jim Zogby, for instance, can't recall a moment of his confirmation. The same with Elie Wiesel and his bar mitzvah. Yet both men are deeply, profoundly religious, and both fight for justice and sanity— impossible goals to achieve, perhaps, *unless* you remember that Judaism teaches that the world rests on justice, peace, and truth and that the Gospels say that Jesus loved the poor and the weak and scolded the rich and the powerful. These lessons can be academic exercises—Comparative Religions 101. But Zogby and Wiesel take them to heart because church and shul seeped into them at an early age: as an altar boy in Utica, Zogby saw the magic of the Eucharist; as a student of the Talmud and the Kabala in Romania, Wiesel learned dangerous secrets and hidden mysteries. By the time their rites of passage arrived, they were witnessing holy splendor and divine glory *every day*. Initiations were superfluous. They did not need the jolt of a bar mitzvah or a confirmation to bind them to their faith. They lived that jolt. But today, so many people are not steeped in faith. They are steeped in cynicism, and it will take more than an isolated ceremony to keep them in their religion. For that matter, it will take more than an isolated ceremony to *bring* them to their religion.

In many communities, these rites are still central and still indispensable. But often, especially in the West, they've turned into afterthoughts—empty exercises with little power and even less meaning. So little, in fact, that in Britain, a member of Parliament recently submitted a rite of passage bill that would have required what he called a "nonreligious bar mitzvah for all"—a coming-of-age ceremony at the age of fourteen. The bill, which failed to pass, was an attempt to promote a sentiment of community, as this was not arising spontaneously. In the past, such impulses were channeled through the world of religion, with all that implied: shamans and incantations, prophets and divinations, preachers and Sunday morning fire and brimstone. And now, in quasi-socialist England, at least one politician—oddly from the Labor Party, a group always presumed ready to discard the past—wants the state to pick up the slack.[3]

The prime, overriding assumption I had going into this project was that these ceremonies somehow change us, that those people who really know what they're doing and study hard and pray hard and open their souls and their hearts on this their day of days, experience some kind of quasi-mystical, semi-magical transformation. I assumed that they were irrevocably changed, privy to some secret and power and knowledge that eludes so many of the rest of us.

Does this happen? Not very often, and anyway, to borrow Jim Zogby's mother's favorite phrase, "Would anyone riding by on a horse even notice?" I doubt it. Change, in these circumstances, is barely noticeable to that rider—or to us. And we shouldn't pretend that it is. Such pretensions are arrogant and illusory and, perhaps, serve as distractions from a finer and more subtle truth: each day is an opportunity for a transformation—a nuanced, barely discernible transformation, one that hews to quietude and near invisibility yet nestles in our deepest, truest self. The rider wouldn't notice it. Indeed, *we* barely notice it. But it's there, and it's daily, and it's constant. Conceivably, the only way to apprehend it is to lower our sights from the "big" things (even, if you will, from the enormousness of rites of passage, with their dense weight of obligation and anticipation and import) and attend to the smallness of gestures and the hushed murmurs of whispers and sighs. There's little drama here: it's not the stuff of epiphanies or instant conversions—on the road to Damascus or anywhere else. That happens to few of us, and its very quickness holds the seeds of its probable vanishing. Gradual osmosis—a day-by-day, minute-by-minute absorbing of lessons and truths and wisdoms—lets it seep further and deeper into the very ground of our being.

Obviously, having a rite of passage does not guarantee that you'll like your faith, stay in your faith, or have *any* faith. Which may be why interpretations abound about why we do these rites and how we do them. The Buddhist *jukai* ceremony, for instance, is powerful because it's done *consciously:* teacher and student together decide that it's time for the disciple to take refuge in the Buddha's teachings. The student then brings *all* of himself to the ceremony. Islam, of course, has no rite of passage for teenagers, but someone taking *shahada* brings an awareness to the event similar to a Buddhist taking *jukai.*

For initiations, Buddhists and Muslims only consider readiness and knowledge. Not age. Other religions might consider doing this, even if it means delaying rites of passage for some teens—or hastening them for others. More important than *when* an event occurs is its power to make a dent on the soul. If these ceremonies are opportunities for teens to *seriously* start courting wisdom, then they should do so knowing why they are doing this and what it can lead to. Anything less is a mockery.

In the end, the human longing for ritual is deep, and it surfaces precisely when there are ruptures from the everyday: a birth, a death, a wedding, a divorce, an illness. Gain, loss, joy, despair, confusion: whenever we approach extremes, we need a ritual, a formula, something that relieves us, to some extent, of the burden of figuring out what to do. As the Irish playwright Sean O'Casey said, "All the world's a stage and most of us are desperately unrehearsed." These rites are our stage directions. They provide us with our dialogue and *tell* us what to do. For that, we can be grateful. They knit us into history, even into prehistory; they knit us into ourselves. The need for ritual is so deep that even in our age, when the old ways swiftly become the discarded ways, people are creating their own rites or putting new life into rites that have ossified or lost meaning.[4]

Many synagogues, for instance, especially in Reform Judaism, require that boys or girls choose a social service project that speaks to them—aiding migrant workers, volunteering at food banks, helping Habitat for Humanity build homes for the needy. Catholic dioceses have similar programs for youngsters who plan to be confirmed. And new ceremonies are evolving along the margins of our society. Among Hispanics, the *Quinceañera*—a cross between a debutante's coming-out ball and a full-scale mass in church—acknowledges that a fifteen year old has reached sexual maturity. An old and revered tradition in Latin America and Puerto Rico, the *Quinceañera* has been flourishing in the United States since first introduced in the 1930s. The most important component of the celebration is a *misa de acción de gracias* (a thanksgiving mass). The birthday girl arrives at church in a formal, full-length dress. Flanked by her parents and *padrinos* (godparents), she sits at the foot of the altar throughout the service, accompanied by several *damas* (maids of honor) and *chambelánes* (chamberlains) chosen from family and friends. After the mass, a live band plays *banda, cumbia,* and salsa tunes; the *quinceañera* and her number-one *chambelánes* dance a traditional waltz; and she cuts a multitiered birthday cake that's often dripping in meringue frosting and decorated in hues that match her dress. The cake may be so monumental that the door leading into the reception hall has to be removed to accommodate it.

Another rite—a foot-washing ceremony—is evolving at Quaker-influenced Guilford College in Greensboro, North Carolina. Devised by Will McKindley when he was a nineteen-year-old freshman, the ceremony was intended to mark the transition at the end of the 2004/2005 academic year and everything that came after it for various students: taking summer vacation, then returning to Guilford; or graduating, then punching a clock, earning a salary, and being an "adult"; or dropping out and heading off into entirely uncharted waters. Additionally, McKindley hoped the experience would instill a certain degree of humility. Just as Jesus "poured water into a basin and began to wash the feet of his disciples, and to wipe them with a towel" (John 13:5) after the Last Supper, whoever came to the ceremony might learn that service and compassion are integral to leadership, that lowering yourself to the level of someone's feet also elevates you in the eyes of the Lord.

Raised in a "very liberal, very nontraditional Mennonite family" in Mount Rainier, a Maryland suburb that abuts the District of Columbia, McKindley first encountered foot washing at a Mennonite group in Washington, D.C. Only about nine years old, he was, as he said, "thoroughly confused, but I believe it was toward the end of Lent and we were celebrating Jesus' gesture toward his disciples." Eventually, the ceremony so affected McKindley and his family that they incorporated it into their private religious observances in their home, especially at Easter time. Jesus, in fact, had been so determined to wash the feet of his closest, most intimate, most devoted followers that when Peter balked at Christ humbling himself in this manner, his Lord insisted: "If I wash thee not, thou shalt have no part with me" (John 13:8). For Christ, especially the night before his crucifixion, foot washing was no mere ceremonial act, no formality between leader and follower. It was a pact, an accord between He who was about to depart and those ready to spread the Good News that their Messiah was a man who embodied contradictions, that he could go as low as he could go high, that he knew no limits, and that they, too, could give as much as they could receive.[5]

As he grew older, these foot washings deeply affected McKindley, and by the time he got to Guilford, he was anxious for his new college friends to share in this prodigious cleansing, in their ability to mark a moment in time, to distinguish between "now" and "after now," between "before" and "after," to fill in the juncture that lies between the certainty of knowing and the great, yawning precipice of not knowing. McKindley knew what he wanted, and he knew why he wanted it. He asked several friends, especially a theology major, if this interested them. It did. Then he looked into other faiths and discovered that, at certain Hindu weddings, the father of the groom washes his son's feet and the mother of the bride washes her daughter's feet; and that Buddhists wash feet as a way to symbolize the dispelling of ignorance. And finally, he looked into history and discovered that travelers had their feet washed as they entered and departed cities in the Middle East in the first century. As they entered, because it was feared that the travelers would bring evil spirits into the city; as they departed, as a final act of hospitality, and to be as clean as possible before embarking on the harsh, often hostile roads beyond the city. The people who performed these ablutions did this as their profession.

McKindley tacked up posters around campus, announcing that the foot washing would be held late on a Sunday night, three days after finals started. Around 11:45 that night, McKindley played folk music on his acoustic guitar outside The Hut—a tiny brick building reserved for religious events on campus. Shortly before midnight, he went inside and joined the twenty-five students who had come. Sitting in a circle, they observed silence for a few minutes, then McKindley told them the purpose of the evening, and a friend—the theology major—spoke about foot washing from a Christian perspective, drawing on the Gospels of Luke and John. Finally, McKindley poured warm water into two bowls, distributed towels, washcloths, and bars of Dr. Bronner's soap, and instructed those gathered to wash the feet of the person on their left, using their hands or the washcloths or just by pouring water over the feet. The washing ensued, silently, with each pair of feet taking about three minutes to wash. Afterward, McKindley broke a brief silence by asking people to talk about their joys and hopes and concerns. A graduating senior worried that Guilford was losing its Quaker values; a freshman, aware of how much he had changed over the preceding ten months, was uncertain how he would integrate the "new him" with his family back home; a sophomore whose father had recently died anticipated having a new role back home; a junior said that washing the feet of someone he'd never met before had been "very powerful."

Around 1:15, The Hut began to empty. Some people, invigorated, stayed up all night; most went straight to bed; a few woke up unusually early and, feeling exceptionally fresh, hit their textbooks before they even had breakfast. Over the next few days, what McKindley heard from the two dozen people who had attended the ceremony assured him he'd met his goal. "There's a lot of pressure at that time of year," he told me. "Social pressure. Academic pressure. A lot of people were under stress. There's much Quaker influence at Guilford, and Friends put considerable emphasis on slowing down processes that ordinarily happen so quickly that we barely notice. Washing feet, as simple as it may seem, slowed people down. It made people aware; it made them conscious; it made them humble." He hopes that foot washing will be an annual event at Guilford; ideally, he wants it to be a biannual event, held at the end of each semester.

"If someone like Jesus," he said, "someone so respected by his disciples can do this, then we, too, can bend and lower ourselves, cleansing not just feet but ourselves in the process."[6]

These innovations—foot washings, *Quinceañeras,* bar and bat mitzvahs with a stronger social service emphasis, and so many more adaptations and modifications—lend a modernity to rites of passage while still ensuring that they resonate with our deepest tribal memories, which is where half their meaning is derived. The other half is derived from what we make of them. Keeping them pure and pristine and practicing them exactly as done in the past is a nice nod to everyone who came before us. But that negates our own creativity if done to an extreme.

Margaret Mead, who believed that ritual "has no efficacy without continuity," was shocked when attending a new version of the Anglican low mass in the 1960s. Turning to the congregation, the priest said, "And the Lord be with you," and the people in the pews responded, "And with you." Her dismay, she realized, came from missing "the guarantee that is associated with ritual. The right things must be done in the right way and as they have always been done." By contrast, said Mead, there was no shock at formal dinners in England at the turn of the twentieth century: "No one would start smoking before the port, and no one would drink . . . before the King's toast was drunk." Everyone was secure, certain how the evening would proceed. By extension, the etiquette of the evening reflected the etiquette and the hierarchy that kept society in order. With that in mind, Mead observed, "people fight changes in ritual more fiercely than they fight changes in anything else." Breaking that continuity shatters the illusion of stability that people enjoy, the assumption that what has been will always be. And *that,* in fact, could be the greatest benefit of a coming-of-age ceremony: we aren't just coming into *our* age. We're also coming into the ages that preceded us. Every rite of passage conflates time: "was" and "is" and "will be" fuse into a single, all-purpose tense. There's an out-of-time–ness, a reaching back and forth across the ages, which may be why Abigail Pogrebin had an "out of body" bat mitzvah. She knew that, while time waits for no one, it's never too late to jump on its bandwagon.[7]

For religion to resist the fanatics and the narrow-minded, it must adapt. If not, it'll atrophy and dull, lose its sheen, and forget its own mystery and allure. After the twenty-first century's awkward start, maybe we can do this by paying more attention to rites of passage. They served us well in the past, and they can serve us well now, especially in a world with less ballast and greater confusion: the sand, it seems, is washing away faster than ever from under our feet. As foundations shift, as the bedrock founders, our temptation—maybe our duty—is to turn toward the past, not as a reactionary reflex but as an instinctual assurance that the past is resurrecting itself today as community and as life.

And if we won't embrace these rites, we should at least know why. As Julia Sweeney said before discarding her faith: "I need God because we have a whole history together." True, but she also said, "It's because I take You so seriously that I don't believe in You." Whether we believe in rites of passage, any rites of passage, they deserve to be taken seriously: without them, our sojourn would be more shabby, more diffident; our souls more disheveled, more sundered; our place in the world less rooted, less grounded. These rites are a testimony to our potential, to our possibilities. Our task is to hear them, to heed them, to treasure them. They are our betwixt and our between, the moment when we traverse moments, when we leap from one peak to another, bravely, courageously—ignoring gaps and valleys and gulches, aspiring toward oneness, if not greatness.

Our true worth lies in those moments, in those miniature shards of time that escape us, again and again and again. They are where our soul resides, where these ceremonies flourish, and why they even exist: by summoning a mindfulness that appreciates the vast, spacious present, the moment of a rite of passage will be a multitude of moments, a stunning, subtle galaxy of wonders and amazements and the most ordinary and absolutely down-to-earth visions and splendors.

Short of our own beatitude, we seek our better angels, our own flesh and blood and desire and consciousness—all of our obdurate humanity, even the parts to which we are oblivious, which we are unaware that we possess. For our quest, we summon a certain awe and hope, and both, we pray, will point us toward William Blake's most shining and rudimentary of proclamations: "Everything that lives is holy."

NOTES

PROLOGUE

1. In the end of course, the rabbi in this monolith of a temple in Scranton, with stones so huge they could have been in the Temple in Jerusalem, declared that I was a Jewish adult, and at some point during the service, my father recited the benediction, "Blessed is He who has now freed me from the responsibility of this one." If I'd understood more than a few random words of Hebrew, I would have been insulted.

    And still, we weren't done. More prayers were uttered and more songs were sung and I kept sinking deeper into my overstuffed chair at the rear of the bema. Finally, the congregation burst into "Adon Olam," the song traditionally sung at the end of the service, and for once, I was sincerely thanking God, this time for allowing this ordeal to end.

    After the ceremony, guests enjoyed a lunch, and a gaggle of uncles and aunts praised me with "Nice job" and "Good work." That evening, the out-of-towners came to our house, playing Scrabble in the living room or watching the Miss America pageant on TV, ignoring me as they rooted for Miss New Jersey, Miss Wisconsin, or Miss North Carolina. (They were all wrong. That was the year for Miss Colorado.) Sunday night, my friends went bowling and enjoyed hot dogs at the Jewish Community Center. Over these two days, I received bushels of presents: an illustrated history of Israel, a leather-bound edition of *The Diary of Anne Frank,* ties, shirts, and, inexplicably, a toenail clipper of rather inordinate size.

2.　　Rainer Maria Rilke, *The Notebooks of Malte Laurids Brigge,* trans. Stephen Mitchell (New York: Vintage Books, 1990), 20.

INTRODUCTION: SOMETIMES, THE MAGIC WORKS

1.　　As quoted in Todd Prozan, "Global Warning," *New Yorker,* April 11, 2005, 35.

2.　　Frederica Mathewes-Green more fully considers the consequences of the assumption that youth should be burdened with adult responsibilities, vocational and spiritual, in "Against Eternal Youth," *First Things* 115 (August–September 2005): 9–11.

3.　　Martin Buber, *The Way of Man* (Secaucus, NJ: Citadel, 1966), 40.

4.　　These Native American boys put to shame Gilgamesh, the king in the ancient Babylonian legend who failed miserably when he had to stay awake. Gilgamesh didn't succeed because, unlike those California boys, he was alone; and also because he was looking for something less *real* than what the boys were seeking. He wanted to live forever; the California boys just wanted to be initiated into their tribe. Gilgamesh was doomed from the start, impaled on his own audacity.

　　Near the end of his long quest, Gilgamesh met Utnapishtim, whom the gods had given eternal life. Utnapishtim told Gilgamesh that he would tell him how to live forever if he stayed awake six days and seven nights. Gilgamesh agreed, then sat down next to a river and almost immediately feel asleep as his exhaustion caught up with him. When he woke up six days later, Gilgamesh panicked:

> What do I do now, where do I go now . . .
> Wherever I go, wherever I look, there stands Death!

Utnapishtim felt sorry for Gilgamesh and gave him one more chance. He told the king about a plant that grew at the bottom of the ocean. "Take one bite of that," he said, "and you live forever." Gilgamesh swam to the bottom of the sea, plucked the plant out by its roots, rose to the surface, and soon started traveling home. After journeying a fair distance, he got tired, sat down, and—just like before!—fell asleep. A snake slithered up, ate the plant, and crawled away (quotations from http://www.wsu.edu/~dee/MESO/GILG .htm, accessed February 15, 2005, and May 1, 2006).

Twice, Gilgamesh *almost* had the secret of immortality. And twice, he lost it. By comparison, the Native American kids in California are the real kings. They have the strength to stay awake, the compassion to help others stay awake, and the wisdom to seek what's knowable. No living forever for them. Gilgamesh started out alone and came back alone, empty-handed, having convinced the gods that bestowing eternal life on this monarch, a king who had no qualms about falling asleep on the job, was a total waste.

5.   Willie Morris, *North toward Home* (New York: Vintage Books, 2000), 40.

1. THE DESCENT OF THE SPIRIT

1.   Gene and Sarah Fisher, interviews by the author, Reston, VA, and Washington, D.C., October 3 and 31, 2004.

2.   Gene Fisher, email to the author, December 23, 2004.

3.   The Holy Spirit has also been called the "Counselor," the "Paraclete," and the "Spirit of Christ"—many names for a concept that some Christians have a hard time understanding.

4.   The apostles who presided over the small community of early Christians baptized new members, then anointed them with oil and offered them their first communion—all at the same ceremony. As the church grew, the bishops (the successors to the apostles) could not personally baptize every Christian. There were too many of them and they were too spread out. Baptisms were delegated to local priests, and the bishops, on one of their regular visits to a community, would "confirm" the priests' baptisms with a second anointing.

Eastern churches avoided this splintering of baptism and confirmation by giving priests the authority to administer any sacrament, including communion, to an infant. No church ever considered confirmation necessary for salvation, and some (like the Baptist) don't even bother with it (Hugh Wamble, "Historic Practices Regarding Children," in *Children and Conversion,* ed. Clifford Ingle [Nashville: Broadman Press, 1970], 71–74).

5. Jews and Christians weren't the only ones convinced of water's power to do good—or bad. The Shoshone of the American West, for instance, believe that different spirits reside in rivers and streams. "Water babies," for example, who look and sound just like human infants, can devour a human child and substitute themselves in its place; and in the winter, a full-sized water spirit—the "fish woman"—uses her beauty to tempt people toward her, then drags them down into the water through a hole in the ice. In the American Southwest, the Hopi speak of plumed water serpents that dwell in underground waters or the distant sea which can impregnate bathing women and bring floods, earthquakes, and landslides (Ake Hultkrantz, *Native Religions of North America* [San Francisco: HarperSanFrancisco, 1987], 48–49, 97).

To Zen Buddhists, water is much more benign. The thirteenth-century Zen master Dogen saw water as gloriously transcendent, flowing with purpose and inevitability. "Water," wrote Dogen, "flows over the earth; it flows across the sky; it flows up, it flows down. It flows around bends and into deep abysses. It mounts up to form clouds; it descends to form pools. . . . Water extends into flames; it extends into thought, reasoning, and discrimination; it extends into enlightenment and the Buddha nature. Descending to earth, it becomes rivers and streams. We should realize that when water descends to earth it becomes rivers and streams. And the essence of rivers and streams becomes sages" (John Daido Loori, "Dongshan and Sheshan Cross the River: Dharma Discourse by John Daido Loori, Roshi," http://www.mro.org/zmm/dharmateachings/talks/teisho23.htm).

In a sense, for Buddhists water *is* enlightened, twisting and turning with circumstances, never resisting its predicament, always knowing how to find its way to the oceans. It trusts itself, as Buddhists must trust themselves to twist and turn and face predicaments and the unknown and, ultimately, to return home. The water doesn't second-guess itself; Buddhists don't second-guess themselves.

6. Since Protestants say that communion just *represents* Jesus' body and

blood, Protestants who convert to Catholicism, like Sweden's Queen Christina in the seventeenth century, often balk at the literalism of Catholic communion. According to Christina's biographer Veronica Buckley, the queen, who had been raised a Protestant, was openly "flippant" about her first Catholic communion, apparently figuring that such jests were common among the sophisticated Catholics she knew. Her wisecracking backfired. Her friends who were devout Catholics were appalled, and Spain's royal family—the very people who had arranged her conversion—was convinced she was a fraud. Christina convincingly atoned, and by the time she died in 1688, she was more or less devout, at least if we can overlook her many affairs. For four days, half of Rome filed past her embalmed body. Then the entire college of cardinals said a requiem for her, and she was placed in a crypt in St. Peter's Cathedral. She had come a long way—geographically and spiritually—from being a silly girl who had snickered years before about the transubstantiation that was indispensable to the religion to which she had just converted.

For Catholics, sharing the Host forgives venal sin, the lesser of the two categories of sins. (Venial sins weaken our relationship with God; mortal sins sever it.) The Catholic altar, then, where communion is celebrated, is an altar of grace as much as of sacrifice—God's Son is present, and he is laying himself down for humanity. In some Protestant denominations, communion service is held only twice a year. For Rome, the very purpose of the service *is* the Eucharist: if you miss that, you essentially miss the mass.

7. In a broadcast in the 1960s, Radio Moscow bragged that, under communism, life expectancy rose to sixty-nine years. An announcer attributed this to improved health care plus the virtual disappearance of baptisms. This could explain why Baptists had no success in the Soviet Union: anyone smeared as a health menace probably got a free apartment in Siberia, for life. (Homily by John J. Cardinal O'Connor, St. Patrick's Cathedral, New York, January 11, 1998, http://cny.org/archive/ch/cho11598.htm.)

8. Mark 1:6, 1:10–11. Acts 2:4.

9. Tertullian was one of the first Christians to develop the idea that Adam and Eve had harmed not just themselves but everyone who

came after them. In the early third century he wrote, "We are linked with Adam because all souls were first of all contained in his." Thanks to Adam, wretchedness became the human condition and corruption became human nature. But even Tertullian, an especially dour thinker, was not inclined to baptize children, no matter their age: the *tendency* to sin, which stemmed from Adam's long-ago offense, did not require forgiveness. And anyway, these "young novices," as he called them, were unable to repent or even understand what it meant to live a life of repentance. He preferred that they be baptized after they'd passed through the heat of youth. For Tertullian, baptizing adults for the sins they'd *personally* committed was the only baptism that was valid and worthwhile.

Origen, the next theologian to tackle baptism, essentially fathered "original sin," inventing the term itself ("all are stained with the stain of original sin") and insisting that this universal blot could only be "washed off by water and spirit."

From then on, the call for infant baptism, and the reasons for it, became more strident. A few years after Origen announced that deliverance emanated only from the church, Cyprian, the bishop of Carthage, ratcheted up the consequences of Adam's sin. This "primeval contagion" was transmitted to the entire human race through sexual intercourse, and baptism, the sooner the better, provided the only immunity to our terrible inheritance from Adam. Newborns hadn't sinned, Cyprian knew that. But they were still burdened by the colossal sin which resonated throughout history. Borrowing from Psalms (51:5) to prove his point, "Indeed, I was born guilty, a sinner when my mother conceived me," Cyprian ruled that it was best to cleanse babies so they'd be responsible only for the transgressions *they* committed, not for what they'd acquired from their tainted DNA.

In time, many parents became horrified that if newborns died before being baptized, their souls would go to limbo—a place that's not quite hell but not quite heaven either. There, souls don't bask in God's radiance, but they also don't suffer, as they would in Hell. It took centuries to assure parents that these babies weren't doomed, although not until 1992 did the Vatican officially state that infants who died before they were baptized had been entrusted to "the mercy of God, who desires that all men . . . be saved." If God was so merciful, wouldn't He extend His compassion to Christians who had *not* had their stain from original sin washed away? Further, why would God let such pettiness dominate His goodness? (*Catholic Encyclopedia*, s.v. "Confirmation," http://www.newadvent.org/cathen/04215b.htm, accessed on August 17, 2004, and May 1, 2006; Tatha Wiley, *Original Sin* [New York: Paulist Press, 2002], 44–61.)

10. Especially telling was what was *not* said at the third-century Council of Carthage, which determined when baptisms would be held: no one mentioned the terrible medical conditions of the time. Babies were dying everyday—one out of three died before his or her first birthday. Baptizing them made sense: a lot of them wouldn't be around very long. So many babies died in Rome, in fact, that Latin has no word for "baby." This high death rate inspired Cicero to counsel, "If a child dies young, one should console himself easily. If he dies in the cradle, one doesn't even pay attention." Romans weren't callous, but they were cautious. By not getting attached to their children until they were two or three years old and had a decent chance of surviving, parents protected themselves from grief and sorrow. If you did not "pay attention," as Cicero advised, you did not lose your heart. (Meir Bar-Ilan, "Infant Mortality in the Land of Israel in Late Antiquity," http://faculty.biu.ac.il/~barilm/infant.html; Carrie Boyles, "The Re-creation of a Young Roman Girl," http://cornellcollege.edu/classical_studies/women/boyles/.)

11. David Van Biema, "Life after Limbo," *Time,* January 9, 2006, 68. "Is Limbo in Limbo?" Catholic online news service, http://www.catholic.org/international/international_story.php?id=17813, accessed December 15, 2005, and May 1, 2006. Interestingly, the original head of the commission sanctioned to rethink limbo was Joseph Cardinal Ratzinger, who had written years earlier that limbo was only a "theological hypothesis," not church doctrine. Three years before Ratzinger became Pope Benedict XVI, he wrote that the idea of limbo was "rather unenlightened." In the twentieth century, limbo had become "problematic," particularly when considering the fate of babies who had been aborted. (Van Biema, "Life after Limbo"; Joseph Cardinal Ratzinger, *God and the World* [San Francisco: Ignatius Press, 2002], 401.)

12. Actually, Constantine had been living for a decade with two major sins on his conscience: in 327 he'd had his son and second wife executed. Crispus was killed after his stepmother, Fausta, convinced the emperor that the twenty-one-year-old was conspiring against him. Presumably, Fausta was trying to clear the way for one of her three sons to succeed the emperor. Then in a fit of remorse (fueled by rumors that Fausta was having an affair with a slave in the imperial stables), Constantine had Fausta thrown into a scalding bath. She didn't last long.

Upon his death, lying in a gold coffin covered with purple draperies, Constantine was buried in a mausoleum in the Church of the Apostles in Constantinople. He had built the massive church as a tribute to the apostles and was laid to rest among the statues of these twelve men closest to Jesus—not surprising for a man who had called himself the Thirteenth Apostle.

Almost a thousand miles away, the Roman Senate passed a decree deifying Constantine, and a coin was minted with an image of Constantine ascending toward heaven as God reached out to welcome him. All this was standard practice for deceased Roman emperors, but it does make you wonder how effectively Constantine had eradicated the old pagan ways (Charles Matson Odahl, *Constantine and the Christian Empire* [New York: Routledge, 2004], 268–75).

13. Anonymous Baptist minister, interview by the author, Baltimore, November 24, 2004.

14. "Pastor Electrocuted While Performing Baptism," Associated Press, October 31, 2005, http://www.cbsnews.com/stories/2005/10/31/national/main995829.shtml.

A few years before, another minister—also a Baptist—was standing in an empty baptistery at a Halloween party at his church in the Maryland suburbs of Washington, D.C. With the clouds from the dry ice he'd placed in the baptistery swirling around him, he startled congregants by making spooky sounds and wearing a scary mask. Left alone in the sanctuary for a while, he was soon found dead. Breathing the carbon dioxide had killed him (Rev. John Roberts, interview by the author, Baltimore, November 2, 2005).

15. Leo Damrosch, *Jean-Jacques Rousseau: Restless Genius* (New York: Houghton Mifflin, 2005), 53.

16. Ibid., 56. Or so priests thought. In 1754 a friend who was traveling to Geneva for business invited Rousseau to come along. Rousseau agreed, realizing that the trip might offer him an opportunity to regain his original citizenship: he was famous as a *citoyen de Genève* ("a citizen of Geneva"), but in reality he was a *citoyen sans cité* ("a citizen without a city"), since citizenship was predicated on being a Protestant, and Rousseau had renounced that twenty-six years before. Ordinarily, it was quite difficult to return to Protestantism: you had to endure a series of public humiliations, interrogations before two councils, and three days in prison. But Rousseau was no ordinary returnee, and Geneva's church leaders were eager to welcome back such a celebrity. So a committee of six pastors asked him some vague questions, he offered some vague answers, and they quickly ruled that he had never really abjured Protantism. Instead, they declared—somewhat falsely—that he'd been "taken to France at an early age and raised there in the Roman religion." Now, thankfully, he resolved "to come to his fatherland, make his abjuration and return to the bosom of our church." He was excused from public humiliation and a prison stay on grounds of poor health. He'd already had two baptisms— the first, courtesy of Protestants in Geneva; the second, courtesy of Catholics in Turin. A third was not deemed necessary (ibid., 244–47).

17. *The Lectionary,* s.v. "Louis IX," http://satucket.com/lectionary/Louis.htm. "Saint Louis—Confessor, King of France—1214–1270," Catholic Church Documents Library, http://www.ewtn.com/library/MARY/LOUIS.htm. *Catholic Encyclopedia,* s.v. "St. Louis IX," http://www.newadvent.org/cathen/09368a.htm.

18. Paul Jensi, "Saint Louis—Confessor, King of France, etc." and "Heaven on Earth," http://www.paris.org/Kiosque/jul100/sainte.chapelle.html, accessed January 11, 2005, and May 1, 2006. "The Jewel Box of the Cité—La Sainte Chapelle," http://classes.uleth.ca/200103/art2850b/ste-chapelle.html, accessed January 11, 2005, and May 1, 2006.

19. "On 508 ('I'm ceded—I've stopped being Theirs')," Modern American Poetry Website, http://www.english.uiuc.edu/maps/poets/a_f/dickinson/508.htm.

20. Michelle Duvall (pseudonym), interviews by the author, Baltimore, December 15, 29, and 31, 2004, and email correspondence with the author, January 5, 2005.

21. Duvall, interview, December 15, 2004.

22. *Catholic Encyclopedia,* s.v. "Baptism" http://www.newadvent.org/cathen/02258b.htm. The encyclopedia stipulates that liquids invalid for baptisms are those "not usually designated true water," such as oil, saliva, wine, tears, milk, sweat, beer, soup, and fruit juice: "When it is doubtful whether a liquid could really be called water, it is not permissible to use it for baptism except in case of absolute necessity when no certainly valid matter can be obtained. On the other hand, it is never allowable to baptize with an invalid liquid." While the thirteenth-century pope Gregory IX once declared invalid a Norwegian practice of baptizing with beer, a predecessor five hundred years earlier, Stephen II, approved of using wine for baptisms. That was later declared "void of all authority."

23. For this account of the Montera affair, I'm indebted to the definitive work on the subject: David I. Kertzer, *The Kidnapping of Edgardo Montera* (New York: Vintage Books, 1997). Edgardo's abduction was the most famous of many committed by the Vatican. The Holy See worried that Jewish children who had been covertly baptized yet remained in the homes of their parents would be polluted by the Torah and the Talmud and the Mishnah, sentencing them to eternal damnation and an afterlife far away from the glories of Christ. With that in mind, Rome vigorously fanned the fiction that Jews had killed Christ, and Pope Pius IX, who guaranteed Edgardo sanctuary from his parents, confined Jews to ghettos. One Spanish traveler described Rome's ghetto as a seething cesspool: "One's feet sink into a soft layer of excrement. . . . Half-naked children, covered with scabs of filth which resemble a leper's gangrenous sores, slither everywhere. . . . The houses seem to be true rat holes. And from each of these dens wafts a fetid smell." Jews deserved this squalor; after all, snorted the pope, they were "howling dogs. . . .

There are too many . . . in Rome, . . . and they are disturbing us in all places" (Kertzer, *The Kidnapping of Edgardo Montera,* 50).

Clearly, this was not the best atmosphere in which to be a Jew anywhere on the Italian boot and certainly not a healthy atmosphere in which to appeal for Edgardo's return.

24. Ibid., 118–26, 252, 253.

25. Ibid., 123–29.

26. Ibid., 296–98. Almost a decade after the kidnapping, the pope's attitude hadn't changed. "You are very dear to me, my little son," he wrote Edgardo, blending defiance, self-pity, and whining in the same letter, "for I acquired you for Jesus Christ at a high price. . . . Governments and people, the rulers of the world as well as the journalists—who are the truly powerful people of our times— declared war on me. Monarchs themselves entered the battle against me. People lamented the harm done to your parents because you were regenerated by the grace of holy baptism and brought up according to God's wishes. And in the meantime no one showed any concern for me, father of all the faithful" (ibid., 260).

When Edgardo's mother died in 1890, newspapers printed reports about her deathbed conversion, reports which her son was forced to correct: "I always desired that my mother embrace the Catholic faith, and I tried many times to get her to do so. However, that never happened, and although I stood beside her during her last illness, along with my brothers and sisters, she never showed any signs of converting" (ibid., 296).

27. Information found in this section is taken from the article "Annie's First Communion" by Joan Leonard, http://www.beliefnet.com/ story/23/story_2306.html.

28. Baltimore Catechism, question 46, p. 10; question 516, p. 116; question 1108, p. 216; http://www.sacred-texts.com/chr/balt/index.htm.

A famous humorist told me he didn't do too well with this kind of stand-up exam: "My answer to any given question was 'I don't know'"—not a great formula for guaranteeing a happy afterlife, but apparently pretty good preparation for becoming a funny man (although the humor may have been lost on the congregation that day) (anonymous letter to author from humorist, January 26, 2002).

29. Archbishop William H. Cardinal Keeler, interview by the author, Baltimore, December 30, 2004.

30. Information found in this section is taken from my telephone interview with Brittany Kirsch (pseudonym), Baltimore to New England, May 19, 2005.

31. Rev. Deborah Suess, telephone interview by the author, Baltimore to Greensboro, NC, October 15, 2004.

32. Ibid.

33. Kathryn Summers, email to the author, September 11, 2005.

34. Kathryn Summers, interview by the author, Baltimore, February 27, 2005.

35. Ibid.

36. John Friese, interview by the author, Baltimore, February 27, 2005.

37. Summers, interview, February 27, 2005.

38. If a Mormon confirmation occurs more than one week after baptism, the person is rebaptized before being confirmed. Mormons base this on the account in Acts (19:1–7) of Paul rebaptizing some converts who had been baptized but not given the gift of the Holy Ghost.

39. The Doctrine and Covenants of the Church of Jesus Christ of Latter-Day Saints, 130:22, http://scriptures.lds.org/dc/contents, Official Scriptures of the Church of Jesus Christ of Latter-Day Saints. "Vatican Says Mormon Baptism Is Not Valid," *Denver Catholic Register,* July 25, 2001.

   In July of that year, the Vatican newspaper, *L'osservatore Romano,* reported that Mormons believe the Father "is an exalted man, originating from another planet, who acquired his divine status through a death similar to human death, the necessary way to divinization." The Mormon God has a wife, the Heavenly Mother, with whom he shares responsibility for creation and whose first-born children are Jesus and the Holy Spirit. (In another departure from mainstream Christianity, Mormons teach that God, as well as Jesus, "has a body of flesh and bones as tangible as man's.")

40. Considerably more controversial than the validity of Mormon baptisms is the church's practice of baptizing the dead, also called "baptism by proxy" and "vicarious baptism." Latter-Day Saints believe

that, by baptizing a living person—who is, of course, always a Mormon—on behalf of a deceased non-Mormon, they are granting that individual an opportunity to accept the Gospel in the afterlife. Church leaders insist that they are not imposing Mormonism on the dead; rather, they are granting them a chance to come to the Gospel, since baptism is indispensable for salvation.

Mormons claim that, as late as the fourth century, Christians baptized the dead. Contemporary mainstream Christian scholars dispute this, consigning vicarious baptism among early Christians to several heretical groups, most of which were officially excommunicated from the church. Also arguing against baptism by proxy is many Christians' rejection of the idea that salvation demands baptism and their belief that these Mormon proxies abrogate an individual's personal responsibility.

While vicarious baptisms are primarily intended to offer salvation to the ancestors of Mormons, many other people have been included: the Founding Fathers of the United States, all the U.S. presidents, Christopher Columbus, Joan of Arc, Buddha, Joseph Stalin, Albert Einstein, Sigmund Freud, even Adolph Hitler and Holocaust victims. Anne Frank's entire family, for instance, has been posthumously baptized, with Anne baptized no less than eight times in Mormon temples from Atlanta to Manila and her sister, Margot, baptized six times in six different temples. Their father, who survived the Holocaust, was baptized five times in the same number of temples.

For non-Mormons, the notion that Hitler and Anne Frank could get an equal hearing before God is more offensive than laughable. Helen Radkey, who discovered many of these multiple baptisms, said that Mormons' intentions may be "good, but they're totally out of touch with reality. You don't have to know the mind and will of God to see that there's something out of balance in even offering Hitler the opportunity to share the same destiny as Anne Frank."

In 1999 church leaders agreed to cease proxy baptisms of Holocaust survivors, although research surfaced three years later indicating that the practice had continued. Rabbi Marvin Hier, dean of the Simon Wiesenthal Center in Los Angeles, said, "If these people did not contact the Mormons themselves, the adage should be, 'Don't call me. I'll call you.' With the greatest of respect to them, we do not think that they are the arbiters of who is saved." (*Wikipedia*, s.v. "Baptism for the Dead," http://en.wikipedia.org/wiki/Baptism_for_the_dead; Ben Fulton, "Amazing Grace: Anne Frank and Hitler Share LDS Baptisms," *Salt Lake City Weekly*, August 19, 1999; "Mormons Meet with Jews over Baptizing Holocaust Survivors," December 11, 2002, http://archives.cnn.com/2002/US/West/12/10/baptizing.the.dead.ap/)

41. Kathryn Summers, email to the author, September 6, 2005.

42. Ibid.

43. Ibid.

7. WHAT, *REALLY*, IS A MAN?

1. Elizabeth Bernstein, "More Non-Jews Celebrating Faux Bar Mitzvahs in US," *San Francisco Chronicle*, January 14, 2004, http://www.sfgate.com/cgi-bin/article.cgi?f=/news/archive/2004/01/14/financial1013EST0066.DTL.

2. Ibid.

3. Ibid., and Ralph Gardner Jr., "Bash Mitzvahs!" *New York Magazine*, March 9, 1998, http://newyorkmetro.com/nymetro/urban/family/features/2343/.

4. Jeffrey K. Salkin, *Putting God on the Guest List* (Woodstock, VT: Jewish Lights Publishing, 1992), 3.

5. Cecil Roth, "Bar Mitzvah: Its History and Its Association," in *Bar Mitzvah*, ed. Abraham I. Katsh (New York: Shengold Publishers, 1955), 20.

6. Gardner, "Bash Mitzvahs!"

7. Information regarding Reform Judaism's attempts to end commercialism from Janet Marder, "When Bar/Bat Mitzvah Loses Meaning," *Reform Judaism*, Winter 1992, http://urj.org/worship/letuslearn/s14whenbar/, accessed February 22, 2005, and May 1, 2006.

8. Nathaniel Graham, telephone interview by the author, Baltimore to Auburn, GA, December 7, 2005.

9. Rabbi Debra Kassoff and Dr. Stuart Rockoff, telephone interviews

by the author, Baltimore to Jackson, MS, December 2, 2005. Brenda Goodman, "Always Miles to Go for a Rabbi with 28 Temples in 12 States," *New York Times,* November 26, 2005, B7.

10. Goodman, "Always Miles to Go."

11. Kassoff and Graham interviews.

12. Graham interview.

13. Ibid.

14. Ibid.

15. Alexandra Null, telephone interview by the author, Baltimore to Altus, OK, December 7, 2005; email from Null to the author, December 24, 2005.

16. Alexandra and Lynn Null, telephone interviews by the author, December 7, 2005; email from Alexandra Null to the author.

17. Alexandra and Lynn Null interviews, December 7, 2005

18. Alexandra Null interview; Null email.

19. Lynn Null interview.

20. Alexandra Null's *d'var Torah,* delivered July 23, 2005, The House of Jacob, Wichita Falls, TX; Null email.

21. Information in this section is from my interview with Aaron Lemle, New York, November 5, 2004.

22. Heschel quote from Salkin, *Putting God on the Guest List,* 42.

14. I AM NOT GOD'S POLICEMAN

1. Elie Wiesel, *All Rivers Run to the Sea* (New York: Alfred A. Knopf, 1995), 36.

15. THE THREAD OF LIFE

1. Ajay Kumar, interview by the author, Lanham, MD, April 2, 2005.

2. Ibid.

3. Various interpretations of the sacred thread ceremony from Viswanath Deva Sarma, *The Hindu Rituals* (Calcutta: Viswa Jyotirvid Samgha, 1993), 29; Upen Vaidya, email to the author, September

24, 2005; Ravi Ravichadran, interview by the author, Lanham, MD, April 2, 2005.

4. http://www.gurjari.net/ico/Mystica/html/upanayanam.htm, and J. L. Brockington, *The Sacred Thread* (Edinburgh: University Press, 1981), 200.

5. Hinduism is an exactingly detailed religion. Your caste circumscribes what you will do with your life, and sixty life cycle ceremonies— more than any other religion—commemorate certain key moments in it. For example, three ceremonies just for youngsters are *neskaramana,* which celebrates a baby leaving the house for the first time; *annaprasana,* which celebrates a baby's first solid food; and *chowla,* held when a baby gets his first haircut. Through these multiple ceremonies—all wrapped up in a blitz of colors and smells and endless, mesmerizing chants—Hinduism intends to hasten the end of your many reincarnations and return you to the Godhead (Klaus K. Klostermier, *A Survey of Hinduism* [Albany: State University of New York Press, 1989], 174).

6. Anonymous, interview by the author, Lanham, MD, February 12, 2005.

7. Anonymous, interview by the author, Lanham, MD, February 12, 2005.

8. http://www.indiblog.com/112/desicriticsorg-a-new-chillout-online/ (accessed April 25, 2006).

9. Ramya Gopal, "Bound by the Same Thread," http://www.shastras .org/RamyaGopal.html.

10. Ibid.

11. Dr. Jaishree Gopal, telephone interview by the author, Baltimore to Detroit, November 30, 2005; Rambachan interview.

12. Ramya Gopal, telephone interview by the author, Baltimore to Detroit, November 30, 2005.

13. Mahatma Gandhi, *All Men Are Brothers: Life and Thoughts of Mahatma Gandhi as Told in His Own Words,* ed. K. Kripalani (Paris: UNESCO, 1969), 160, 162.

14. Mahatma Gandhi, *Gandhi's Autobiography: The Story of My Experiment with Truth* (Washington, D.C.: Public Affairs Press, 1960), 479.

15. Ibid.

16. Ibid.

17. Ibid., 480.

18. Ibid., and *Harijan* (English-language weekly journal founded by Gandhi), May 1, 1947, 478.

19. *The Song of God: Bhagavad-Gita,* trans. Swami Prabhavananda and Christopher Isherwood (New York: Penguin Books, 1972), 61.

16. DEEPAK AND GOTHAM CHOPRA, FATHER AND SON: RELIGION IS FREQUENTLY IDIOTIC

1. http://www.skepdic.com/chopra.html.

2. Ibid.

3. Ibid.

4. John Weldon and Stephen C. Myers, review of *Ageless Body, Timeless Mind: The Quantum Alternative to Growing Old* and *Perfect Health: The Complete Mind/Body Guide,* by Deepak Chopra, *Christian Research Journal* (Winter 1994): 43.

5. Kawina Melwani, "Deepak Chopra: Vedantic Evangelist," *Hinduism Today,* July/August 2000, http://www.hinduismtoday.com/ archives/2000/7–8/2000–7-09.shtml, accessed December 20, 2005, and May 1, 2006.

17. WAKING UP

1. John Daido Loori, interview by the author, Woodstock, VT, September 18, 2005.

2. John Daido Loori, "Dongshan and Sheshan Cross the River: Dharma Discourse," http://www.mro.org/zmm/dharmateachings/ talks/teisho23.htm, accessed January 2, 2006, and May 1, 2006.

3. Ibid., and also the winter 2004 issue of "The Hazy Moon," newsletter from the Green Mountain Zen Center, Lafayette, CO.

4. Loori interview.

5. Huston Smith, *The World's Religions* (New York: HarperSanFrancisco, 1991), 82.

1.   Imam Yahya Hendi, interview by the author, Washington, D.C., March 16, 2005.

2.   Ibid., April 28, 2005.

3.   Ibid.

4.   "If you become Muslim while you're on your way to death," Imam Hendi told me, "then God only holds you responsible for what you do in the time left to you on this earth. All God wants is for you to acknowledge His glory and your willingness to live by His laws. The time factor does not matter."

Scholars only seem to differ over saying *shahada* in the bathroom: you don't want to pollute the sacred. But as the imam told me, "For me, the *shahada* has two forms. There is the outer *shahada,* which you can hear; and the inner *shahada,* which is spiritual. Even if you say it in the bathroom, you're saying it in your heart. I don't leave my heart outside the bathroom, then put it back in when I come back out." While Islam has no specific criteria for who can utter *shahada,* for who can be a convert, Imam Hendi always assigns readings to these potential newcomers: "They need to know what they're getting themselves into, then we discuss the readings for one hour, two hours, three hours. We talk until I feel that they are comfortable knowing what Islam is all about. Then I say, 'Okay. Come back. We will do it.'"

Despite his efforts not to judge potential converts—"It's really between them and God"—Hendi has turned some away. He wants to be certain that they are not running away from something, especially their own religion. He also wants them to understand the basic concepts of Islam, especially the *umma,* or community. "To be a Muslim," he said, "you are part of the *umma.* You go to the mosque [for communal prayer]; you participate in the social life of the community. You contribute to the community. [Muslims are obligated to contribute 2.5 percent of their net worth to charity each year.] If they say they want to become a Muslim but prefer to keep their money to themselves, something is wrong" (Hendi interview, April 28, 2005).

5.   Amira Qureishi, interview by the author, Baltimore, April 8, 2005.

6.   Hendi interview, March 16, 2005.

21. COLEMAN BARKS: JUST BEING SENTIENT IS CAUSE FOR RAPTURE

1.   Coleman Barks, introduction to *The Essential Rumi,* by Jalal al-Din Rumi, trans. Coleman Barks (San Francisco: HarperSanFrancisco, 2004), xvi.

2.   Rumi, *The Essential Rumi,* 99.

23. MICHAEL WOLFE: I FEEL LIKE A MONOTHEIST WITH EXTRA CREDENTIALS

1.   Michael Wolfe, *Hajj* (New York: Atlantic Monthly Press, 1993), 7.

EPILOGUE: WOULD ANYONE RIDING BY ON A HORSE EVEN NOTICE?

1.   William James, *The Varieties of Religious Experience* (New York: Modern Library, 1929), 378–79.

2.   Maurice Friedman, *Encounter on the Narrow Ridge: A Life of Martin Buber* (New York: Paragon House, 1991), x.

3.   Christopher Caldwell, "There Ought to Be a Law?" *New York Times Magazine,* May 22, 2005, 18.

4.   O'Casey quote from "The New Rites of Passage" by the editors of *Utne Reader,* July/August 2004, 63.

5.   Will McKindley, telephone interview by the author, Baltimore to Greensboro, NC, September 1, 2005. McKindley, email to the author, September 11, 2005.

6.   McKindley interview.

7.   Margaret Mead, "Ritual and Social Class," in *The Roots of Ritual,* ed. James D. Shaughnessy (Grand Rapids, MI: William B. Eerdmans Publishing Co., 1973), 92, 94.

ACKNOWLEDGMENTS

I love viewing the credits at the end of a film. They're the final census of brains, imagination, talent, ego, and ambition behind a motion picture: the gaffers and the best boys, the second unit directors and the foley artists, the doting sycophants to the stars and the many people who want to be stars. They're all here. Just as film credits are a testament to the elaborate collaboration demanded by a few hours of celluloid, books, especially nonfiction books, have their own credits, otherwise known as "acknowledgments."

My name may be on the front cover, just as a film director's name leads the roster of a movie's credits. But behind the six syllables of my name is a mighty corps. Their numbers may be scant compared to the legions employed in filmmaking, but without them, this book would not have progressed beyond a half-baked germ of an idea.

Deeply essential were those people whose interviews get a chapter to themselves. They deserve particular thanks. All were unexpectedly generous with their time, their ruminations, and most important, their frank revelations of self and soul, with all that implies: Bob Abernethy, Chinua Achebe, Coleman Barks, Leon Botstein, Roz Chast, Deepak Chopra, Gotham Chopra, Dr. Yusuf Islam, Rabbi Harold Kushner, Roshi John Daido Loori, Abigail Pogrebin, Letty Cottin Pogrebin, Ram Dass, Huston Smith, Julia Sweeney, Robert Thurman, Elie Wiesel, Michael Wolfe, and Jim Zogby.

My deepest regret regarding this book is that I could not interview two friends who suffered untimely and tragic deaths: Iris Chang in November 2004 and Peter Jennings in August 2005. Both had agreed to be interviewed; both, I believe, would have enjoyed the interview, since religion intrigued them. Iris's books mined the convoluted origami of certain, often disturbing histories; her excavations of Japan's wartime atrocities in China will forever do credit to her name. Peter had staggering curiosity, empathy, and wisdom. A reassuring presence to millions of Americans during some of our most scarring crises, he was a caring and thoughtful gentleman. We are all the less without his knowledgeable, calming, comforting presence.

My agent, Amy Rennert, and her able first mate, Dena Fischer, muscularly championed this project. Editor Reed Malcolm and *his* able first mate, Kalicia Pivirotto, and Marilyn Schwartz and Jimmée Greco all shepherded the manuscript through the shoals of editing and production, offering sage advice along the way. Alex Dahne then gracefully navigated the vagaries of media, a sphere with its own unique culture and tongue.

I am grateful for the First Amendment of the Constitution, which provides for three essential freedoms: freedom of religion, freedom of the press, and freedom of expression. As Americans, this is our creed, regardless of our belief or disbelief in a faith—any faith. It defines us as a people, and it allows us to remain a people. It also allows us to say and write what we wish about religion, much as I have in this book. As a nation founded on tolerance, we cannot forsake tolerance to suit prevailing fashions and fads. That is no less than an invitation to embrace the very tyranny the American Experiment was established to rebuff.

Thanks to Hazel Gurland for meticulous and thorough research. A bouquet of really expensive flowers to the impressively indefatigable Katherine Michaud—your transcribing was always accurate and amazingly swift. A salute to Anne Stone for squeezing in some transcribing before Katherine came along.

Marlene Roeder, Ryushin, and Zuisei: you run interference with finesse and skill.

William Cardinal Keeler and Mark Pacione of the Archdiocese of Baltimore and Gene and Sarah Fisher: may the Holy Spirit strengthen you, wherever you may be.

Revs. John Roberts and John Ballenger of Woodbrook Baptist Church in Baltimore: may those waters always refresh you.

Ian Joyce, Deborah Suess, Max Carter, and Will McKindley, all in Greensboro, North Carolina: you're friends among Friends.

Imam Yahya Hendi and Amira Qureishi kept me on a straight path.

Ravi Ravichadran, Ajay Kumar, Shilpa Rajan, Anantanand Rambachan, Jaishree Gopal, Ramya Gopal, Vikram Masson: Shri ram shri ram.

Mickey, Aaron, and Beth Lemle: I wish I'd known you sooner. I would have given Aaron a fine present.

Nathaniel Graham, Alexandra Null, and their well-traveled rabbi, Debra Klassoff: The bright lights of the big city might get all the attention, but treasure what you have. Trees, quiet, and clear skies have their virtues, too.

Mulan in Los Angeles: do yoga with Babar, please. He's more flexible than ordinary elephants.

Roz in Connecticut: enjoy *The Daily Show*. And your own show: someday maybe?

Joel and Alice: thanks for your spare bedroom.

Jacqueline Seaberg: good idea, that guy in upstate New York! Gina Matthew: good idea, those guys in California! Who says a teacher doesn't learn from his students?

Diane Finlayson, keep your eyes fixed on God, even while in the studio giving dire weather predictions.

Jane Redmont helped put this book to music. When Jane asked what song I'd like people to hum while reading *Opening the Doors of Wonder*, I immediately burst into "Zip-a-dee-doo-dah, zip-a-dee-ay. My oh my what a wonderful day. . . . Wonderful feeling, wonderful day!" When these rites and rituals really work, when they take you closer to yourself and your God and your faith than ever before, then why not burst out with a little "Zip-a-dee-doo-dah"? That's the spirit speaking. That's your heart speaking. That's the wonderful feeling of a wonderful day.

As usual, Ichabod guarded the home front, Desdemona purred, Zefius (the world's fattest cat) still needs a girdle, Helen kept the fires burning, Molly listened to my babbling, Sarah stayed cool 'cause she is cool, and Amy provided free room, although I had to provide the board. Still: not a bad deal.

All this is not to slight the three girls who sat next to me at a confirmation in Reston, Virginia. Glancing at my fevered note taking as the bishop delivered his homily, one of them nudged me gently, then whispered into

my ear: "Are *you* preparing to be a bishop?" After scribbling my answer—
"Think about it: Do *I* look like a bishop?"—we covertly passed notes back
and forth, something I haven't done with a twelve year old since I was . . .
well, since I was twelve. I wasn't being initiated that day, but thanks to those
three girls, I felt like a kid, a rejuvenation that, for all I know, was a gift
from the Holy Spirit itself. I'm a devout non-Catholic, yet I must admit:
if youth and silliness are among the attributes the Spirit sows, then worshipping at the sign of the cross is mighty tempting indeed.